The Confusing World of Benny Hinn

G. Richard Fisher
and M. Kurt Goedelman

with
W.E. Nunnally
and Stephen F. Cannon

D1248949

A
Personal Freedom Outreach
PUBLICATION

The Confusing World of Benny Hinn

Published by
Personal Freedom Outreach
P.O. Box 26062 • Saint Louis, Missouri 63136-0062
(314) 921-9800

Compiled from the pages of
The Quarterly Journal
Keith A. Morse, Editor

Ninth Edition
Revised and Updated
December 2002
ISBN: 0-9716247-3-9

Acknowledgements

In 1991, Personal Freedom Outreach published its first critique examining the doctrine and practice of Benny Hinn. Stephen F. Cannon, the ministry's Arizona director, was the man who inaugurated what has turned out to be a decade-long investigation. It was Steve's research and desire to expose the corruption he saw, which, in turn, whetted the appetites of other directors to further investigations of the dubious faith healer's claims. Chapter 2 contains the greater part of his original work. Echoes of his research can also be found throughout the book.

Special acknowledgement must be given to Wave E. Nunnally for his valuable insight into areas relative to his personal expertise in the studies of Judaism, the Hebrew language, and biblical hermeneutics. Wave is responsible for Chapters 15 and 16, which examine Hinn's regrettable biblical interpretations.

Particular appreciation goes to Keith A. Morse, editor of Personal Freedom Outreach's newsletter, *The Quarterly Journal*, from which material in this book has been acquired. His talents and professionalism have given PFO integrity in its publications and helped it to earn respect from both laity and clergy in the Church, and from our colleagues in apologetic and counter-cult ministries.

A very special thanks goes to Jill Klein who invested her competent literary skills to examine the final draft of the manuscript which is the basis for this ninth edition. We are grateful for her valuable suggestions and meticulous proof-reading of this publication.

Finally, even in the age of computers with spell and grammar checkers, the human eye is still a necessity. A word of acknowledgement also is extended to Dr. Robert L. Griffin, David Stamps, and Angela Goedelman, whose time and expertise of the final proofread are deeply appreciated.

Table of Contents:

Foreword

Today there is a growing "signs and wonders" movement among professing Christians which far surpasses in scope and impact anything previously seen. Its followers number in the tens of millions and their appetite for what they imagine to be miraculous is seemingly insatiable, causing multitudes to cross continents and even oceans in pursuit of the latest supposed miracle worker or prophet. Through mass meetings broadcast worldwide on radio and TV, the leaders of this movement wield an almost incalculable influence over vast segments of both the Church and world.

If miracles are indeed exploding and true prophets are speaking for God to His glory, these blessings ought to be made known. But if false prophets are leading millions astray with bogus "miracles" and pretended "revelations" which actually bring reproach upon our Lord, then the warning concerning such grave deception ought to be made known clearly and vividly in order to deliver as many as possible from their snares. The unsaved, strangely enough, seem to have clearer discernment than many Christians in recognizing fake signs and wonders. Sadly, they tend to write off Christianity as a whole because of a few frauds.

The secular media has, in many instances, done a work that Christian leaders who should have been warning the flock have neglected. Its many exposés of false "prophets" and phony "miracles" have been devastating. Yet much of the Church—and not just the charismatic portion of it—continues to hail what it calls "the last days great revival promised in Scripture." In fact, no such revival is foretold. Instead, whether one likes it or not, the Bible prophesies that the Church age will culminate in apostasy and unprecedented spiritual deception.

Christ's solemn question, "When the Son of man cometh, shall he find faith on the earth?" indicates the very opposite of a last days revival. When asked what "signs" would herald the nearness of His return, Christ three times emphasized: "Take heed that no man deceive you ... many false prophets shall arise, and shall deceive many ... and shall shew great signs and wonders; insomuch that, if it were possible, they shall deceive the very elect" (Matthew 24:4, 11, 24). Christ was very explicit, and if words have any meaning, there is no doubt that His description fits many of today's popular healers and televangelists:

> "Many will say to me in that day, Lord, Lord, have we not prophesied in thy name? And in thy name have cast out devils? And in thy name done many wonderful works? And then will I profess unto them, I never knew you: depart from me, ye that work iniquity" (Matthew 7:22-23).

In view of numerous biblical prophecies to the contrary, how is it possible that so many professing Christians, and even Church leaders, insist that the last days before Christ's return are to witness the greatest revival in Church history? That this deluded hope persists is itself one more sign that the very deception Christ foretold is upon us.

The proliferation of false miracle workers who fit the descriptions of those about whom Christ and the New Testament writers warned has been almost breathtaking. If some of today's most popular preachers and Christian talk show hosts are not among those to whom Christ will say, "I never knew you; depart from me...," then His words are meaningless.

Unquestionably, the best known and most popular "miracle worker" performing today is Benny Hinn. He claims to have had more revelations and seen more visions than anyone, even in Bible times, including John who wrote Revelation. Hinn has rebuked "the spirit of cancer" and the "devil of death and of debt" so many times without result that it would be laughable, if only so many weren't deceived. His bizarre heresies, false prophecies, contradictions, and outright occult involvement are uncovered and thoroughly documented in the following pages. Yet the more outrageous

Hinn becomes, the more his popularity grows and the larger the crowds he attracts.

All over the world, record-breaking crowds of up to a million eager seekers after the miraculous gather expectantly to witness the open display of supernatural power which Hinn pretends to have at his command. Many attending Hinn's healing meetings leave not only with empty pockets, but worse off physically than when they came. His devastating effect upon gullible believers who are easily led astray, is more than sufficient reason for the authors of this book to present us with the terrible truth about Benny Hinn.

The number of Church leaders is astonishing who, in spite of his well known false prophecies and bogus miracles, publicly praise and flatter Benny Hinn. This includes, of course, the usual coterie of false prophets such as Oral Roberts, Kenneth Hagin, Kenneth Copeland, and others associated with Paul and Jan Crouch's Trinity Broadcasting Network. Many of TBN's stars, including Jack Hayford and Rex Humbard, were among the 3,000 who gathered to applaud Hinn at the 25th anniversary of his ministry.

Humbard praised Hinn as "the most illuminating man ... [for] detecting and feeling the moving of the Holy Spirit that I've seen in my 68 years of God's work [and] one of the greatest Bible teachers that God ever let live." That "68 years of God's work" could leave a man so blind says volumes for the whole signs and wonders movement of which Humbard has long been a highly respected leader. On TBN, Hinn, this "greatest [of] Bible teachers," scorned doctrine and theology as "sick stuff" and said, "I don't discuss doctrine." That broadside met with approval from Paul Crouch, who himself has referred to sound theology as "doctrinal doodoo." The following pages will document just how heretical and ignorant a Bible teacher Hinn really is.

In 1999, a 25th Anniversary celebration to fete Hinn included some respected non-charismatics. Among them was Jerry Falwell, who had the following to say:

> "Pastor Benny and I are friends. ... He came [to Lynchburg] and we had a wonderful day together. He

met the 6,000 students of Liberty University as we walked from building to building. Most of them knew him. Many of them are your partners [Benny]. ... We spent a lot of time in conversation about what God is doing. ... I am a Baptist. ... When I look at your crowd in those coliseums, all I see are the 18-year-old high school seniors. Now I know the rest are important, but I want all of them at Liberty University to train them to be champions for Christ!"

In view of such widespread delusion, this book is invaluable. It has been completely revised and updated. Those who feel they don't need the information it contains should at least buy a few copies to pass on to friends and acquaintances. It could save someone's life, both physically and spiritually. I commend it highly.

Dave Hunt
Bend, Oregon

"I'm an artist, ... I've always been an artist. And people want drama in a situation like this."

Benny Hinn
February 15, 1978

"But I'll tell you honestly, I think I'm going to quit preaching healing and start preaching Jesus."

Benny Hinn
May 20, 1993

"My children are afraid of me under the anointing. What they do not know is I'm afraid of the anointing too."

Benny Hinn
September 10, 1999

"The word will spread that if some dead person be put in front of this TV screen, they will be raised from the dead—and they will be by the thousands."

Benny Hinn
October 19, 1999

Myth Maker, Myth Maker

Time and again, preachers burst onto the scene, attracting attention and capturing followers with what they claim are new insights into Scripture and new powers from God, only to be exposed as being not only unoriginal, but false.

Benny Hinn, who has risen to unprecedented worldwide popularity as a healing evangelist, is one of the most prominent examples of this phenomenon. His incredible rise to a heretofore unequaled celebrity status among many within Charismatic and Pentecostal camps came during the 17 years he was pastor of the Orlando Christian Center (later called World Outreach Center and World Outreach Church).

The Florida-based charismatic church Hinn founded in 1983, at one time claimed a weekly attendance of 12,000. He is also the author of numerous best-selling books, and his daily television programs are said to reach a potential audience of nearly 100 million homes in 128 countries. In all of this, Hinn epitomizes the kind of histrionics, emotionalism, and hysteria that can bring reproach to the Gospel of Jesus Christ.

Humble Beginnings with Supernatural Hype

Born in Jaffa, Israel, on December 3, 1952, Toufik[1] Benedictus (Benny) Hinn's biography is replete with the same supernatural events described by most of the luminaries of the mystical Christian movement (MCM).[2] While all of them allege scriptural precedence, Hinn's claims are typical of those in the MCM who want special attention: William Branham, Paul Cain, Bob Jones, and Kenneth Hagin, for example. Hinn's experiences include:

- visitations by Jesus at an early age (age 11, in his case);[3]
- dreams and visions with visitations by angels;[4]
- protracted times of private worship and prayer;[5]
- one-on-one dialogues with the Holy Spirit;[6]
- out-of-body experiences with accompanying angelic warfare.[7]

These claims portray Hinn as a man of God who has seen "revelations" and "visions" unparalleled since biblical times. In fact, if one assembled Hinn's purported visions, dreams, angelic visitations, and direct revelations from God into one book, they would exceed that of Jesus' Revelation to the Apostle John on Patmos!

Hinn says that this goes on all the time. He says: "Someone asked me, 'Benny Hinn, do you still have those mountain tops when you see angels and God visits you still? Is it still happening?' My answer is, 'It's been greater!'"[8]

Hinn's extrabiblical extremes border on fantasy, if not occultism. He says there are little angels who look like children. In his testimony he says,

> "I'm telling you the truth, you could literally sit there in total shock. ... If you think I'm crazy, go on. Angels would appear in my bedroom at night and just stand and look at me. I would wake up to see angels in my bedroom. All sizes. Call me crazy but I would even see little boys in my bedroom with beautiful white robes. Like, little, they almost looked like girls but they were male. You say, 'Do you mean there are little angels?' I believe that 'cause I saw them. ... There must be little angels in heaven. I think so."[9]

Compare this with the description of angels made by occultist Emanuel Swedenborg in 1758 which he claimed lived in the "inmost heaven":

> "Externally they appear simple, and before the eyes of the angels of the lower heavens they appear like children, that is, as very small, and not very wise, although they are the wisest of the angels of heaven."[10]

Supposedly, even God Himself can't get enough of Hinn and yearns for time alone with the superstar faith healer. Hinn tells the story that:

> "Once, in England, I was staying at the home of a Christian family. My room was at the very top of the house. One evening I was lost in the Spirit, having the greatest time in the world talking to Him. The woman of the house called up, 'Benny, supper is ready.' But I was bubbling over and didn't want to leave. She called again, 'Supper is ready.' *And as I was about to leave, I felt someone take my hand and say, 'Five more minutes. Just five more minutes.' The Holy Spirit longed for my fellowship.*"[11]

Dr. Jay Adams denounces such nonsense. His description and censure of mysticism fits Hinn with incredible accuracy:

> "Mysticism is a selfish as well as an arrogant approach to life because the mystic believes his special access to God is the most important thing in life, and while he wallows in it, the world can go hang! There is a self-centered absorption in one's self that few other activities can approximate. Of course, the so-called 'Christian mystic' is no more in some special relation to God than the Muslim or the Indian mystic. All have an experience that is similar, but it is of their own manufacturing. They fabricate this experience which, they maintain, is so ethereal and blessed they cannot describe it."[12]

Adams continues his powerful assessment:

> "At length the mystic, having entered into his esoteric experience, finds it difficult to think of himself as anything but in a class of his own. While he may speak of the experience as humbling, humility does not seem to be his outstanding characteristic. Rather, he is inclined to look upon those who have not entered into such experience as spiritual peons. There is nothing about mysticism in the Bible. It is a movement in many religions that has (wrongly) been incorporated into Christianity. But it does not fit."[13]

Moreover, Hinn's stories and tales of the supernatural keep shifting, changing, and metamorphosing until one wonders if he ever will get them right. Parts of Hinn's 1999 autobiography get closer to the truth, while other parts carry on his mystical deception and give new versions of old stories.

Altered States of Unconsciousness

For example, Hinn admitted that some boyhood tales in *Good Morning, Holy Spirit* were not recalled correctly. In the book he told of a "dream" his mother had in which she had "six beautiful roses."[14] In this dream, Jesus appeared and asked for one of the roses. In the version of the dream Hinn told to his Orlando church in 1987, he said, "There were eight roses in her hand and Jesus came and said, 'One of them belongs to me.'"[15]

In the retelling of the purported vision, Hinn explains that his mother more recently "explained it was about lilies,"[16] not roses. Despite the change in number and flower species, Hinn's interpretation of the dream remains consistent — and herein lies the question as to its divine source and precise interpretation. Hinn now explains the dream of "six beautiful lilies" in his mother's hand as:

> "When she awakened, [his mother] Clemence asked herself, What does this dream mean? What can it be? Eventually, our family was to have six boys and two girls, yet my mother never forgot her bargain with God. 'Benny,' she said, 'you were the lily I presented to Jesus.'"[17]

Hinn suggests the single flower requested by Jesus in the dream symbolizes his call and life as a minister. The problem with Hinn's (or his mother's) interpretation lies in the fact that Benny is not the only member of his family to have become a minister. Four other of Clemence's sons — Willie, Henry, Sammy and Michael — are pastors and evangelists. Why then did Jesus only ask for one flower when five sons would eventually devote themselves to full-time ministry work? Perhaps Hinn's Jesus is a casualty of open theism or process theology — not knowing what the future would hold. Some may say that the number and type of flowers, and the dream's interpretation type, is a minor issue. Perhaps, but it still does not answer the question: How could one misconstrue a vision from God?

The Patriarchal Christening

Another instance of Hinn's inconsistency with fact is his original telling of his christening. As he recounts his christening in the Greek Orthodox Church, he says he was christened "by the patriarch of Jerusalem, Benedictus." "In fact," Hinn writes, "during the ceremony he gave me his name."[18] Eugene Hoade, in *Guide to the Holy Land*, writes on page 89 that Patriarch Benedictus I was elected in 1958. The December 11, 1980 *Jerusalem Post* indicates his election was in January 1957. Either date reflects that Vasileios Papadopoulos (Benedictus) was not installed as the "Patriarch of Jerusalem" until several years after Hinn's birth.

Hinn now admits, "My baptism took place at the residence of the Greek Orthodox priest in the historic area of Jaffa known as the Old City. Officiating was Benedictus, a friend of our family *who became the patriarch of Jerusalem.*"[19]

The Schooling

Another problem with Hinn's story is his reputed completion of basic education in Canada. Hinn says: "During my senior year at Georges Vanier. ... I had an encounter with the Lord. ... in February 1972."[20] Yet, he was not a "senior" in February 1972. Hinn is pictured as an "undergraduate" in the 1972 yearbook, *Vestigia*, of Georges Vanier Secondary School.[21] There, Hinn is listed under his birth name: "Toufik Hinn."

Hinn's use of the terminology "my senior year" in *Good Morning, Holy Spirit* is incorrect on two counts. First, the terminology was not used. During the time Hinn attended school in Toronto, there were 12th and 13th grades in secondary school. According to an administrator, the terms freshman, sophomore, junior, and senior were not used because of the grade structure. Second, if the term had been used for the benefit of a United States reading audience, it could apply only to the 12th or 13th grade. Hinn completed only the 11th grade before dropping out.

According to the manual *Recommendations and Information for Secondary School Organization leading to Certificates and Diplomas 1972-1973*, one can only graduate from secondary school by completing, with proper credits, either grade 12 or grade 13.[22]

It appears that as early as 1976, Hinn tried to portray himself as a secondary-school graduate. His then-hometown newspaper, the *Toronto Globe and Mail*, reported:

> "He finished Grade 12 at Georges Vanier Secondary School on Don Mills Road and planned to take a Seneca College course to become a travel agent. On his way to pay the tuition fee, an inner voice told him to go home and he realized God wanted to meet him."[23]

This story is not told in any of Hinn's newer books or tapes. Hinn could not have attended Seneca College, anyway. Its admissions policies, obtained from a 1971-1973 course catalog, would have prohibited him from applying for admission to the college without a secondary-school diploma.[24]

When confronted with the falsehood, Hinn backtracked on the account of his schooling. In the October 5, 1992, edition of *Christianity Today*, Hinn says,

> "I never said I was a senior, period. Anywhere. It's not in my book. All I mentioned in my book is that I got saved in high school in February of 1972."[25]

However, on page 28 of *Good Morning, Holy Spirit*, he says, "During my *senior year* at Georges Vanier" (emphasis added). And even as late as 1999, he continues to claim for himself what he denied to *Christianity Today* magazine. In *He Touched Me*, he writes: "During my senior year at Georges Vanier...."[26]

Additionally disturbing is the fact that this high school drop-out frequently portrays himself as having been an excellent student:

"I was very clever in school. I always had high marks."[27]

"Amazingly, the principal really liked me. ... I will never, never, never forget the principal coming in and saying, 'We're gonna pass you this year without exams.'"[28]

"And because I lacked in my personal life, I put everything in my school life."[29]

"I was a good student."[30]

His Bedroom Seminary

However, for the Christian, more objectionable should be the absence of any formal Bible training in Hinn's education. This inadequacy is a critical factor in both his constant theological malpractice (as other chapters in this book detail), and in his appeal to supernatural and divine revelation. Hinn will use his "lack of formal Bible training" as an excuse for his unscriptural convictions and as a way to respond to the criticism.

Despite the clear biblical injunction against a novice being set in a prominent position within the Church (1 Timothy 3:6), the rapid growth of Hinn's ministry precluded him from pursuing a Bible education. During an interview, Hinn told reporter Randy Frame:

"When I begin in the ministry, my problem was I had no training. I had no Bible school training. And, again I don't know why the Lord launched me into a healing ministry almost really overnight. But I do say this, that I have longed for years, I have looked for the chance to have some kind of Bible training of some sort in my life. Yet, it just never seemed to happen. The ministry grew so fast and it's still growing and today we are running some of the largest crowds anywhere in America, plus the large church we have."[31]

In *The Anointing*, Hinn sounds unapologetic for his lack of formal Bible training. He writes: "The Holy Spirit became real to me. He became my Companion. When I opened the Bible,

I knew He was there with me as though He were sitting beside me. He patiently taught me and loved me."[32]

He further explains away his lack of formal Bible training by claiming that during his purported early encounters with the Spirit: "I was receiving an education greater than any university or seminary could offer. My teacher was the Spirit Himself."[33]

It is a wonder then how Hinn can be so mired in heresy.

Christians should not be so willing to excuse Hinn for an insufficient biblical schooling. Apologist Robert M. Bowman, Jr., in his book, *Orthodoxy and Heresy*, amply debunks the idea that a "lack of formal Bible training" absolves one of guilt for repeatedly teaching false doctrine. Bowman writes:

> "Some people, confronted with criticisms of certain teachers in the church, dismiss those criticisms by saying that the teachers in question don't claim to be theologians. The critics, they suggest, are imposing a standard on the teachers that is unfair. ... There is much truth in these observations. Not everyone is a trained theologian and is capable of making all of the distinctions and qualifications that theologians regard as important. It would be unfair to ask everyone involved in ministry to expound in detail on various minor points of doctrine or to discuss subtle points of New Testament Greek grammar. The problem is that certain persons *are* teaching on doctrinal or theological matters beyond their competency."[34]

Bowman further stresses:

> "It is one thing to express errant opinions on theological matters in a private setting. It is another to present oneself to the body of Christ as a teacher and then express the same sort of errant opinions. Especially if people write a book, or distribute cassette tapes of their sermons, or publish a newsletter, in which they offer teaching on doctrinal matters, they have to expect to be held accountable for teaching false doctrine. In some cases, a teacher who is generally sound doctrinally will express a false opinion on doctrine out of sheer

ignorance, and once confronted will gladly retract the error. Such a person should not be criticized or labeled a heretic or a false teacher. On the other hand, ignorance cannot excuse continued teaching of false doctrine. A person who is confronted about teaching doctrinal error and who refuses to retract the error cannot legitimately hide behind the disclaimer of not being a theologian. Nor can someone whose doctrinal teaching is generally unsound hide behind such an excuse."[35]

The Kathryn Kuhlman Connection

Much of what could be said about Hinn's teachings and practices might sound familiar to people who have studied American evangelists over the years. That study would reveal that Hinn's teachings contain very little that is new or original.

Hinn acknowledges that three women "evangelists" made a profound impact on him. The three are Maria Woodworth-Etter, Aimee Semple McPherson, and Kathryn Kuhlman. All three were controversial in ministry, both from within and outside the Church. Each was divorced during her life as a believer, with McPherson having two divorces. None was a good role model for an aspiring evangelist. Out of this threesome, Kuhlman had the greatest influence on Hinn. He has borrowed many of his stage techniques from Kuhlman.

An examination of much of Hinn's material reveals his high regard for Kuhlman. He attended some of her meetings and sang in her stage choir, so he had ample opportunity to observe her. Hinn's books, sermons, video and audio tapes, and magazine interviews are replete with quotations and recollections of the late faith healer. Kuhlman died in 1976, just long ago enough for people to forget her quirky style and flamboyant stage presence.

Hinn became enamored not so much with Kuhlman as with her effect on people. Her ability to control a group fascinated Hinn. Based on viewing films of Kuhlman's services, it would appear that her chief ability was whipping a crowd into a frenzy. An associate of Hinn says that he adored her. It is probably closer to the truth to say he adored what she could do. In his book, *The Anointing*, Hinn presents a glamorous, almost mythical picture of parts of Kuhlman's life.

The Source

Also in the volume, Hinn tells about going to Kuhlman's meetings, and then admits,

> "I had been in the ministry only three months and I had never seen anything like it. ... I went back to Canada and thought about it. 'I'm going to try this,' I said."[36]

Hinn's notion hardly sounds like the call of God. Imagine Paul saying, "Boy, I have watched that Peter get the job done. I am going to try that."

Later, Hinn writes,

> "As I've said for many years, Kathryn Kuhlman was a minister of the Gospel whom I followed very closely."[37]

After watching footage of Kuhlman's meetings and comparing her method and message with Hinn's, one can conclude that Hinn sounds like he is regurgitating many of her statements, mimicking her style, and copying her practices. For example, there is video footage of her teaching "slaying in the spirit" from Acts 9. It is obvious that Hinn's view of that topic is not straight from heaven, but straight from Kuhlman.

In *The Anointing*, Hinn says he learned about "holy laughter" from Kuhlman.[38] "Holy laughter," or "laughing in the Spirit," occurs when one "under the power" gets hysterical with laughter and the laughter spreads to others in the meeting. Hinn practices that just as Kuhlman did. He tried it and it works.

Laughter is contagious. Anyone who has ever been in a group where someone starts really laughing and that laughter spreads out to the rest, knows the experience. Holy laughter is just more group dynamics lifted from Kuhlman's repertoire. The Bible does not once refer to "laughing in the Spirit."

Lifting the Cover

Kuhlman was no model of the Christian life, even though Hinn says God used her "to teach and inspire me in those early days."[39]   What he learned from Kuhlman was a workable package of group dynamics that she herself might not have understood. Her biographer and friend, the late Jamie Buckingham, took off the wraps in *Daughter of Destiny*. There was much in Kuhlman's life to hide, and Buckingham works overtime to smooth out and paper over her faults and foibles.

Buckingham makes light of Kuhlman's materialism, but reveals that she had a special vault in her basement to store her valuables. She died with considerable wealth, but constantly told her followers that she had "died to self." She spent huge amounts on clothes while paying her staff notoriously low salaries.[40]

After her death, her fortune did not go back into Christian work. A small portion of her more than $2 million personal estate was divided among 20 employees of Kuhlman's foundation and three relatives. The balance was bequeathed to a couple who had entered into Kuhlman's life a scant eight months before her death.[41]

Even more disturbing is Kuhlman's 1938 marriage to evangelist Burroughs Waltrip, who abandoned his wife and children to marry Kuhlman. Six years later, Kuhlman abandoned him.[42] She spent her life refusing to speak to others about these issues and treated the events as though they had never happened. Kuhlman lied about her age, and while in her late 60s made her announcer introduce her as a "young woman." Even from the grave, she refuses to disclose her age, as her burial plaque provides only the date of her death. Conspicuously absent is the date of her birth.

Another Divorce for Kathryn?

In a 1999 book, Hinn appears to be distancing himself from Kuhlman, the woman whom he has said meant so much to his life and ministry. Here Hinn writes:

"Many times, I've been asked, 'Benny, tell me about Miss Kuhlman. What was she like?' They are surprised when I say, 'Oh, I never had the opportunity to meet Kathryn personally.' Looking back on my journey to Pittsburgh, I believe what happened that day was in God's providence. As I told members of my staff recently, had I met Kathryn it is possible that I would have forever believed she gave the anointing to me, or that God may have used her in some way to transfer it to me."[43]

This, now, from the man whose life and ministry was so indebted to Kuhlman's influence. In the past, Hinn visited her grave at Forest Lawn Cemetery in Southern California, where he claims her anointing still lingers — even to the place where people are actually healed from visiting the grave.[44] Hinn also says Kuhlman appears to him in dreams and visions. In one report, she supposedly gave him a revelation of a heightened level of the miraculous — "greater things for the glory of God" — coming to his ministry.[45] (A fuller treatment of the bizarre claims made by Hinn about Kuhlman's influence in his life and ministry can be found in Chapter 13.)

If Hinn is truly beginning to downplay the significance of Kuhlman in his ministry, one can only wonder if Oral Roberts will be next. A three-hour video, *Miracles: Yesterday, Today & Forever*, produced in 1994 by Hinn's organization, emphasizes the influence of Roberts' life and healing ministry on Hinn and suggests that Roberts has passed his mantle to Hinn.

Avoid the Myth Maker

To some people, even some professing Christians, facts are like putty, to be molded into whatever shape they want. They are immune to the command, "Lie not to one another" (Colossians 3:9). Despite this, sometimes the bending of the truth is amusing enough that others dismiss or excuse it.

A myth can be defined as a tale, a legend, or a fable. It is the opposite of truth. The Apostle Paul warns: "Neither give heed to fables" (*muthos*/myths) (1 Timothy 1:4). The Apostle Peter declares as well: "We have not followed cunningly devised fables" (*muthos*/myths) (2 Peter 1:16). Again, Paul warns of a day when "they shall turn away their ears from the truth, and shall be turned unto fables" (*muthos*/myths) (2 Timothy 4:4).

Gerhardt Kittel calls myth, "The fairy tale or marvel as distinct from credible history."[46] He also emphasizes: "The position of the New Testament regarding what it calls myth is quite unequivocal. The only occurrences of the term are in negative statements. There is obviously a complete repudiation of myth. It is the means and mark of an alien proclamation, especially of the error combated in the past."[47] Finally, he stresses: "The firm rejection of myth is one of the decisions characteristic of the New Testament. Myth is a pagan category ... myth as such has no place on Biblical soil ... as a direct impartation of religious truth."[48]

Christians have a right to expect clear, consistent testimony from a man who says that his salvation experience was foretold in an angelic vision and that he regularly hears revelation knowledge directly from God.

Hinn has proven himself to be unfaithful in the little things and the big things. His message is not to be trusted. His methods are borrowed. His spiritual gift — his "anointing" — is counterfeit. His doctrine and practice are suspect.

"Get Ready for Revelation Knowledge"

James 3:1 warns, "Let not many of you become teachers, my brethren, knowing that as such we shall incur a stricter judgment." Benny Hinn's theological revelations strike at the very core of Christianity. One can never be sure if Hinn will generate tritheism, modalism, or Arianism when he speaks — under alleged divine unction — about God's nature. Occasionally, he even makes a Trinitarian point.

Not only does Hinn put great confidence in his revelations, but he expects everyone else to do so. They are not mere opinions. They are the very words of God:

> "Revelation knowledge, what is it? It leads you to eternal realities. We're not talking today about some idea or some philosophy. We're talking about an eternal reality."[1]

With Hinn's "revelation knowledge" comes the ability to reveal things about God never known before:

> "Well, let me tell ya — we're not here to tell ya things you've heard for the last fifty years."[2]

> "Please, please, please don't think OCC is here to repeat something you've heard for the last fifty years. ... If we quit giving you new revelations, we're dead."[3]

Historically, we have seen this appeal to special spiritual insight used to produce doctrine contrary to the Word of God. This is true not only in the traditional cults, but also in the mystical Christian movement (MCM).[4] It is also true of Hinn.

Out of these "revelations," Hinn has repeatedly promoted a blatantly defective view of the Triune Godhead, a defective Christology, and a defective view of man. Yet, despite his assertion that these revelations are something "you hadn't heard before," they are, for the most part, a rehash of the standard Word-Faith party line that was made popular by the writings of Essek W. Kenyon.[5]

As do the mystical Christian teachers, Hinn wishes to make his eternal realities compatible with Scripture:

> "If I say something that's not in the Bible — believe the Bible, don't believe me. So let's make a deal, can we? That if I say anything that is not in this book, dismiss it. But if it's in this book, then pay attention to it! ... I told you earlier, if I say something [and] the Bible says something else, you believe the Bible. Say, 'The Bible is always right.'"[6]

But, in fact, such a statement is merely lip service to the accuracy of the Scripture. The doctrines examined here are not found in the Bible, yet Hinn's followers accepted them without question.

"Now are you ready for some *real* revelation knowledge?"[7]

One need not listen long to Hinn's tapes before hearing his unorthodox teaching on the nature of the Triune God:

> "God the Father is a person and He is a triune being by Himself separate from the Son and the Holy Ghost. ... God the Father is a person, God the Son is a person, God the Holy Spirit is a person, but each of them is a triune being by Himself. If I can shock you, and maybe I should, there are nine of them. ... God the Father is a person with His own personal spirit, with His own personal soul and His own personal spirit body."[8]

> "God the Father is a person separate from the Holy Ghost. Totally separate. ... Do you know the Holy

Spirit has a soul and a body separate from that of Jesus and the Father?... God the Father then is a triune being within Himself. He's a person, He has His own Spirit, He has a soul. ... A soul is my intellect. ... God thinks. ... separate from the Son and separate from the Holy Ghost. ... God the Father is a separate individual from the Son and the Holy Ghost, who is a triune being who walks in a spirit body and He has hair ... has eyes ... has a mouth ... has hands."9

Cult researcher Bill Alnor submitted copies of the above transcript to two professors at the Philadelphia College of the Bible in October 1990 and their opinions were the same: Hinn's view of God in the message is "heretical." Gary Johnson, professor of Church History, said:

"For one thing his concept of the Father, the Son, and the Holy Spirit each having a spiritual body was condemned at [the councils of] Chalcedon [A.D. 451], Constantinople [A.D. 381] and Nicea [A.D. 325]."10

"He says the Trinity is nine persons and that's heresy. What he's advocating is not a whole lot different than what is advocated by Kenneth Copeland as reported in the book *The Agony of Deceit*."11

According to doctrine professor Dr. Glen Goss:

"He [Hinn] doesn't understand theology. Yes, it's very clearly heretical. Each member of the Trinity is also a Trinity? That's really far out and it's not orthodox in any way, shape or form. He has no theological basis for what he's saying."12

Hinn has no theological basis for his view of God, nor does he have any biblical basis. His view that God the Father and God the Holy Spirit have a body with "eyes, hands, a mouth, etc." is more concurrent with Mormonism than it is with orthodox Christianity. The only way to produce a tri-triune Godhead is with the convoluted logic of Benny Hinn.

While Hinn stresses the personality of the Holy Spirit, he frequently appears to become unclear himself as to the details

of this biblical truth. During a service at Grace World
Outreach Center in St. Louis, part of Hinn's illustration on
the person of the Holy Spirit paralleled the teachings of the
Watchtower Society:

"Listen church, God the Father, God the Son, and God
the Holy Spirit are one. How are they one? You'll never
understand the oneness until you understand the work.
Well, let me say this to you. It's like the sun in the sky.
That's probably the closest thing we can use so we can
understand. And don't try to figure it out, whatever
you do. It's just like the sun. You could say the Father
is like the sun, Jesus is light that comes out of it, and
the Holy Ghost is the heat you feel when you stand
there. But when it comes to the work now, whenever
we see the Father in the Godhead, we see Him having a
special job that the Son and the Holy Ghost do not do,
but the Father only. We see the Father as the great
commander. He's always saying, 'Let there be light.'
'Let's make man in our image.' 'Isaiah, go tell that
king.' 'Moses, go to Pharaoh.' He's always giving
commandments. Say after me, 'The Father is the
commander.' [Congregation repeats.] Now when you
look at Jesus, what is His job? Every time He moves He
is doing, doing, doing, doing. Well, the Father says,
'Let's do.' So the Father says, 'Let there be light.' Jesus
does it. 'Let's make man.' Jesus does it. 'Let's save the
world.' Jesus does it. 'Let's heal their bodies.' Jesus does
it. He's the doer. The Book of Acts says Jesus began to
both do and teach. He, Himself, said 'I came to do the
will of my Father.' So say after me, 'Jesus is the doer.'
[Congregation repeats.] But how about the Holy Spirit?
Every time you see Him, He is the power behind the
doing. Say after me, 'The Holy Spirit is the power.'
[Congregation repeats.] 'He is the power of the
Trinity,' say it. [Congregation repeats.] It's like this,
my dear brother, if I said to someone sitting here,
'Please turn on the lights.' Suppose the lights were off. I
said 'Turn them on.' So the guy goes and puts on the
switch. Watch, I'm the one who said, 'Turn them on.'

He did it. But who brought the light? The electricity. The Father says, 'Switch, put on the switch." Jesus goes and does it. And the electricity, the Holy Spirit, brings it up, shines."[13]

Moreover, Hinn's comments show his ignorance of both theology and science, since the sun's heat is not the sun and the sun's rays are not the sun. As well, electricity is not the light and vice versa. On the other hand, Scripture affirms that each of the three persons of the Godhead is equally God.

In his book, *Good Morning, Holy Spirit*, Hinn makes another incorrect illustration when he writes that the Holy Spirit is "the breath of God,"[14] and a "person."[15] Both of these cannot be true and the Holy Spirit is not God's breath.

Hinn's unorthodoxy goes on: "The first person Adam met was the Holy Ghost. You say, 'Really?' Don't you remember it was the breath that came through him and opened his eyes feeling the breath of the Spirit. He's the first manifestation of the Father to humanity."[16]

Hinn also appears to call into question his own purported visitations from Jesus Christ. In the same message, delivered to Larry Lea's Church on the Rock, Hinn cautioned:

"You say, 'I had a vision of Jesus.' I'm gonna shake you even further now. ... You say, 'I've seen Jesus.' Oh, have you? John saw Him and fell like a dead man. Whom have you seen? You say, 'Really?' Don't you know? He is His Spirit. Jesus hasn't left heaven to meet you anytime yet. But He has sent His Spirit into the earth. He'll come and sup with you through the Holy Ghost. He'll speak to you through the Holy Ghost. He'll manifest His presence through the Holy Ghost. And the Holy Ghost will always testify, and magnify, and glorify Jesus. You say, 'But it looked just like Jesus.' Well, what do you think the Holy Ghost looks like? The Holy Spirit is His Spirit. How often have we closed our eyes and seen a figure in white. You say, 'Who is that?' The Holy Ghost. 'Oh, I didn't know that.' Oh, you should. He is the manifestation of Jesus to your mind. He's the manifestation of Jesus to your spirit."[17]

"So don't question this teaching.
Only the immature question it."

The above quotation comes from a sermon tape titled, "Our Position in Christ." The teaching that Hinn doesn't want questioned is what is commonly known in MCM as the spiritual death of Jesus (SDJ) teaching. Popularized by Kenyon in his book, *What Happened from the Cross to the Throne*, it has been taken up by others and expanded. Hinn has jumped onto the bandwagon.

> "Before He died, I should say, on that cross, something happened to Him which began the wheels of the New Creation moving and that was this: He died spiritually! ... Jesus Christ understood that spiritual death is union with the satanic nature. ... What is spiritual death? Separation from God."[18]

> "He who is the nature of God became the nature of Satan when He became sin."[19]

> "First, He died spiritually, and then He died physically, and He was carried for three days and three nights into the underworld as a prisoner."[20]

> "Jesus Christ knew the only way He would stop Satan is by becoming one in nature with him. ... He [Jesus] did not take my sin, He *became* my sin."[21]

> "Jesus Christ had to die spiritually to understand what it means to be dead spiritually. He could not have been a perfect Savior had He not experienced all you'll ever experience."[22]

According to Hinn, there were two deaths of the cross: a spiritual death, then a physical one. Jesus died first spiritually. At that point He literally took on the nature of (or became one with) Satan. Also at that point, Jesus lost His deity and God the Father deserted Him. Then Jesus died physically and His spirit (which at that time was only the spirit of a man) was taken into hell.

"When Jesus Christ went down to the underworld ... He did not face Satan in hell as God! For had He faced him as God, the devil would have said, 'Not fair. Not fair.' ... If Jesus went to the underworld as the Son of God, He did not need the Holy Ghost then to raise Him from the dead; He would have raised Himself!"[23]

At the end of His three days of torment, it was time for Jesus to be born again!

"He's [Jesus] in the underworld now, God isn't there. The Holy Ghost isn't there, and the Bible says He was 'begotten.' You know what the word 'begotten' means? It means 'reborn.' Do you want another shocker? Have you been begotten? [Congregation shouts "Yes!"] So was He. Don't let anyone deceive you. Jesus was reborn. ... Did the Father leave Him? C'mon, did the Father leave Him? [Congregation shouts "Yes!"] That's death! ... Did the Holy Ghost come back on resurrection morning? [Congregation shouts "Yes!"] That's rebirth! He was reborn! He had to be reborn! ... If he was not reborn, I could not be reborn. ... Everything I've gone through He went there first. [Congregation cheers and applauds.] So don't question this teaching. Only the immature question it."[24]

It is impossible to produce from the Bible, verses that detail any of the above "doctrine." It is only through Hinn's so-called "revelation knowledge" — rehashed Kenyon and a few misapplied biblical texts — that it can be done. Let us now turn our attention to a couple of these verses.

The first example is 2 Corinthians 5:21: "For He hath made Him to be sin for us, who knew no sin; that we might be made the righteousness of God in Him." SDJ advocates say this proves that Jesus took on the sin nature, or Satan's nature.

The second is Matthew 27:46: "And about the ninth hour Jesus cried with a loud voice, saying, 'Eli, Eli, lama sabacthani?' that is to say, 'My God, my God, why hast thou forsaken me?'" Hinn and others claim that this verse demonstrates spiritual death and the turning away of the Father from the Son, causing Jesus to lose His deity.

If the above verses teach what Hinn and others say that they do, then we have at least two serious problems. First, if Jesus had the satanic nature before His physical death, then the sacrificial sin offering was unholy. Yet the sacrifice as typified in the Old Testament and openly revealed in the New must have been Holy and sinless — without spot or blemish. Secondly, if Jesus took on the satanic nature, was forsaken by the Father and lost His deity, then there was a fundamental change in the Godhead. Yet, both Testaments assert that God does not change and specifically singles out Jesus as being the same, past, present, and future.

The confusion generated by 2 Corinthians 5:21 most likely stems from an unclear translation of the Greek word for "sin," *hamartia*. As it is in Hebrew, so it is in Greek that the word for "sin" and "sin offering" is the same. It is the context of the passage that fixes the proper translation of the word (Hebrew: *chatta'ah*; Greek: *hamartia*). In Leviticus, for example, the word *chatta'ah* is translated "sin" 20 times, but is translated "sin offering" 63 times, wherever the context demands it.

When the Old Testament was translated into Greek by the Alexandrian Jews in the third century B.C., the Hebrew word *chatta'ah* was rendered *hamartia* by the translators. Again the context would fix the proper translation.

The Apostle Paul, being schooled in both languages, no doubt followed the same rules of language of the Septuagint translators and used the single Greek word *hamartia* for both sin and sin offering in 2 Corinthians 5:21.[25]

Therefore, we see that the verse could be translated: "For He hath made Him to be a 'sin offering' for us, who knew no sin; that we might be made the righteousness of God in Him." This translation is consistent with the rest of Scripture and with Old Testament typology concerning sacrifice for sin. It also clears up the aforementioned contradictions.[26]

So, we see that this verse cannot be used to teach the spiritual death of Jesus. There is not one verse in the Bible that either states or implies that Jesus died spiritually or united with the satanic nature on the cross or anywhere else.

What of the assertions that Jesus lost His deity when the Father forsook Him on the cross? Christian Research Institute's Brian Onken points out:

> "It is of great importance to note that this passage is not didactic but narrative; that is, this verse in Matthew is not a specific teaching about Christ's atoning work but is rather a record of what transpired before the eyes of witnesses. Caution is needed because, although we have a record of what Christ said, what He meant by these words is open to question."[27]

As previously shown, Christ became the legal substitute for sinners, receiving in His own person the punishment that was due them. As the wrath and judgment of God were unleashed on the Son, the Father could not share the fellowship with Him that they had so long enjoyed. The Son was treated as if He were a sinner, because He was standing in our place. This, however, does not necessitate a change in His nature or that He was essentially severed from God.

T.J. Crawford explains:

> "In order to give its just meaning to His language, we can hardly suppose less than that, amidst His other sufferings, the sensible joys and consolations of His Father's fellowship and countenance were withheld from Him. Nor is it any very difficult matter to conceive that even in the case of the beloved Son of God some such spiritual privation may have been endured. For it is not beyond the bounds of human experience that the favour and love of God should actually be possessed, while no felt support and encouragement are derived from them. Although it be an unquestionable truth that 'the Lord will never leave nor forsake His people,' and that 'nothing can ever separate them from His love,' yet there are times in the history of His most devoted servants, in which we find them bitterly deploring that the light of His gracious countenance is hidden from them, and that they derive

no conscious satisfaction from the joys of His favour and the comforts of His fellowship. May we not say, then, that this was the main source of the Savior's lamentation on the cross? It certainly appears to be the kind of affliction which His words most naturally and obviously suggest."[28]

It is also worthy to note:

"In New Testament times for one to cite the opening words of an Old Testament passage such as Psalms 22 was equivalent to citing the entire passage. We can be sure that these words of Jesus would have been understood by His disciples as equivalent to His saying, 'Remember the 22 Psalm.' Christ's enemies had just quoted another saying from this Psalm in taunting Him, 'He trusted in God; let Him deliver Him now if He will have Him, for He said, "I am the Son of God."' (Matthew 27:43, quoting Psalm 22:8.) This fact would give weight to Jesus citing this Psalm."[29]

Jesus did not die spiritually and there was no change in the nature of the Godhead. Jesus Christ is the same yesterday, today and forever, says Hebrews 13:8. Even the Psalm cited by Jesus Himself proves the contrary. Psalm 22:24, "For he hath not despised nor abhorred the affliction of the afflicted; *neither hath he hid his face from him*; but when he cried unto him, he heard."

Hinn and other Word-Faith teachers would do well to heed the Word of God and repent of the foolish speculation that they erroneously label "revelation knowledge":

"But I say unto you, That every idle word that men shall speak, they shall give account thereof in the day of judgment" (Matthew 12:36).

"So, I'm Benny Jehovah!"[30]

The above quote leads us to yet another theological error of Hinn's: that a born-again person actually becomes God on the earth. True to previous form, this doctrine follows closely Kenyon's *New Creation Realities* and elevates man to deity. It also reduces the position of Jesus Christ of being the unique incarnation of God on the earth by putting believers on the same level as Jesus.

According to Hinn, when a person becomes born again and the Holy Spirit comes to dwell in his spirit, then that person becomes deity, literally a God-man:

> "His Spirit and our spirit man are one, united. There's no separation. It's impossible. The new creation is created after God in righteousness and true holiness. The new man is after God, like God, Godlike, complete in Christ Jesus. The new creation is just like God. May I say it like this? You are the little god on earth running around."[31]

Despite occasional denials that he is teaching that men literally become gods, Hinn continued to use unambiguous words to teach that we do:

> "Say after me: 'Within me, is a God-Man.' Say it again: 'Within me, is a God-Man.' Now, let's say [it] even better than that. Let's say, 'I am a God-Man.' ... This spirit man within me, is God—is a—is a God-Man. Say after me: 'He's born of heaven. He's a super being.'"[32]

> "God came to earth and touched a piece of dust and turned it into a god. ... Are you a child of God? Then you're divine! Then you're not dust anymore. Are you a child of God? Then you're not human!"[33]

That is, Hinn says, a person's spirit is not human. The body is the only thing about the Christian that is human, and that will pass away. However, that part which is really real is the same on earth as Jesus Christ.

> "When you say, 'I am saved,' what are you saying? You're saying, 'I am a Christian.' What does that word mean? It means 'I am anointed.' You know what the word 'anointed' means? It means 'Christ.' When you say, 'I am a Christian,' you are saying, 'I am Messiah' in the Hebrew. I am a little Messiah walking on earth in other words. That's a shocking revelation."[34]

"Now ladies and gentlemen, you are on earth exactly what Jesus was on earth. ... As He is so am I, on earth. ... When you walk, Jesus is walking. When you talk, He's talking. When you move, He's moving."[35]

"When I stand in Christ — I am one with Him; united to Him; one spirit with Him. I am not, hear me, I am not a part of Him, I am Him! The Word has become flesh in me! ... When my hand touches someone, it's the hand of Jesus [that] touches somebody!"[36]

"I [Jesus] loved you enough to become one of ya! And I love you enough to make you one of me!"[37]

If equating believers with Christ is not bad enough, Hinn goes one step further. In one of the most bizarre examples of scripture misinterpretation ever, Hinn wants to give all believers the last name "Jehovah."

"This new man inside of you is just like Jesus — has God's last name. You people missed just what I said. The new man has God's last name. For the Bible says about him, in Isaiah, 'I have surnamed thee.' You all have the same last name, you know that don't you? You know what your last name is? Jehovah. So, I'm Benny Jehovah; Dick Jehovah; have the same Daddy."[38]

The only place that the phrase "I have surnamed thee" occurs in the Bible is Isaiah 45:4. However, the verse has nothing to do with Jehovah giving his children a last name. It has nothing to do with believers whatsoever. Isaiah 45:4 announces: "For Jacob my servant's sake, and Israel mine elect, I have even called thee by thy name: I have surnamed thee, though thou hast not known me."

The antecedent to the word "thee" in the phrase "I have surnamed thee" is Cyrus, King of Persia. One has only to go back to Isaiah 45:1 to see that the subject of conversation is the anointing of Cyrus for the great task of letting the Israelites go back to Israel.

The Hebrew word for "surname" is *kanah* and is often translated "to give flattering titles" (see especially Job

32:21-22). So, for the sake of the descendants of Jacob, elect Israel, God set aside Cyrus for a purpose and gave him a flattering (honorable) title. Yet Hinn has this verse saying that Jehovah has given all believers the last name "Jehovah."

If Hinn will take such a clear-cut verse as this and twist it into such an outlandish interpretation, then it becomes necessary to carefully examine any scriptural assertion that he makes. This is exactly what Christians must do.

It is clear that Hinn's teachings are a theological quagmire emanating from biblical misinterpretation and extrabiblical "revelation knowledge." This has led him to a defective view of the Godhead, a flawed Christology, and a faulty anthropology.

Christians rightly criticize Mormonism when it speaks of men becoming gods, and when they talk about God the Father having a physical body. We throw up our hands in disgust when they use scriptures out of context to try to prove these things. Yet hundreds of thousands of Christians are accepting Hinn's similar pronouncements without question.

There was a time that if believers were equated with being "God on the Earth," or if they were elevated to being a manifestation of Christ on the earth, the cry of blasphemy would have been deafening. It is sad that the lack of biblical knowledge in the contemporary church has brought us to the point that such challenges to orthodoxy are accepted so readily.

It is also sad that a major Christian publisher will accept, publish, quietly re-edit, and defend Hinn's pronouncements.

The Curious Case of Thomas Nelson Publishers

When a publisher has a controversial best-seller, there are several directions it can take. It can ignore the critics and hope the controversy goes away, it can withdraw the book from publication, or it can make corrections to the controversial areas and try to put a positive spin on the whole affair. Thomas Nelson Publishers has chosen to do the latter.

In an article published in *Christian Retailing* magazine titled, "Thomas Nelson Clarifies Hinn's Holy Spirit Book,"

Nelson's Bruce Barbour "called the changes 'clarifications' rather than 'corrections,' because the term 'corrections' makes it look like something was wrong with the first editions. ... Thomas Nelson believes Hinn's theology is correct, but that it should have been stated more clearly. For Thomas Nelson's part, Barbour said 'we should have been more careful in the initial editing.'"[39]

He also told the magazine that "12 to 15 clarifications had to be made because the book led some readers to think that Hinn teaches there are 'three separate Gods.'"[40] Barbour further stated:

> "...it is not that unusual to make clarifications in a book after it has been published, and after the publisher receives feedback from readers. However, he said the intensity of the feedback — and the confusion — concerning Hinn's book makes this occurrence unusual."[41]

Lack of space prohibits a detailed examination of the changes in the book, but we will examine three substantive ones:

- Page 86, paragraph 5. Old: "I am told a little of what the Father looks like." New: "I am told a little of how the Father reveals Himself."
- Page 135, paragraph 4. Old: "And let me add this: Had the Holy Spirit not been with Jesus, He would have sinned." New: "And let me add this: Had the Holy Spirit not been with Jesus, He may have likely sinned."
- Page 146, paragraph 4. Old: "Do you know that every unbeliever is filled with a demon spirit?" New: "Do you know that every unbeliever is greatly influenced by demons?"

It is amazing that Nelson would put its imprimatur on this aberrational theology. By defending Hinn, Nelson is helping Hinn propagate his unorthodox teaching.

The statement in *Christian Retailing* magazine that "12 to 15 clarifications had to be made" is troubling. Thomas

Nelson's senior editor, William D. Watkins,[42] wrote to several of Hinn's early critics. In Nelson's attempt to squelch charges of heresy, Watkins wrote:

> "Enclosed you have a set of these corrections, which contains two groups of material: one group displays the clarifications we made in pencil on the uncorrected book pages; the other group shows those corrections typeset."[43]

Even if there had been only one "clarification" per page, the 12 to 15 number would have been exceeded. However, there are multiple changes on most of the pages. There were at least 10 changes on page 87 alone.

While it may not be unusual to make post-publication changes in a book, those revisions are usually noted. The title page or copyright page will carry a notation that the book has been revised or updated. Beginning with the eighth printing of *Good Morning, Holy Spirit,* many "clarifications" have been made but no revision notices have been included. On two different occasions, bookstore managers were shocked and troubled when this writer told them that the book had been revised and showed them the nature of the revisions. Christians need to be asking Nelson why these revisions were done so quietly. Concerned Christians should also be asking Nelson if they really believe that Hinn's theology is "correct," or are they trying to do some damage control on a best-selling book?

And lastly, Christians should not allow Nelson to turn the controversy into a charismatic vs. anti-charismatic argument. An article in *The Orlando Sentinel* stated that, "[William] Watkins said the criticism rises from a difference between Christians who, like Hinn, are charismatic and those who are reformed."[44]

Many critics of Hinn's theology have Charismatic backgrounds, this writer included. The issue is not spiritual gifts. The issue is extrabiblical "revelation knowledge" vs. the sufficiency of the Holy Scripture.

Perspective

Certainly Hinn is not unique in his approach to Scripture and the Gospel. He is just another powerful voice in the movement trying to push Christianity into a thoroughgoing mysticism.

Those in the mystical Christian movement pay lip service to the accuracy and authority of the Bible, but cast serious doubt on its sufficiency by introducing new doctrines through extrabiblical "revelation knowledge." Hinn and others raise the question: "Has God really told us enough, or do we need newer, more comprehensive revelations?" Scripture makes the claim that in His Word, God has told us everything we need to know pertaining to life and godliness (2 Peter 1:3,4).

Hinn is already experiencing the fact that building a theology on "revelation knowledge" is building on a foundation of shifting sand. First there were the "clarifications" in the book. Now he is supposedly backing off on certain aspects of the SDJ doctrine:

> "Hinn explained: 'I no longer agree that Jesus was born again in Hell. That I did teach. I no longer agree that He went down to the underworld under the control of Satan, which at one time I did teach.' Now, when he teaches the spiritual death of Christ, he only means 'Jesus was separated from the Father.' He said he's dropping this teaching altogether for at least a year, to give himself time to study it further."[45]

If Hinn had only been teaching the SDJ as a doctrine that he believed was derived from Scripture, then the matter could more easily be forgiven. But he did not and it cannot. Hinn taught the SDJ as "revelation knowledge." Statements from revelation knowledge are supposed to be "eternal realities." Discerning Christians must ask Hinn: "Which is untrue, that revelation knowledge is not opinion or philosophy but an eternal reality; or that you ever received revelation knowledge on the SDJ doctrine?"

Christians must hold accountable anyone who names Christ as Savior and publicly teaches the Word of God. Any proclaimer of the Gospel, be he pastor of the smallest church or the most renowned Christian TV evangelist superstar, should be held subject to the Berean test (Acts 17:11).

Such a preacher might contradict himself for several reasons. He might himself be confused. He might be a deceiver. He might be trying to create an impression, a persona, or some other type of image. Or he might be untaught and unable to process detail. One thing is certain, God is not behind the confusion.

The thought of Christians seeking titillation through demonstrations of supernatural power, rather than the truth of God's Word, brings to mind the words of the Apostle Paul:

> "I marvel that ye are so soon removed from him that called you into the grace of Christ unto another gospel: Which is not another; but there be some that trouble you, and would pervert the gospel of Christ. But though we, or an angel from heaven, preach any other gospel unto you than that which we have preached unto you, let him be accursed. As we said before, so say I now again, If any man preach any other gospel unto you than that ye have received, let him be accursed" (Galatians 1:6-9).

3

Born Again, Again and Again

Benny Hinn's conversion to the Christian faith is equally as confusing as his theology. Hinn has given a number of different accounts describing his conversion experience. There are varying and significant differences between cassette tapes containing Hinn's testimony and those found in his writings, including his early books, *Good Morning, Holy Spirit* and *The Anointing*.

The most standardized version of his conversion is found in his 1990 best-seller, *Good Morning, Holy Spirit*. Here Hinn indicates his conversion occurred in February 1972 during a morning prayer meeting at his secondary or high school library with "twelve or fifteen" of his fellow students.[1]

Several years before his book was published, Hinn was describing a conversion which he said had taken place years prior to 1972. In a 1983 message in St. Louis, he related a simple story of how he was converted right after his immigration to Toronto from Israel in 1968:

> "Then in 1968, I was only about 13 or 14, we moved to Canada and it was in Canada that I was born again right after '68. ... Someone witnessed to me and I got saved — right then — which was right after '68."[2]

Two years prior to the conversion narration he delivered in St. Louis, Hinn was promoting still another varied account. In the 1981 publication, *The PTL Family Devotional*, printed by the PTL Network, the January 17 devotional is by Benny Hinn. His photograph appears with it. He is identified as: "International Evangelist, Healing Ministry."

Here Hinn writes: *"I got saved in Israel in 1968."* (See page 42 for a reproduction of Hinn's devotional/testimonial.)

The varied accounts prompt the question: Does Hinn really know where or when he was converted? Yet Hinn's confusion is not only limited to the time and place of his conversion. Conflicting details of even his more widely used, February 1972, rendition are easily observed.

In *Good Morning, Holy Spirit*, Hinn tells of a dream the night before his conversion in which an angel rescued him from a deep, endless chasm. After his escape from the abyss, Hinn says the angel "dropped me on Don Mills Road — right at the corner of Georges Vanier School. He left me inches from the wall of the school, right beside a window."[3]

In a 1987 taped message, Hinn told of an angel who took him *inside* the high school room where he was saved:

> "And I was now with the angel flying. I saw myself in this dream flying with the angel holding my hand and he took me right to my school. The next morning at ten of eight I got saved *in the exact spot* where the angel took me in a dream. ... This angel takes me by the hand in my dream and I'm *in my school*."[4]

In the taped version, the particulars of Hinn's invitation to the prayer meeting also conflict with his later narratives. Hinn first told of being led by a lone schoolmate from his locker to a room off the library:

> "I go into the school, open my locker, get my books, a girl shows up called Michelle. ... Took me by the hand and pulled me to the prayer meeting. ... and I tried to stop her, please understand when you stutter you can't talk, you'd just better keep quiet and just follow. ... She takes me to a room in the exact corner where the angel had dropped me in my dream. I get into this room and there's six fellas. ... One of them called Bob Tadman. ... Another fella called Paul Pynkoski. ... All I know was I was feeling something and I said, 'Jesus.' I remember my words were, 'Come back.' I didn't know what to say. Nobody told me, say 'Come into my heart.' So I said, 'Come back.' When I said come back this feeling

just went, shhhhhhhhhh. And when it did I said take
my life. And from that day till this I've never been the
same."[5]

In *Good Morning, Holy Spirit*, Hinn tells of a group of
students who invited him to a prayer meeting. Michelle, the
sole player in the 1987 account, is not mentioned. Hinn
writes:

> "As I sat there [in the library] not even thinking about
> the dream, a small group of students walked over to my
> table. ... They were the ones who had been pestering
> me with all this Jesus talk. They asked me to join the
> morning prayer meeting."[6]

Later, in the meeting, Hinn remembers: "I don't know
why I said it. ... I repeated those words again and again, 'Lord
Jesus come back. Lord Jesus come back.'" He then adds
something missing from the cassette tape account: "Suddenly
I saw Jesus with my own eyes."[7]

As Hinn assembles his narratives, he has repeatedly
demonstrated a propensity to misstate or confuse facts stated
in previous accounts of the same event. Perhaps his problem
stems from an inability to accurately recall what he said in his
earlier versions of a story. Yet it appears that Hinn — or his
editors — have begun to finally make an effort to stay
consistent.

A subsequent description of the event, as told in his 1999
autobiography, *He Touched Me*, now more closely parallels the
account found in *Good Morning, Holy Spirit*. Hinn writes in
this new volume:

> "The next morning I awoke early and rushed off to
> school before class began. I needed to study in the
> library. I was seated at a large table, concentrating on
> my work, when a small group of students approached
> me. Immediately, I knew they were the same ones who
> had been giving me all this 'Jesus talk.' 'Would you like
> to join us in our morning prayer meeting?' one of them
> asked. They pointed to a room that was just off the
> library. I thought, *Well, perhaps I'll get them off my back if*

I agree. After all, one little prayer meeting isn't going to hurt me."8

Whether one accepts Hinn's former narrative of a single-student encounter at a school locker or his latter evolved tale of a multi-student confrontation in the school library, it is significant to note that none of the key players mentioned by Hinn remembers the meeting where Hinn says he was converted. During interviews and conversations with several high school friends, none could recall how, when, or under what circumstances Hinn was converted. Everyone assumed a conversion, but none remembers Hinn ever giving them details.

Regardless of which report Hinn says is true, the more serious concern is lack of a clear Gospel presentation at Hinn's "prayer meeting" conversion. Each and every version is grossly inadequate when it comes to this vital issue. Hinn's current description of the episode states:

> "Suddenly, every member of the group raised their hands toward heaven and began to pray in languages I'd never heard before. My eyes became the size of saucers. These were students I had known in my classes — now talking to God with sounds I did not understand. ... My mind flashed back to Bob in the kiosk, saying, 'You've got to meet Jesus. You've got to meet Him!' Meet Him? I thought I already knew Him. ... In the middle of the room, I closed my eyes and spoke four words that changed my life forever. Out loud I said, 'Lord Jesus, come back.' I had no idea why those were the only words that came out of my mouth. Again, I said, 'Lord Jesus, come back.' ... Then I said to the Lord, 'Come into my heart.' And what a glorious moment that was! His power was cleansing me from the inside out. I felt absolutely clean and pure. Suddenly, in a moment of time, I saw Jesus. There He was. Jesus, the Son of God."9

As his classmates babbled in tongues, Hinn suggests a genuine conversion experience. Absent, however, from the event is any distinct presentation and understanding of man's sinfulness and God's offer of forgiveness through the sacrifice of Jesus Christ, our need for repentance and faith, and the cost of our faith and obedience. Hinn's chronicle is nothing but a mystical, easy-believe conversion. But, perhaps this, like other facets of his life profile, may well change and evolve in the coming years and in its retelling.

Confusing Family Conversions

Hinn's confusion does not stop with his own conversion testimony. In 1984, he self-published *War in the Heavenlies*. In this early volume, Hinn describes struggles with his family's unwillingness to respond to the Gospel. "One night...," he writes, "the Lord spoke to me **instantly** by revelation." The Lord's "revelation" informed Hinn that he was "the KEY" to the salvation of his family members and that he should "Take Authority."[10] Hinn then writes:

> "The Lord opened my eyes one night to a great revelation that brought salvation to my entire family. My mom, my dad, five brothers and two sisters came to the Lord in a most miraculous way *all at the same time* because of what I began to understand."[11]

Six years later, in *Good Morning, Holy Spirit*, he again addressed the redemption of family members:

> "One by one, they came to me and began to ask questions. They'd say, 'Benny, I've been watching you. This Jesus is real, isn't He?' My sister Mary gave her heart to the Lord. And within the next few months my little brother Sammy got saved. Then came Willie."[12]

He then writes that in April 1975, on an "unforgettable night" he "opened the Scripture and led [his] parents to the saving knowledge of the Lord Jesus Christ." Then, following the conversion of his parents, his brothers Mike, Henry, and Chris "got saved."[13]

"All at the same time" or "One by one" over a period of several months — which account is accurate? And as with his own personal testimony, Hinn's confusion of his parents' conversion is not just limited to the time and place of conversion, but conflicting details are likewise conspicuous.

The initial conversion account, as detailed in *War in the Heavenlies*, tells of his family's resistance to the Gospel wherein Hinn, by "revelation," found himself to be the key to his parents' salvation. He was to "take authority," and he immediately did that. By doing so, his parents, along with all of his brothers and sisters, "came to the Lord." Boldness and "authority" mark the first conversion story. Hinn "took authority."

However, the story and the picture later changed drastically in *Good Morning, Holy Spirit*. As noted above, although Hinn often claims direct revelation from God, his memory again obviously fails him here.

Hinn wrote in *Good Morning, Holy Spirit* that one "unforgettable night" he opened the Bible and led his parents "to the saving knowledge of the Lord Jesus Christ." Here he now is clear to give the precipitating factors as:

- They came to hear him preach at a church service,
- At home they asked: "how can we become like you?" and
- His father was convinced by his preaching.[14]

In this 1990 or second version, there is nothing about taking "authority" and Hinn says he "tiptoed" into his parents' house hoping not to encounter them for fear of their displeasure. In fact, Hinn recounts that he drove the streets of Toronto until after two o'clock in the morning to avoid facing his mother and father. When he saw his parents waiting for him, he was "startled," "began to tremble," and described his condition as "even worse" than being "panic-stricken."[15] So according to his best-selling publication, it is timidity, fear, and surprise — *and a total lack of "taking authority"* — that mark the second story. The only commonality between the two vastly different versions is that they both occurred at night. The other details are totally different.

And then, some years later, Hinn would revisit the description of his parents' conversion — only to further muddy the episode. Hinn appeared on the May 12, 1999 installment of Trinity Broadcasting Network's *Praise the Lord* show. As the program progressed, he digressed into unfounded biblical interpretations of the demonic and a wild tale of the conversion of his father, which found him mired in more documented lies and fabrications.

Hinn apparently now has three conversion stories for his deceased father, just as there are three contradictory conversion stories for himself.

In Hinn's third attempt to describe his father's conversion, there again is no mention of "taking authority." But here, too, his parents' attendance of a church service to hear young Hinn preach also falls by the wayside. There are now new wrinkles and new details totally unlike the previous two reports. In fact, the father's conversion in this new story is totally different by way of Hinn having to *destroy a mysterious black book* that had amazing properties. But let Hinn tell the story as he did that evening on the TBN broadcast:

> "My father, right before he got saved, he used to always enjoy smoking a hubbly-bubbly. Hubbly-bubbly is a big water bottle that you smoke and it brings — it causes bubbles. Well, he brought this hubbly-bubbly thing from Israel to Canada. And when he quit using it 'cause he had a new one, he stuck some stuff in it and put a book in it. A little book in it. I prayed for my parents to get saved for a long time, nothing happened. One night in prayer, the Lord said, 'Go destroy the book!' Well, I knew I could not because it was inside this bottle. So the Lord said, 'Destroy the bottle!' I said, 'Lord, if my daddy finds out, I'm in trouble.' That's what I said to God. And the convicting power of the Holy Spirit was so strong, I had to go and smash that thing. Now saints, you believe this; you don't, it don't matter. Because I'm going to tell you what happened. I—I—I destroyed that hubbly-bubbly thing, when my daddy was sleeping, took the book, threw it in the fireplace, it would not burn. I'm telling you, that book would not burn. Now I'd only heard about those things happening. I thought they were lying to me. I

have preachers talk about — oh, yeah, bunch of — I saw it. So I thought, 'Now, come on.' So I'm looking at this thing in the fireplace not burning. So I picked up a little thing there by the — by the — by the fireplace and took the book back out with these tongs. And that thing, not even smoke on it. Ahh, now that can't be, come on, you know, this is not a dream here. It was paper, just like any book. Threw it back in. That thing just laid there with the — with the fire and the fire was hot in there. And something said to me, something said to me, 'Say in the name of Jesus.' And when I said, 'In the name of Jesus,' that thing burned. But the biggest miracle was my — my dad and mom were saved the next day. And — and this is when I began realizing the importance of destroying things that can keep demons in our homes."[16]

The Importance of Truth

In all of this, we must never lose sight of the importance of truth. God the Father is a God of truth (Deuteronomy 32:4). Jesus the Son is truth (John 14:6). The Holy Spirit is the Spirit of truth (John 15:26). However, the Apostle Paul warned that people would turn from truth to fables and lies (2 Timothy 4:4). Anyone claiming to represent God should tell the truth at all times. There should be no question about their honesty and genuineness. The spokesman for Hinn's ministry, David Brokaw, currently speaks to the media for him. Hinn is wise to have a public spokesman because he constantly contradicts himself and cannot keep his stories straight. Brokaw told the news media that "critics have hounded the pastor but have yet to turn up evidence of any impropriety."[17]

Is Brokaw's remark truthful? It is, but only if you exclude Hinn's lies, fabrications, myths, exaggerations, fables, tall tales, and unbiblical teachings, all of which have been documented.

The dictionary defines truth as: "The quality or state of being true. ... sincerity, genuineness, honesty. ... correctness, accuracy."[18] That which is true corresponds with reality and facts.

In the Greek New Testament, the word used for truth is *alethes*. Akin to it is *alethinos*. Both are adjectives. W.E. Vine describes the meanings: "actual, true to fact, ... of things, true, conforming to reality, ... denotes true in the sense of real, ideal, genuine; ... of Christ, ... God's words."[19]

Vine then explains the verb form (*aletheuo*): "signifies to deal faithfully or truly with anyone ... Eph. 4:15, 'speaking the truth;' Gal. 3:16, 'I tell (you) the truth,' where probably the Apostle is referring to the contents of his Epistle."[20]

Greek authority Kenneth S. Wuest says this about those who twist or refuse the truth:

> "When people avert their ears from the truth, they lay themselves open to every Satanic influence, and are easily turned aside to error. Instead of being in correct adjustment to the truth, namely, that of seeking it for the purpose of appropriating it, these people have put themselves out of adjustment and have been consequently wrenched out of place. They have become dislocated, put out of joint. Like a dislocated arm which has no freedom of action, they have given themselves over to a delusion which incapacitates them for any independent thinking along religious lines which they might do for themselves."[21]

God wants truth externally as well as deep within us (Psalm 51:6). If we cannot trust men who claim to be men of God to tell the truth, whom can we trust?

Apologist Craig Hawkins reminds us:

> "God is not glorified nor Christianity benefited by Christians, no matter how well-meaning, who proclaim untruthfulness, even in the attempt to defend and advance the truth."[22]

_____ January 17

The Person Of The Holy Spirit

"He that spared not his own Son, but delivered him up for us all, how shall he not with him also freely give us all things?"
Romans 8:32

I got saved in Israel in 1968, but the person of the Holy Spirit didn't become real to me until 1973 at a Katherine Kuhlman meeting. I had heard of the Holy Spirit, had received the baptism, spoken in tongues, but every time I heard Him mentioned, it was in relation to the gifts. I had never heard the Holy Spirit, Himself, mentioned as a real person.

While we waited that night to hear Miss Kuhlman, I could feel the presence of the Lord. I literally shook at His closeness, and it became more intense. When Katherine came out on the platform, I felt a rush of wind. There were no open windows or doors, it was the Holy Spirit sweeping over the auditorium.

She began by asking, "Do you know Him?" I knew she meant the Holy Spirit, and I knew I didn't know Him. Tears started streaming down my cheeks as I asked the Lord to take my life and use it. That day I was introduced to the Holy Spirit, the Third Person in the Holy Trinity. I felt like I was charged with electricity. This experience caused me to remember a similar experience I had as a child. I had seen a vision of Christ and felt this same sensation, one of power, excitement, and expectation. I spent hours in prayer and communion with my new found friend. Even the speech impediment I was born with disappeared, causing my parents to become believers. Discover for yourself this mighty, comforting person, the Holy Spirit.

Benny Hinn
International Evangelist
Healing Ministry

The PTL Family Devotional, entry for January 17
published: December 1981

The Miraculous Claims of Benny Hinn

There is no doubt that lies sell and are more popular than truth in this day and age.

Benny Hinn is a phenomenon of our times. Sadly, many Christians demand heroes and icons, and for many of them, Hinn answers the call. His books and television broadcasts are full of self-serving tributes to his claimed spiritual stature and impact. In spite of his many goofs, gaffes, and media troubles, he still manages to enchant people. False prophecy, heresy, and necromancy do not slow the *Hinn Express*. He continues to sweep thousands off their feet — literally, as his followers succumb and are willing to fall on command.

Hinn claims not only to transmit the supernatural, but also to have, himself, been a recipient of divine healing from a severe stuttering problem. However, those who knew Hinn during his youth in Toronto can't recall a speech impediment as severe as he says he had.

The Stutterer

Hinn describes himself during his teen years as growing up in Toronto, Ontario, as a lonely young man with few friends. He says his "stuttering problem" made him shy and reclusive:

> "It destroys your image. ... brother, that's it, no friends, nobody talks to you, and if you do talk to anybody they're gonna mock you."[1]

> "I was stricken in early childhood by a severe stutter that made oral communication unbelievably difficult,

almost impossible. ... I was a loner — quiet, shy and uncertain."[2]

"Benny Hinn had stuttered *all* his life."[3]

"Now when I grew up, I stuttered so bad that nobody would talk to me. Because when they did, they could not make out what I was saying."[4]

"If I'd tried to speak, words just didn't come out."[5]

"From my earliest childhood I was afflicted with a severe stutter. The smallest amount of social pressure or nervousness triggered my stammering, and it was almost unbearable."[6]

"For twenty-one years of my life, for twenty-one years of my life, I stuttered. For twenty-one years of my life I couldn't talk. And now I begin to preach so fast, I spoke so perfectly that I was telling myself, 'slow down, slow down, slow down, slow down.' Do you know why I speak so fast sometimes? I'm not aware of doing it. It's because for twenty-one years I couldn't talk."[7]

"Because of my stutter, I didn't get into many conversations."[8]

"With my severe stuttering problem, I knew that it would be useless to argue with the usher."[9]

Hinn says God commissioned him to preach the Gospel, but he protested, "Lord, you know I can't talk." Hinn then says that his "severe stutter" was eliminated when he stood up to preach for the first time to a church youth group in Oshawa, Ontario. This purportedly happened December 7, 1974, nearly three years after his conversion in February 1972.[10]

During that time, Hinn had contact with many people, including friends he made at a church called The Catacombs. At this church, Hinn performed with a group that sang and did interpretive dancing. Hinn also was in regular contact with people who would have noticed his stutter.

Hinn has made public a September 18, 1992, letter from Friar Henri, Director of the College des Freres in Jaffa.[11] Friar Henri taught Hinn religion there in the early 1960s. In his letter, Friar Henri states that as a child Hinn stuttered. Nonetheless, not one person interviewed about their contact with Hinn in Toronto, including people he named in his testimony, recalled him having a severe stutter. The only allusion to a speech complication was a reference to Hinn's jumbling of words when he would speak rapidly while anxious or under stress. These people attributed his speech difficulties more to difficulties with the English language.

David Lockwood, who was youth pastor at Trinity Assembly of God in Oshawa, remembers meeting Hinn at a Kathryn Kuhlman appearance in Pittsburgh. Lockwood is the man who invited Hinn to address the youth group, called Shilo Fellowship, on December 7, 1974, the night Hinn says he was freed from stuttering. "I can't recall him stuttering," Lockwood said.[12]

Jim McCalister was co-pastor of The Catacombs church, which met every Thursday evening in downtown Toronto at St. Paul's Cathedral. The Catacombs grew out of the efforts of Merv Watson, a school music teacher. The nucleus of the fellowship was young people from the Jesus People movement of the mid-1970s. Hinn and schoolmates from Georges Vanier Secondary School regularly attended services there. McCalister, who now lives in Florida, said he did not remember Hinn as a stutterer, but that he "spoke very rapidly and he wasn't always with it. Benny was a little bit of a problem to me in terms of his exuberance for anything that was a little bit frothy."[13]

Watson remembers Hinn, too, but not as a stutterer. "When Benny got excited, he had kind of a repetitive thing, like: uh, uh, the, the, uh. But to the extent that he describes it, I was quite surprised. Because it wasn't that pronounced that it was difficult for him to speak. He would get excited, but, you know, we all get a little tongue-tied."[14]

Also during the time frame Hinn asserted to be a stutterer, Watson further recalled: "We used Benny in a production where he shared the dramatic antiphonal declaration of a Psalm which required clear speech and clear rhythm."[15]

Mike MacLean was another personal friend of Hinn's during The Catacombs years. MacLean roomed with Hinn during a church trip to London, England in 1974. When MacLean was asked if Hinn had a stutter, he said, "No, in fact I can remember saying to my wife when I read [Hinn's] book, 'Do you recall Benny having a stuttering problem?'" He added, "The biggest thing that threw me in the book — the one comment I made immediately — was the stuttering. He talked as if he could hardly communicate."[16]

When MacLean was asked what happened at Oshawa, he responded: "It was one of the first meetings he [Hinn] had, people were just falling over."[17]

Paul Pynkoski, whom Hinn identifies as being present at his conversion experience, said, "I don't remember a stutter of any pronouncement."[18]

A Georges Vanier Secondary School administrator does not recall Hinn stuttering, but said he was someone who "loved to perform." Even after 20 years, this administrator recalls Hinn stopping him in the hallway to remind him of an interpretive dance program he was performing in. He remembered Hinn asking him, "Are you going to come and see me dance?"

Hinn told Norman Snider in the *Toronto Globe and Mail Fanfare* magazine: "'I'm an artist,' he told me in a quiet voice. 'I've always been an artist. And people want drama in a situation like this.'"[19]

In a *Toronto Globe and Mail* article dated December 25, 1976, Hinn told reporters Peter Whelan and Aubrey Wice that his call was based on his power to knock people over. The article relates: "On December 7, 1974, he first spoke in public at Trinity Pentecostal Church in Oshawa."

Then Hinn's own words: "I held up my hands to pray and the 100 people present fell on the floor. That's when I became aware of my tremendous power." It is noteworthy that he told Whelan and Wice nothing about being freed from stuttering, which he now cites as the prime event in his call to the ministry.[20]

Perhaps disclosure of the statements by Hinn's high school classmates and of the early newspaper articles raised his ire. Hinn went on the *Praise the Lord* show with the specific purpose of denouncing his critics and their declarations. Hinn told the viewing audience:

> "And then people begin to say things that aren't true, it must be addressed and we need to come and say, 'That's not true.' ... One of them said, 'Well, he never did stutter.' I had to produce documents to show that I did."[21]

Here again, Hinn exhibits his ability to deceive, distort and misquote — and then easily respond to a straw man argument. Hinn's shyness or reticence as a child was never questioned, only the story that he was healed of stuttering at age 21 in Canada.

Hinn then implies that numerous affidavits are available to refute PFO's findings. On the program he stated:

> "It's really so sad that I had to get 25 students, who knew me when I was a teenager in school, to sign affidavits to say, 'He did stutter.'"[22]

He also later enlisted the support of his friend Stephen Strang. In a *Charisma* magazine editorial, Strang wrote that Hinn "has obtained numerous affidavits from the people with firsthand knowledge of his childhood."[23]

Despite requests for these documents, these "numerous affidavits" never have been produced. It most likely is a safe judgment to maintain that the "affidavits" never existed. In a later issue of *Charisma*, Hinn himself said, "But my family will tell you that I stuttered, and many friends who knew me back then are ready to sign affidavits that I stuttered."[24]

In October 1992 and June 1993, Hinn claimed he *had* "numerous affidavits" to confirm his stuttering as a teen and young man. Then in August 1993, he said only that he had friends *ready* to sign affidavits.

Faced with a lack of evidence for his tale of a miraculous healing, his claim was finessed even more. He said in the *Charisma* interview:

> "I did stutter right up until the Lord healed me at the age of 21. I would stutter terribly when I was asked to say something in public, or when I was in the presence of my dad or some other authority figure. *The only time I didn't stutter was when I prayed or when I was with people I was comfortable with. So maybe some acquaintances don't remember me stuttering because I didn't stutter in their presence.*"[25]

Hinn tried, albeit inadequately, to face and answer the impartial and collaborated testimony of former friend's recollections of young Benny Hinn as a man who loved to perform and be in the limelight. A perspective which, years later, Hinn himself would (perhaps unknowingly) admit.

While Hinn continues to assert what he labels "a horrible stuttering problem"[26] and still maintains he was a reclusive, shy, backward stutterer as a child, Hinn now admits that as a boy he put on shows, productions, and song-and-dance routines.[27] He tells how he loved to strut among his mother's family and rattle off memorized parts from TV shows. He writes:

> "At their house I became an extrovert. 'When are you going to put on the show?' my little cousins begged. They were talking about a skit, or a 'production' I organized every year during our visit. During those years there was a popular television comedy program in the region titled, *Doctor, Doctor, Follow Me!* We did our own version of the show — complete with song-and-dance routines. You should have seen us — me, Willie, Chris and our cousins entertaining a room full of cheering, exuberant relatives."[28]

At his relative's home, gone is the fear and reclusive behavior that he claimed dominated his youth. Just like the way his teenage friends remember him in Canada. A showman — sometimes rattling off memorized material — not the fearful, tongue-tied, shy, inhibited, reclusive, backward child Hinn repeatedly claims to have been.

Hinn goes on to say, "When I was seventeen or eighteen, I believed that some day I would go into politics, or perhaps find employment in the travel industry."[29] Both occupations are quite ill-suited for a young man allegedly crippled with a shattered self-image and humiliation.

Flight of Fantasy

Hinn also tells stories that indicate he has tremendous supernatural powers. Even his critics don't always know that he's telling a fantasy version of an event. Truth is sacrificed for impression as exaggeration takes over.

In May 1983, Hinn and five others survived the crash of a small airplane. Hinn has led people to believe that he escaped injury and that through his prayers and actions another passenger had an injured eye restored. Hinn creates this impression by what he says and leaves out. He gives the distinct impression that the healed man walked away from the crash site with no problems.

During a *Praise the Lord* broadcast, Hinn tells the story to Paul and Jan Crouch, the show's hosts:

Benny Hinn: Paul, you know, you probably heard I—talking to you in a private—I probably shouldn't be telling you this but, you do know I was in a plane crash once?

Jan Crouch: Um hum. Yes.

Paul Crouch: Oh, yes.

BH: In a private plane crash.

JC: Yes, yes.

PC: Yes, yes, yes. ...

BH: And then sitting on a plane, a Cessna jet, which they tell you never to fly single-engine at night, but I did. One o'clock in the morning over Avon Park, Florida, the engine quits, you know.

PC: Yes.

BH: Eleven thousand feet in the air and the—and the pilot looks back and says, "We're in trouble." And he didn't say it with calm lips, you know.

Audience: [Laughter]
BH: When the pilot's lips move, you're in trouble.
JC: [Laughs]
PC: [Laughs] Yeah, right.
BH: And there was another fella with him, a Baptist young man, he was just as nervous. And what was amazing is the Lord spoke on that plane and said, "Nothing will happen to you."
Audience: [Someone shouts: "Glory"] [Applause]
PC: Mmmm. [Applauds] ... Where did you land?
BH: In a farm.
PC: [Laughs]
BH: We didn't land. We—we hit—we—we crashed and missed the runway and thank God we did, because had we not missed the runway, we would have hit some wires right in front of us. We hit the tree and that thing rol—rolled four times. And whan—when I walked out of that plane, Paul, I didn't have not a scratch on my body. We remember that. *Not a scratch.*
Audience: [Applauds]
PC: I had almost forgotten that, Benny, but I—it all comes back to me now. Yes.
BH: And—and—But you know, Paul, faith is vital to our existence. And on that plane, I, too, spoke back and said nothing will happen. The Lord just spoke to me, we're gonna all be all right. And not one of the six people on that plane either died, of course, there were some—some injuries, some serious injuries. But nobody died.
PC: Um hum.
BH: And you know God gives you boldness, when things like this happens, it's amazing. And when we crashed, there was a young man with us named R.C. Hill [Robert Hill] who sells motorcycles in Orlando. Or did at that time, now he sells cars, who knows what he sells now. But anyway—
PC: [Chuckles]
BH: His eye was out of his—
PC: Socket.

BH: —came out of his, yeah. And I—and he said, "Pray for me." And there was a lot of injuries, my own wife was injured a little bit. And I took that eye and stuck it back in his face.
PC: Really.
BH: And prayed and God healed him.
PC: Would that be—
BH: And that is a fact.
PC: —one of the early miracles, then, that the Lord—
BH: Well, that was one of the big ones. [Laughs]
PC: [Laughs]
Audience: [Laughter]
BH: I would have never laid my hands on anybody in that condition before, you know.
PC: No, no, I know.
JC: I had a chicken whose eye was out—
PC: Ohh, please!
BH: I believe it, Jan.
PC: Get out of here![30]

Facts documented in two newspapers, reports by the Federal Aviation Administration, National Transportation Safety Board, the Highlands County Sheriff Department, the Florida Hospital in Orlando, along with a conversation with passenger Robert C. Hill, reveal a different picture.

The accident occurred in Avon Park, Florida (south of Orlando) on (Thursday morning) May 26, 1983, at approximately 12:35 a.m.[31] Hinn, along with his wife, Suzanne, a pilot and co-pilot, and two other passengers were returning to Orlando from a religious service held Wednesday evening in Naples.[32] Approximately 20 minutes from Orlando, the aircraft experienced power loss due to "fuel starvation."[33] The pilot turned the plane around and attempted to land at the nearest available airport, Avon Park Municipal Airport.[34] Due to the loss of power, the aircraft hit several trees during its landing approach and crashed into a field about 200-300 yards short of the runway.[35] The plane had flipped over from impact, lying on its topside.

The Orlando Sentinel newspaper reported all six occupants were injured and admitted to the hospital. Five remained in the hospital for treatment.[36]

The *Avon Park News Sun* reported the following information on Hill:

> "Hill was the most seriously injured person in the crash, having to be transported to Florida Hospital in Orlando for plastic surgery. ... Reports have it that Hill suffered serious injuries to the head in the accident. He was never admitted to Walker Memorial Hospital as were the other passengers, as he was transferred almost immediately. ... The Hinns were transferred from Walker Memorial to Florida Hospital so they could be closer to their homes."[37]

The Avon Park paper also reported Hinn "said he was in a state of shock" and that he said "It will be the last time I will ever fly in one of these (single engined airplane) again."[38] Hinn did not report any miracles at the scene, neither did the newspapers, sheriff, other victims or witnesses to the crash. The Florida Hospital in Orlando confirmed the admission and stay of both Hinn and his wife, Suzanne. Their records show both were admitted on May 26, 1983, with Benny released on May 28 and Suzanne on May 29.[39]

If anyone could rightfully claim that God said "Nothing will happen to you," it would be pilot Ricky Mathis and passenger Moniquey Mabry. Both were released from the hospital the same day they were admitted.

Hinn may not have "had a scratch on his body" but, according to the sheriff's report, he had "multiple contusions, abrasions, lacerations." Suzanne was listed as having "multiple contusion, abrasion and intercrannial [sic] injuries (Concussion)."[40]

A phone conversation with Hill further proves that Hinn embellished the story. Hill said the crash "ripped my eye and the side of my face; they rebuilt the whole thing. Broke three ribs and a lumbar vertebrae."

When asked how long he stayed in the hospital, Hill said, "I was in and out for various operations." When questioned as to whether he had to return to the hospital for subsequent surgeries, Hill replied, "Yes." Hill, who said he occasionally attended the Orlando Christian Center, said:

> "When we hit I went into an air vent. It destroyed the left side of my face. My eye was like a scrambled egg. When Benny came to. ... I never was unconscious. ... My thought was, my God there's so much blood. ... I said, 'Benny, I'm blind.' He came around and laid hands on me and prayed and sight came into my left eye. ... What happened was on the right eye. We hit so hard it pulled the vitreous jelly from the eye and put a hole in my eye. They said if it moved at all I'd be blind in that eye. In the other eye they had to build the skin and all that, all around it."

When asked if his eye did not actually come out, Hill replied:

> "It was mushed like an egg. It went into the air vent. The air vent is like a cookie cutter."

Hill reports that he has perfect vision today, thanks to surgery.

The comparison of Hinn's version with the facts can only raise questions about his other claims.

Benny Who?

Schmidt's Girls College is an all-girls Catholic elementary and high school in East Jerusalem, the only Arab girls' school that has been open since the 1950s, having anywhere from 300 to 600 students. Another school, St. Joseph's School, is inside the old walls of Jerusalem and is virtually unknown.

Hinn, in his 1987 taped testimony, makes astounding claims about preaching at an all-girls school in Jerusalem in 1976.[41] While not directly named, Hinn's description of the school clearly identifies it as Schmidt's.

Hinn tells the story this way:

> "Never forget, I was preaching in Jerusalem in 1976. ...
> I was invited to preach at a Catholic school, all girls in

> Jerusalem. So I went there. And there must be two or three hundred gir—Arab girls. And on the front row sat all these nuns, you know with their big black robes. And I looked at one of them and I said, 'My, I know this woman.' So I looked at her, I said, 'Don't I know you?' She said, 'Yeah, I know you too.' To discover she was the same nun who taught me as a child. Sat in my meeting. ... I began preaching and every single girl in that school got saved, including all the nuns. And that precious nun — [congregation applause] that precious nun — that precious nun, that taught me the Bible as a child came up for salvation. You don't know what that did to me."[42]

In March 1993, members of the Schmidt's faculty were asked if they remembered the incident. Those asked agreed that based on Hinn's description, he had to be talking about Schmidt's. Still, everyone questioned said, "Benny who?" and insisted that no such event ever had taken place at their institution. Sister Nunciado, the school's mother superior, personally knows the nuns who were there in the 1970s.

"It is incredible. It is impossible, I know the sisters who were here at that time and none gives any report of this," she said.

Father Dusind, chaplain since 1955, oversees anything having to do with religious instruction at the school. He had never heard of Benny Hinn and laughed out loud when Hinn's account was read to him.

> "This is nonsense, real nonsense. I know Sister Constancia and Sister Angelina, who was Mother Superior at the time, and Sister Radigundus. They were all there in the '70s. They are retired at [this] time, living in Jerusalem and I visit with them. I can assure you that they are still very much Catholic nuns. They have never hinted at such a thing."

> "It never happened and could not happen because a Charismatic healer or Protestant preacher would never ever be let in to talk to the girls. Something as dramatic or radical as suggested would be remembered by

everyone in the school. In fact, it would be known in all Jerusalem. Ask anyone. No one knows of it."

Is He Lying Again?

According to Hinn, God moves in "marvelous" ways — even to the extent of calling off professional sporting events. Or does He? On one of his daily broadcasts of *This Is Your Day*, Hinn claimed divine intervention for his ministry over the (Miami) Florida Panthers, the city's National Hockey League team.

The faith healer asserted that: "The Lord spoke to me while in Miami, here the first day, and said, 'Come back here for Good Friday.' We were supposed to go somewhere else. And I said, 'Lord, open the way.' And guess what? The manager of the Miami Arena canceled the hockey game so we can have the arena for Good Friday, April 10th, 1998. And I think that's marvelous, don't you?"[43]

Author and critic of Hinn's ministry, Yves Brault, contacted the Miami Arena concerning the alleged cancellation. His call was directed to the "special events" department of the facility and he was told that "no" hockey game was ever scheduled for April 10. Brault was informed that a game slated for April 9 between the Panthers and Philadelphia Flyers remained on the schedule.

The arena spokesperson further stated, "We can't cancel a game because the tenants take preference and the Panthers are the tenants in our building. But right after the hockey game, we'll start setting up for Benny Hinn."

The 1998 schedule of the National Hockey League was released in July 1997. Hinn's Miami Miracle Crusade, where he claims God spoke to him concerning the Good Friday service, was held October 8-9, 1997, at the arena.

Truth is Better Than Fiction

In the past, Hinn, through his attorneys, has threatened litigation for the disclosure of his exaggerated and false claims, labeling them erroneous and defamatory statements. Yet, throughout it all, it has been Hinn, not his critics, who has had to conform, nuance, and modify statements. And, all too frequently, they are the very stories and tales which his lawyers said had been misrepresented.

His propensity for exaggeration and embroidery can and has been well documented in his public statements and writing. Then, too, one must ask: How many other tales and claimed revelations were misremembered, embellished, or complete fiction? Hinn's more bizarre stories often have no witnesses or support whatsoever. And when there are claims of videotape evidence, none actually exists.

As one Canadian journalist reported:

> "Almost everything that Hinn has ever said about his personal history has been scrutinized by a small but intense army of Christian critics, affiliated with 'anti-cult' organizations in the United States. ... His most outrageous claims — that the Holy Ghost gives him visions of the future, visits him regularly, and heals the afflicted in his presence — are all described in the Bible and thus cannot be faulted in themselves. So the spiritual quarrel has shifted onto the terrain of investigative journalism. If it can be shown that Hinn has lied about the mundane details of his life it follows, although the connection is rarely spelled out, that he is also lying about his spiritual connections."[44]

All of the above cries out for answers and discernment. Is Hinn confused and therefore confusing? Does he make statements just for impression and effect? Is it lack of precision or outright deception? Whatever it is, we must continue to listen to him discerningly.

The Mythological Mayor Hinn

Sometime following the 1982 death of his father, Benny Hinn began to claim repeatedly that when he was a young boy living in Israel, his father, Costandi, was the "mayor" of Jaffa. For example, in his books, *Good Morning, Holy Spirit*,[1] and *The Anointing*,[2] as well as on two audio cassettes of his personal testimony recorded at his former church,[3] Hinn purports his father was the mayor of Jaffa during his childhood.

Historical fact easily confirms that neither before nor after 1952 (the year Benny was born) was there a mayor of Jaffa named Hinn. Israeli historian Dan Kurzman tells us that at the time of the 1948 War in Israel, "Jaffa was left virtually leaderless."[4] From that point on, Kurzman states, "Jaffa ... became a Jewish suburb"[5] with *Jewish* mayors. Costandi Hinn was an Arab, which alone precluded him from such an office.

Perhaps, there is one plausible explanation for why Hinn would create the myth that his father was mayor of Jaffa. It gives him one more characteristic to share with his idol Kathryn Kuhlman, whose father, Joe, had been a mayor.[6] As Hinn developed his "calling" as a faith healer, he so patterned his methodology after Kuhlman that maybe this was just one additional aspect of her life which he borrowed for his own story. In Arab culture there is a propensity to copy, to imitate, and to take on desired superficial traits in others. Saying what they think others want to hear and blending in is an obsession in Arab culture. Stating a wish as an accomplished fact is quite common.[7]

A History Lesson for Benny Hinn

Jaffa technically did not exist after 1948 because it was merged with all-Jewish Tel Aviv, forming one municipality called Tel Aviv-Jaffa. Details of the merger of the two cities, which became formal and final in 1950 under Mayor Israel Rokach, are readily available in numerous accounts of that period. There was no distinct city of Jaffa when Hinn was born two years later.

This fact appears to be foreign to Hinn. In Chapter 2 of *Good Morning, Holy Spirit*, Hinn refers to Tel Aviv and Jaffa as separate cities. To the reader unfamiliar with the history of the two municipalities, Hinn adds to the confusion by writing: "During my childhood, the hundred thousand people of Jaffa had become engulfed by the exploding Jewish population of Tel Aviv to the north. Today the metropolis has the official name of Tel Aviv-Jaffa."[8] Indeed, Hinn needs a history lesson.

In April 1948, about 70,000 Arabs fled Jaffa when Israel's army pressed in. All Arab rulers and authorities abandoned the city, leaving a leadership vacuum. The Israelis eventually conquered Jaffa. A tiny remnant of Arabs signed an official surrender on May 14, 1948.[9]

The story of Arab Mayor Haikal's hasty exit out of Jaffa is found on the front page of the *Palestine Post*, May 11, 1948 ("Jaffa Capitulates: An Open City"). The Tel Aviv regional commander took control. Menachem Begin wrote a first-hand account of the fall of Jaffa in his book, *The Revolt* (pp. 363-371). On page 371, Begin writes, "The conquest of Jaffa was one of the fateful events in the Hebrew war of independence."

Jaffa then was taken over by the municipality of Tel Aviv and the two cities were merged. The Israeli government made this merger final, official and irreversible on April 24, 1950, when the municipality was officially named, "Tel Aviv-Jaffa."[10]

Tel Aviv-Jaffa shifted from military rule to mayoral rule in the merger and became one city. Therefore, since there was no city of Jaffa after 1950, it would have been impossible for there to have been a mayor of Jaffa during Hinn's childhood. In addition, all the mayors of Tel Aviv-Jaffa have been well-known Israelis.

Politically Impossible

Zionism is about a Jewish state, not a bi-national one. Reading through *The Journal of Palestinian Studies* and Arabic newspapers readily shows that the Arab citizens of Israel are regarded as second-class and are tolerated as a despised minority, a fifth column and outsiders. They cannot, even in the wildest scenario, be part of the mainstream. They are viewed as a serious internal threat never to be trusted.

For example, David K. Shipler, in his work, *Arab and Jew*, writes:

> "Today, one out of every six Israelis is an Arab, but the Arab is not Israeli in the full sense. His citizenship is shallow. It taints his self-identity with complication. He exists at the edge of a society that can never, by its nature, accept him as a complete member in disregard of the religious and ethnic identities that set him apart. He is an alien in his own land, an object of suspicion in his own home, torn between his country and his people."[11]

Shipler further writes that the Arabs "were seen as inherently hostile to the state, deserving of subjugation, and dangerous to educate" and that they became "automatic targets of scrutiny, distrust, and restriction in the understandable obsession with public safety."[12]

He's Not on the List — Any List

Both the Mayor's Office in Tel Aviv-Jaffa and the Museum of the History of Tel Aviv-Jaffa in Israel furnished a list of all the city's mayors for the past six decades. One worker at the Tel Aviv Foundation was insulted that the suggestion of an Arab mayor for Tel Aviv-Jaffa was even made. The names and dates provided were also confirmed with *The Jerusalem Post*. As well, numerous *Palestine Post* articles from

1932 and on, and numerous biographies of government officials and notables in Israel to reconstruct the Jaffa-Tel Aviv merger and the people involved were checked.[13]

Here is what the facts unquestionably establish: Israel Rokach was elected mayor of Tel Aviv in 1936 and was the "mayor of the merge" in 1950. Rokach was well known to James McDonald, U.S. ambassador to Israel.[14] Haim Levanon was mayor of Tel Aviv-Jaffa from 1952 until 1959. His term covers the period Hinn says his father occupied that post.

The balance of the list, well past the time the Hinn family relocated to Canada, is as follows: Mordekhai Namir, 1959-1969, and Yehoshua Rabinowitz, 1969-1974.

Moreover, all of the former mayors of Tel Aviv-Jaffa achieved greater status in the Israeli government and all their biographies appear in *Who's Who in the World? 1975*, further confirming their mayoral service.

Even a list of the Arab mayors of Jaffa who served from 1918 to 1948 — before Benny Hinn was born — reveals there never was a Costandi Hinn or any other person surnamed Hinn who was mayor of Jaffa.

The Evidence Continues to Mount

There are other arguments that refute Hinn's assertion that his father was mayor of (Tel Aviv-) Jaffa. Consider the following:

1. *Arab Minority.* By the time Israel's army took Jaffa in April 1948, 95% of the Arab population had fled. There were 3,600 Arabs left who were leaderless, docile, and all virtually illiterate.[15] The fact that the Arabs were overtly pro-Nazi during World War II stuck in the minds of the Israelis.

Tel Aviv itself was founded (in 1909) and grew as a reaction to the antagonism and mounting hostility of the Jaffa Arabs against the Jews.[16] *The 1936 Year Book and Almanac of the Holy Land* says that the Jaffa Arabs were "fanatical."[17]

So, in 1948, when the all-Jewish council of Tel Aviv became the council of Tel Aviv-Jaffa, it kept Israel Rokach as mayor until 1952. The council then elected Haim Levanon as his successor. This practice continued until the 1970s. Under this system, an Arab never could have been elected mayor. The idea of Golda Meir being mayor of Tel Aviv-Jaffa once was floated by Israeli leader David Ben-Gurion. The opposition from the orthodox community was so great that the idea was dropped. If a Jewish woman was unacceptable as mayor at the time, certainly any Arab would have been, too.

Ben-Gurion was noted for his distrust of the Arabs. In 1936, he wrote in his diary words that have been called "the curse on Jaffa":

> "I have never felt hatred for Arabs, and their pranks have never stirred the desire for revenge in me. But I would welcome the destruction of Jaffa, port and city. Let it come; it would be for the better. This city, which grew fat from Jewish immigration and settlement, deserves to be destroyed for having waved an ax at those who built her and made her prosper. If Jaffa went to hell, I would not count myself among the mourners."[18]

And just following the capture of Jaffa, Ben-Gurion stated his official policy: "Jaffa will be a Jewish city. War is war."[19]

2. *The threat of assassination.* Arab hostility against Arabs would have been the strongest deterrent to an Arab being mayor of an Israeli city. After the war, Arabs hated anyone of their kind they considered a collaborator. On July 20, 1951, King Abdullah of Jordan was murdered in Jerusalem because he was negotiating with Israel. Arabs considered the execution — carried out by Arabs — justifiable. An Arab mayor of an all Jewish city would have been dispatched quickly either by Israeli extremists or the Arabs themselves. There was an "Arab Blood Society" operating in the slums of Jaffa, set up to retaliate against any Arab who had any dealings with Jews.[20]

Yet Hinn would have readers believe, "Even though my father was not Jewish, the Israeli leaders trusted him. And they were happy to have someone in Jaffa who could relate to such an international community. We were proud of his circle of friends, which included many national leaders. He was asked to be an ambassador for Israel in foreign nations but chose to stay in Jaffa."[21] It happens that Israel Rokach, the mayor of Tel Aviv-Jaffa during Hinn's childhood, was the international ambassador.

The evidence presented shows all of Hinn's claims to be false. If his father had been mayor of Tel Aviv-Jaffa during the 1950s, there would be pictures, newspaper accounts, government documents confirming the fact. There is nothing.

3. *The explosive nature of Jaffa itself.* For many years the Jews of Yemen were persecuted, abused, mistreated, and afflicted under Arab rule.[22] Throughout 1949 and 1950, Ben-Gurion ordered airlifts of Yemenite Jews. Almost all the Jews in Yemen were settled in Israel and realized that they now could tell the Arab minority in Israel what to do. They could "get them back" and "teach them a lesson."

The Yemenites were known to be Arab "haters" and hostile because of the years of persecution. The Yemenites also tried to throw off their oriental stereotype and prove to the European Jews that years in an Arab land did not make them favorable to the enemy. Many of those Yemenite Jews settled in Jaffa, a city that is only about one mile square. Add to this the other oriental Jews from Iraq and other Arab states who settled in Jaffa, and it becomes very obvious that the minority of Arabs still there would have kept a low profile.

To suggest that these Jews would have tolerated an Arab mayor is too much to imagine. Hinn's proclamation shows him too ignorant of all these matters. It is easy to understand why. Arabs in Israel are taught little of Israeli history.

When is a Mayor Not a Mayor?

The possibility was even considered that "mayor" could mean something else in Israel. We knew that "sheikh" means a respected man, an elder in a notable family, but has no political meaning whatsoever. But Hinn does not call his father "sheikh." He calls him "mayor" and says he was politically powerful.[23] "My father had been a mayor," he repeatedly wrote.[24]

Vivian Ajlouny of the *Al Fajr Jerusalem Palestinian Weekly* was contacted. Ajlouny is a Jerusalem Arab, Greek Orthodox by faith, and knowledgeable about Arab culture. She said "mayor is mayor." It is a political term and nothing else. It can be understood in no other way. It is "Al-Baladiyeh" in Arabic — literally, the "head of a municipality." Israel or America, wherever, a mayor is a mayor.

Little Response

A phone call was made to the Orlando Christian Center on April 21, 1992. It was eventually directed to a man who would only identify himself as "Steve." The call was placed to discuss the disparity between Hinn's claims and the facts documented above. At first Steve said the "mayor" claim was true. When confronted with the facts, he said that Hinn was neither Arab nor Jew. When told that this only heightened the contradiction, he said, "We'd be glad to respond to that." A response in writing was requested, but no response from Steve has ever been received.

Two weeks later, on May 8, Bruce Barbour of Thomas Nelson Publishers was called. He, too, was presented with findings about the mayors of Jaffa and how they contradicted Hinn's claims published by Barbour's company. Barbour responded by saying that the information and sources cited against Hinn's claims were wrong. He said Thomas Nelson had irrefutable proof of Hinn's claims but refused to be specific. When asked if all of the official Israeli sources solicited were wrong, he responded with an emphatic "Yes."

When asked for copies of his "proof," Barbour said, "I don't have it, Benny will send it." When informed of the response previously given by Hinn's representative "Steve" and his subsequent failure to provide the promised evidence, Barbour said Hinn was busy. After further discussion, Barbour said he would send proof. Barbour's pledge has also gone unfulfilled. Nothing was ever received from Thomas Nelson Publishers regarding Hinn's claims.

Faced With the Facts

When Hinn's untruth was publicly exposed, he scrambled for excuses and alibis. For a while, he retreated to the claim that his father was only the "unofficial mayor" of Jaffa, and further blamed his book's publisher, Thomas Nelson, for inserting the word "mayor" into his two books. He alleges he tried to correct it prior to publication:

> "[Thomas] Nelson [Publishers] and I discussed it. And I even told Nelson, I said, 'Look, we better not say "mayor." Let's kind of give the whole picture politically.' And Nelson said, 'People aren't interested to know all those politics and this and this and this. If he functioned as mayor, he was.' And basically he was."[25]

These claims also can be easily refuted.

First, keep in mind that Hinn twice made the "mayor" claim on the 1987 audio cassette tape of his testimony, three years before publication of *Good Morning, Holy Spirit.*

Second, the original manuscript copy of *Good Morning, Holy Spirit* which Hinn submitted to the publisher read: "My father was the Mayor of Jaffa during my upbringing."[26] The sentence was published as: "My father was the mayor of Jaffa during my childhood." Thomas Nelson, therefore, is not to blame.

Hinn further orchestrates his fabrication by writing: "We lived comfortably. Dad's position in government made it possible for us to have a home in the suburbs. It was a wonderful home that had a wall around it with glass along the top for security."[27]

Hinn's real childhood home was nothing like that. In March 1993, Hinn's evangelistic organization, with the aid of his brother Christopher's travel agency, took 2,000 people to Israel on a ten-day tour. A tour guide named Tzvika Chulakov took one of the 50 buses for Hinn's tourists. Chulakov told how the buses briefly rolled through Jaffa, slowing at the corner of Yafet and Pasteur streets. Hinn's organization had placed a sign on the sidewalk pointing to the French Hospital with the words, "Benny Born Here." Another sign, on the same corner, pointed across the street to Number 23 Yafet Street. It said, "Benny Went to School Here."

One place the buses did not go was another half-mile south to Hinn's "wonderful home in the suburbs" at 12 Ibn Rashad Street. It was and is the site of a small three-story building owned by the Greek Orthodox Church. The second level housed the church's boys club, and the top floor was used by the church's treasurer.

That neighborhood is home to a people who appear to care little for their property or where they throw their garbage. Its cramped quarters and garbage-filled empty lots reek of poverty and lack of influence.

Costandi Hinn rented the ground floor, which consisted of two bedrooms, a bath and kitchen — hardly comfortable quarters for a family of nine. One can readily understand why the elder Hinn relocated his family from Jaffa to Toronto, Ontario.

Hinn says his father knew national leaders as close personal friends. Yet, few residents of the neighborhood, among the many asked, remember Benny or Costandi Hinn.

Brother Chris to the Rescue

With repeated requests for documentation having been ignored, Hinn's younger brother, Christopher, finally provided documents in an attempt to substantiate the mayoral claim. However, these materials did more to undermine than support it.[28] The papers included two documents in Hebrew and a certificate from the Greek Orthodox Patriarchate Ecclesiastical Court. When the Hebrew documents were translated by two independent sources, they turned out to be nothing more than work permits from Tel Aviv-Jaffa. One of the documents indicated Costandi Hinn's status was being changed from that of a temporary worker to a permanent one. The permits said he was a minimal security risk and one revealed an $8.00 a month raise. The second also contains the provision that Costandi Hinn could be fired with only two weeks notice. These are hardly conditions and provisions that would be placed upon the mayor of a city.

The latter certificate was a proof of employment. It said that the elder Hinn worked from 1939 until 1948 as a "Telephone, Radio, Technition [sic]" at the Jaffa Post Office. From 1950 until 1964, he served as "Secretary for Labour Exchange in the Labour Ministry for Jaffa." In 1964, he was appointed "Liason [sic] Officer for the Minorites [sic] and Public Relations of Tel-Aviv Jaffa Municipality." The latter position was held through 1967. There is still no indication, whatsoever, that Costandi Hinn ever was mayor of Tel Aviv-Jaffa, and no list of the mayors of Tel Aviv-Jaffa contains his name.

Using *Charisma* to Answer His Critics

Hinn next tried to silence the mounting evidence against him by using *Charisma* magazine to respond. In a cover story interview, he told editor Stephen Strang:

> "On a recent trip to Israel, we videotaped an interview with Dany Avrahami, the director of the Jaffa municipality, who worked with my dad. We asked him bluntly, 'Was my father mayor? Did he do the work of the mayor?' He answered that, though my father did not have the title of mayor, 'his function was like a mayor of Jaffa.' He even provided me with documentation."[29]

Yet, when asked to be allowed to view the Avrahami interview, both *Charisma* and Hinn's ministry refused to make the tape available. George Parsons, a spokesman from Hinn's former Florida-based church, said during a phone conversation that documenting the claim was "not important."

Strang's response was similar. He was asked to: "Please show us with whom, for whom, and over whom Costandi Hinn functioned as mayor." Four months and two letters later, a reply was received in which Strang concluded: "I am not interested in engaging in a debate over Benny or the validity or the lack thereof of your claims."[30]

With such resistance by Hinn and his colleagues to supply the Avrahami evidence, an inquiry to the Office of Mayor of Tel Aviv-Jaffa was made. There it was learned that Dany Avrahami is no official, but part of a team or committee that oversees "Southern Villages" (cities), and this shared responsibility is considered low-level.

The Jerusalem Post also responded to a request for information on Dany Avrahami with: "Unfortunately after searching in our Archives we were unable to find any articles written on Dany Avrahami. We tried various spelling possibilities, searched in pasted copies of old archives material as well as our database, all to no avail."

No Longer a Mayor

In his new autobiography, *He Touched Me*, Hinn now says his father "can best be described as a liaison between the community and the Israeli government."[31] Throughout the book, he then ascribes to his father a host of various occupations and responsibilities: postal service employee,[32] Red Cross worker,[33] fruit inspector at the Jaffa port,[34] president of the Greek Orthodox Club,[35] movie projectionist for the club,[36] and, following the family's 1968 move to Canada, insurance salesman,[37] all of which are a far cry from the political position once claimed for him.

Yet, Hinn maintains the pretense that his father held a "unique position in the community" and persists in describing him "as a liaison between the community and Israeli government."[38] He also maintains he "was deeply touched that my father had earned such respect and trust from the Israeli government,"[39] which is still an undocumented claim.

Hinn has now — perhaps unknowingly — provided for readers insight into the socio-economic status of his father and family when he writes: "My father didn't own an automobile the entire time we lived in Israel — he either walked to work or took public transportation."[40] A mayor or even a "government liaison" would be expected to have a car and driver (as do politicians in Israel today) and not be left to walk or take a bus to work.

Moreover, Hinn says, "We were not a wealthy family."[41] Hinn's family left Israel for Canada virtually penniless and was dependent upon the sponsorship and goodwill of agencies recommended by the Greek Orthodox Church and a neighboring family.[42] There was no status or good life, but rather, as described by Hinn himself, just the opposite. This is not to say that poverty is bad, but that one should tell the truth, the whole truth, and nothing but the truth.

Benny Gibran?

Hinn in some ways resembles the late Kahlil Gibran. Gibran was a charmer who used others for material gain. Both Gibran and Hinn are best-selling authors (with good editors) who have gained a large following. Gibran composed a tall tale of being a child of "fortune" growing up in a very well-to-do home of culture and love. Many still hold onto Gibran's myth. However, in fact, Gibran was raised in "a harsh life of poverty, with a cruel overbearing father, a drunkard who bullied his family."[43]

Gibran, like Hinn, was born in the Middle East in an Arabic culture. Gibran was Lebanese, Hinn is Palestinian. Exaggeration of pedigree is a way of life all over that region. While a Bible believer would say one should not lie about his parentage, the Middle Easterner is conditioned in a tradition (of fabricating) that is looked upon as honorable. Even conversion to Christianity does not change that for some. For believers, words cannot be spoken just to appease others, but must correspond to reality.

This Old House

Hinn now also admits that his nine-member family lived in three rooms on the ground floor of a building owned by the Greek Orthodox Church.[44] This is a far cry from the previous description of: "We lived comfortably. Dad's position in government made it possible for us to have a home in the suburbs. It was a wonderful home."[45] Strangely though, Hinn qualifies his admission by interjecting, "there was ample room."[46] Once again, we are confronted with Hinn's ongoing childhood delusions since the reality of nine people living in three rooms would hardly be "ample room." One can only imagine the conditions with seven children living in one bedroom.

Moreover, the location was less than "wonderful" in a minority Arab area of a run-down and neglected section of the city. PFO visited the building that housed the Hinn basement home in Jaffa. The visit confirmed the idea that conditions were crowded. Jaffa neighbors interviewed by PFO talked of poverty there. The only attractive thing about the neighborhood is that at the end of the street one has a magnificent view of the Mediterranean Sea. And even though the house is within view of the Mediterranean, the harsh realities of life in Jaffa in that era cannot be wished away. The oppression of the Arab minority is well documented and easily proven.

When Hinn's claims went unchecked, he was able to refer to the house on Ibn Rashad street as "a home in the suburbs. It was a wonderful home." The truth that Hinn has been forced to confess is that his family only occupied the ground floor of the building which housed the Greek Orthodox Club. He further admits, "By the time I was a teen, our bedroom in Jaffa began to resemble a hospital ward."[47]

Hinn's early biographies are not factual. Even his 1999 effort continues to take serious liberties with the truth. He has in the past and continues to create a fanciful and distorted story that does not square with logic or history.

Perhaps, as earlier suggested, the Kuhlman connection is plausible for his fabrications. The Arab bent toward rhetoric and overstatement and the drive for honor and pedigree might have added to it. Only Hinn knows for sure all the reasons. But one thing is certain, his claims are refuted by the facts and an understanding of the culture he grew up in. What the Christian world needs is increasing integrity, honesty, and truth, not fables and fiction.

The Anointing of Benny Hinn

Benny Hinn claims that God has powerfully anointed him and says that this "anointing" gives him the power to knock people down, or "slay them in the Spirit," by touching, waving, or blowing on them. So serious is Hinn about this anointing that he warns his critics:

> "You'll never go unpunished touching the anointing. You can mock Benny Hinn's hair, clothes, eyes and shoes, and socks, I'll let you. Go ahead. I will laugh with you. You can mock the way I talk, you can mock anything you want, I'll probably laugh with you. Never mock the anointing. 'Cause the day you do, I won't have to do a thing about it. I'll just say, 'Lord, take care of them.'"[1]

Spiritual intimidation has been an incessant methodology used by Hinn. He, like most in the mystical Christian movement, is quick to revile with the anthem, "Touch not God's anointed!" when criticism of his doctrine and practice surfaces. And in most cases, Hinn is even more vicious than others in his judgments.

On a *Praise the Lord* telecast in 1990, Hinn said:

> "You wonderful people of God quit attacking men of God by name! Somebody's attacking me because of something I'm teaching! Let me tell you something brother, You watch it! ... I don't mind if they attack Benny and the way he is and the way he walks, but don't attack the anointing on my life... Don't attack this man of God [speaking of Paul Crouch]. There is a group here in California that thinks they are the judgment seat of Christ! They judge everything that

you do. Listen here fellah, let me tell you something, you're not my judge. Jesus is my judge! You walk around with your stiff lip and collar on your neck — dear God in heaven I wish I could just — oooh! They call it a 'ministry,' my foot! You know I've looked for one verse in the Bible, I just can't seem to find it, one verse that says 'If you don't like 'em, kill 'em.' I really wish I could find it!... Ladies and gentlemen, don't attack God's servants! Don't publicly attack them by name! ...don't mention people's names on your radio program and your TV program — thinking you're doing God's service — you're not! You stink — frankly that's the way I think about it!"[2]

Moments later in the same telecast, he asserts:

"Paul [Crouch], it angers me to no end — there's no power but judgment; no life but death! Quit it! I'm sorry, I'm not exactly the normal kind of guy you know, I'm from Israel. Sometimes I wish God would give me a Holy Ghost Machine Gun — I blow your head off!"[3]

It is appalling to note not only the harsh, unloving, intimidating tone of these statements, but also that the audience responded to these statements with laughter and applause. Also, while Hinn cautioned his critics not to mention names[4] on their broadcasts, he apparently does not feel constrained to do the same:

"There's a man called Harry, that has just said, 'This man is phony!' Be careful Harry, I'm not a phony man. I'm God's servant. Be careful — you don't know what you're playing with. Your first name is Harry. You're Harry Albert, and your last name is Krey — K-R-E-Y, that's your name. And the Lord gave me your first, middle and last name to warn you. ... You're shaken that I have your name — you're right. You better be shaken because God's presence is on my life and I know things by the Spirit."[5]

Speaking at the 1992 "World Charismatic Conference," Hinn again scourged his critics, particularly Christian

Research Institute, saying:

> "Be careful! Your little ones may suffer because of your stupidity. Now I'm pointing my finger today, with the mighty power of God on me, and I speak. You hear this, there are men and women in Southern California attacking me. I will tell you under the anointing now, you'll reap it in your children unless you stop. You'll never win. You'll never win. ... And your children will suffer. If you care for your kids, stop attacking Benny Hinn. You attacking me on radio every night, you'll pay and your children will. Hear this from the lips of God's servant. You are in danger. Repent! Or God Almighty will move His hand. Touch not My Anointed."[6]

His friend and avid supporter, Paul Crouch, president of the Trinity Broadcasting Network, eliminates those who question Hinn from the Body of Christ. On a broadcast of *Praise the Lord* where Hinn appeared to answer his critics, Crouch asserted:

> "Who knows, even some of the heretic hunters might get saved tonight. We could dare to believe that together, could we not? Would somebody say me an 'Amen' out there?"[7]

Hinn agreed. During the same telecast the faith healer asserted:

> "Had someone told me a few years ago I would be fighting so-called Christians, I would never have believed it. The unbelievers have been kinder to me than these so-called Christians. Do you know what they really are? False brethren. That's what Paul calls them."[8]

Further, Hinn does not reserve his wrath for theological critics. During an August 1992 sermon at his Orlando Christian Center, Hinn told of an unpleasant encounter with a customs supervisor at a Chicago airport. Hinn said of the man, "If I could have killed him, I would have."[9]

Two months later, in a phone conversation with Hinn's younger brother, Christopher, and attorney Stephen W. Beik, who said he represents Hinn, the preacher's ghastly statement was dismissed as a joke. "And you took him seriously?" Beik asked.[10] Apparently someone did. A cassette tape from that service was later obtained and found that the angry comments had been edited from the sermon.[11]

The Curse Goes On

Years later, in Denver, Hinn continued his exploit of "speaking judgment" on his opponents. His justification was simple: His critics had blasphemed the Holy Spirit and he now had the right to tell God what he wanted to see done. Supposedly, his judgments came with a divine backing. "Under the anointing not one word falls to the ground," he told Paul Crouch and the TBN viewing audience.[12]

So powerful is his new level, he warned:

"I am not the same man under the anointing as I am now. ... Believe me when I tell you, I do not even identify with the Benny Hinn you see on television. Because it's a different man, it's not me. My children are afraid of me under the anointing. What they do not know is that I'm afraid of the anointing too. I'm not afraid of myself, I'm afraid of what the anointing can do to me if I mistreat it. Or if I abuse it or if I misuse it."[13]

He further readied the audience for the video segment of his Denver crusade they were about to watch:

"I've been preaching 25 years almost. I've never seen the anointing as frightening as I saw in Denver Friday night. And so when you hear me in just a little bit give blessings and cursing and basically all I say, is each, any who attacks this anointing, and I speak ... a judgment on them."[14]

As the crusade highlight is shown, the TBN viewers witness what most would describe as a "man possessed." Hinn growls:

"The glory! The glory! If I don't release it I'll blow up. If I don't release that anointing I'll blow up. I got to release it on somebody. ... Yes Lord, I'll do it! I place a curse on every man and every woman that will stretch his hand against this anointing. I curse that man who dares to speak a word against this ministry. But any man, and any woman that raises his or her hand in blessing towards this ministry, I bless that man. I bless that home. I bless that family. Any man, any woman, any person that raises his tongue in blessings toward this work, raises his tongue in blessing toward this anointing, raises his tongue in blessing toward this servant of the Lord, I bless them. ... I rarely ever do what I'm doing now. This is the Holy Ghost on me telling me to do this. I bless you. I bless your homes, your life, your future, your children. May every attack of Satan against you be destroyed. May every plan of hell be destroyed against you and every plan of God be established in Jesus' name. Amen, amen, amen."15

A Few Words on Methodology

Hinn has long shown himself adept at crowd manipulation. He consistently urges his audience to be demonstrative by using the device of asking repeated questions and having them shout back the answers with increasing emotional intensity until they are ready to agree with almost anything he is saying:

"N-Now-hey-are you really — do you really want truth? Hey! Do you want truth?" [and the congregation shouts "Yes!"] "Are you ready for some heavy stuff?" [and the congregation shouts "Yes!"]16

and:

"Now, lets get to something a little heavier — are you ready for something a little heavier?" [and the congregation shouts "Yes!"] "How many of you can handle a lot more?" [and the congregation shouts "Yes!"]17

Those who have studied crowd dynamics know that a group of people is more easily influenced by a dynamic speaker than are solitary individuals. Someone who is normally not very emotional can be worked to a fever pitch in a crowd. One who would be more analytical of what is being proposed by the speaker is intimidated by the emotional, positive response of those around him. The psychological pressure is to be accepted by the group, and so the individual tends to conform to the response of that group. Once a psychological commitment has been made to what has been said, it is difficult to reverse that commitment later.

Knocking Them Down

Hinn claims that his anointing has given him supernatural powers, so that he can knock people off their feet without touching them, a phenomenon in Charismatic and Pentecostal circles commonly called being "slain in the Spirit." Hinn supports this claim by referring to Acts 9 and the story of Saul's conversion. Here Hinn proves that he is a poor exegete of Scripture. Acts 9:3 describes Saul's conversion encounter with Christ. Saul fell down — or was knocked down — but stayed conscious and alert as he conversed with the resurrected Christ. He was not out or in a fog or "slain in the spirit," as Hinn suggests.

Nowhere does Paul or anyone else in Scripture suggest that all conversions happen in this way. Nowhere in Scripture is Acts 9 suggested as a pattern for sanctification or as a norm for the Christian life.

There is no question that people fall over at Hinn's services. But there is also no question that God is not the one knocking them over. More likely the tumbles can be explained by the predictable and traceable principles of group dynamics. The explicit or implicit expectations of forceful leaders, especially if these leaders convince the followers that they are the voice of God, can greatly influence an audience.

Go With the Flow

Marc Galanter, in his book, *Cults: Faith, Healing, and Coercion*, talks about group psychology and the intense pressure in some meetings to conform to group expectations.

Those expectations often dictate behavior. People do not have to be long in a group before they know what is expected. Conforming to expectations is the key to acceptance. There are group tasks and group rituals that are essential for cohesiveness and full acceptance.

Galanter writes, "Often they are implicitly aware of their style of behavior in an unexpected situation since it is based on previous instruction to the group." Of course, that instruction may be verbal or modeled by repetition in all the services and meetings. Galanter goes on to say, "In these groups, transcendental experiences, often hallucinatory, are quite common. ... Intense emotional experiences are reported, such as profound euphoria or malaise."[18]

A further enlightening statement on being "slain in the Spirit" is found in *The Dictionary of Pentecostal and Charismatic Movements*, which says:

> "It is generally acknowledged that in addition to God, the source of the experience can be a purely human response to autosuggestion, group 'peer pressure,' or simply a desire to experience the phenomenon."[19]

Another expression of group dynamics is easily demonstrated by the fact that a comedy movie is much funnier when seen in a large theatrical setting than at home on television viewed by one or two people. Additionally, television situation comedies are broadcast with "laugh tracks" to induce the desired reaction in the audience.

The emotional intensity at Hinn's services can also be demonstrated outside religious circles. Many can easily recall the vivid pictures from the 1950s and 1960s of youths swooning at the feet of rock music idols such as the Beatles, Elvis Presley, and others. The fame surrounding such entertainers would cause the devoted fan, meeting the star face to face, to achieve a nearly hypnotic state of hysteria, causing physical changes in the body. This excitement readily explains the fainting by the groupie. Therefore, it is not difficult to ascertain that for many of the ardent devotees of Hinn who come face to face with him, a completely natural explanation can be cited for what is claimed to be the "power of the

Spirit." Yet, it is hard to believe that the Lord would imitate and circulate behaviors produced by the unsaved world.

The church at Corinth's emulation of the pagan frenzies practiced in the Temple of Apollo caused Paul deep concern. The apostle warned that disorder and chaos would cause the unsaved to say believers were mad (1 Corinthians 14:23). Paul also reminds us that God is a God of order and of peace, not of disorder and confusion (1 Corinthians 14:33,40).

When Hinn's followers call out for him to "wave" or "throw" the Holy Spirit at them, they know exactly what they are expected to do and how they are to respond. They "go with the flow," as many ex-practitioners readily confess.

Child-evangelist-turned-Hollywood-actor Marjoe Gortner questioned the validity of faith healers in his 1972 Academy Award-winning documentary film, *Marjoe*. Gortner has claimed the title of "The World's Youngest Ordained Minister," being officially ordained in 1948 at age four. He conducted revivals and healing services across the United States. His disillusionment with the deceptive techniques he presented as divine direction led him to expose the big business of faith healing.

In Flo Conway and Jim Siegelman's book, *Snapping*, Gortner offered this revealing account:

> "'I lecture in about twenty colleges a year,' he began, 'and I do a faith-healing demonstration — but I always make them ask for it. I tell them that I don't believe in it, that I use a lot of tricks; and the title of the lecture is "Rhetoric and Charisma," so I've already told them how large masses are manipulated by a charismatic figure. I've given them the whole rap explaining how it's done, but they still want to see it. So I throw it all right back at them. I say, "No, you don't really want to see it." And they say, "Oh, yes. We do. We do!" And I say, "But you don't believe in it anyway, so I can't do it." And they say, "We believe. We believe!" So after about twenty minutes of this I ask for a volunteer, and I have a girl come up and I say, "So you want to feel better?" And I say, "You're lying to me! You're just up here for a good time and you want to impress all these

people and you want to make an a-- out of me and an a-- out of this whole thing, so why don't you go back and sit down?" I really get hard on her, and she says, "No, no, I believe!" And I keep going back and forth until she's almost in tears. And then, even though this is in a college crowd and I'm only doing it as a joke, I just say my same old line, *In the name of Jesus!* and touch them on the head, and wham, they fall down flat every time."[20]

Hinn's "Freedom"

Hinn asserts another benefit from his anointing: freedom from worldly desires. He says, "In my case, I know I have lost complete desire for anything to do with the world. My worldly desires are gone."[21]

This is quite a claim, in light of revelations throughout the years of Hinn's lavish lifestyle. As early as 1991, Hinn was being indicted with an excessive way of life. *Orlando Sentinel* reporter Mike Thomas writes:

> "This comes from a man who just turned in his Mercedes for a Jaguar and recently moved from the exclusive Heathrow development to the even more exclusive Alaqua, where he now lives in a $685,000 home. His suits are tailored, his shoes are Italian leather and his wrists and finger glitter with gold and diamonds. ... Hinn also gets gifts in the form of cash, jewelry and other valuables. He makes no secret of these excesses. He wears his diamond Rolex, diamond rings, gold bracelet and custom suits for all to see. He drives a Jaguar and his wife drives a Cadillac. He seems flabbergasted that anyone might question this. ... He sits in his expansive patio overlooking the Alaqua golf course — while the pool man cleans the pool and the housekeeper feeds his baby son — talking about what he considers a modest lifestyle, as if everyone lives like this."[22]

In 1997, a *CNN/Time* report also focused upon the financial. The news feature explained, "The money is managed by Hinn's self-appointed board of directors ... but their secrecy raises suspicions among critics." A significant portion of the program then detailed some of the excesses in his life and ministry. These included:

- Hinn and members of his entourage flying the Supersonic Concorde to Europe at nearly $9,000 per ticket — almost double the cost of first class tickets to save four hours flying time.
- Hinn and his personal bodyguards staying in some of the most exclusive and expensive hotels in the world — in Presidental Suites costing as much as $2,200 a night.
- Hinn paying one of his former bodyguards — who threatened to go public with allegations of his extravagant spending — over $100,000 to keep quiet.[23]

The news media has long questioned if Hinn is really "reaching for God — or wallets?"[24] A Dallas newspaper pointed out that at his crusade in its city, "Donor cards distributed Friday night had donor blocks pre-printed for amounts that started at $100,000 and went down to $1,500."[25]

Hinn wants his followers to believe that he is superior to most Christians by virtue of his anointing. His life and ministry is portrayed in subjective and emotional terms encompassed in his own make-believe world. He warns his critics to "touch not the Lord's anointed," all the while he denounces and curses those who question him. Hinn is also confusing and contradictory with his declarations that we must abandon self, die to self, and empty oneself to get the anointing, while he lives in exorbitant luxury.

Hinn's anointing is much like the formidable wizardry of the Wizard of Oz — intimidating at first sight, but really only a façade. "Pay no attention to the man behind the screen," thundered the Wizard when he was exposed by Toto the dog. Christians would do well to pay no attention to the false anointing of Benny Hinn.

A New Road for Benny Hinn?

In the decade of the 1990s, Benny Hinn promised to reform as often as an election-year politician. News articles (both Christian and secular),[1] a substantial three-hour video compiling many of the television news investigations of Hinn,[2] along with this book[3] all help to spell out the dilemma of a man in a world of deep confusion.

While still actively pastoring his Orlando Christian Center, Hinn closed his May 30, 1993 sermon by saying he was about to take his ministry and congregation "on a new road." Hinn said:

> "Lately there's been a lot of questions about things I've taught, things I've said. Now let me also clear this out. There's been certain teachings that I taught in OCC years ago I no longer believe."[4]

And then admitted:

> "Unless changes are made now, this ministry won't last another three years. I'm telling you what the Holy Ghost told me. Unless we make changes now, not only with what I teach, but with what we do with what God has given us."[5]

Hinn vowed to make some changes. He began by ditching the souffle hairdo, his Mercedes-Benz, and his Rolex watch and other pricey jewelry. Many took Hinn at his word, accepting his claim to be taking a "new road."

Hinn also offered clarifications of his aberrational or heretical teachings on the Trinity, faith, healing, and prosperity. He also recanted his belief that Christ had to die spiritually after dying physically on the cross at Calvary. Hinn noted:

> "Some of my friends, whom I still respect, I'm beginning to disagree with."[6]

Criticism began to wane despite his history of making similar claims. While it was hoped that Hinn would change, others adopted a "wait and see" attitude.

One critic who reacted positively to Hinn's recantations was Ole Anthony of the Dallas-based Trinity Foundation. Anthony, who worked with ABC's 1991 *PrimeTime Live* investigation of Robert Tilton, first applauded Hinn, saying that because of his "openness and willingness to correct mistakes ..., Benny Hinn offers the promise of accountability."[7] A short time later, Anthony returned to become one of Hinn's chief critics.

Others lauded his professed changes as repentance, a theme Hinn began stressing at "miracle crusades." The media took notice. The *Chicago Tribune* ran a story with a headline that read, "Turnabout: Benny Hinn repents."[8] *Charisma* magazine carried a seven-page interview with Hinn in which he responded to his critics and tried to explain the changes in his ministry and teachings.[9]

But one has to ask if those applauding Hinn's repentance are familiar with similar turnabouts the evangelist-healer has announced in the past. A careful examination of what he now says with what he has said in the past could prompt skepticism.

Dissecting Hinn's "Repentance" Sermon

Hinn's May 30 sermon easily could be summarized: "I used to believe that. I used to teach that. I no longer believe that. I no longer will teach that."

By Hinn's own standard of godly repentance, he has missed the mark. In a 1987 sermon, Hinn said:

> "Do you know what repentance means? Godly sorrow. Most of us don't even know what repentance means.

We think, 'I'm sorry. Forgive me. Amen. Go mess up again tomorrow.' That's not repentance! Repentance is a completely changed life. It's when you break because of sin, godly sorrow takes hold of you and you say, 'Never again.' That's repentance."10

In the *Charisma* interview, Hinn says that while he formerly taught things such as believers being "little gods" and Christ's spiritual death, he says, "I never taught heresy."11

No responsible orthodox Christian teacher subscribes to either of those doctrines. To call believers "little gods" — even to the point of requiring his congregation to repeat after him: "I am a God-man"12 — is to discount the uniqueness of Christ's incarnation. To teach that Christ didn't finish man's redemption on the cross attacks the heart of the Christian message.

Hinn tries to pass off another heresy of his as a joke. Hinn told *Charisma*:

> "In Finis Dake's book *God's Plan for Man*, he teaches that each member of the Trinity has his own spirit, soul and body. One Sunday when I was speaking on the Trinity, I repeated that teaching. As soon as I did, I could feel tension in the congregation because people sense when you say things that aren't right. So I tried to clear the air. Jokingly, I said, 'There must be nine of them.' Well, the people laughed and I thought, Boy that was a dumb thing to say. Then I forgot about it. The next Sunday, I apologized to my congregation for saying such a thing. I told them it wasn't right for me to teach this nor was it right to joke about it. The people acted like they didn't even remember it. They had dismissed it because they know me."13

Hinn's recollection of the sermon differs from what is on tape:

> "I feel revelation knowledge already coming on me. ... God the Father is a person, God the Son is a person, God the Holy Ghost is a person, but each of them is a

triune being by himself. If I can shock you and maybe I
should, there are nine of them. ... God the Father is a
person with his own personal spirit, with his own
personal soul and his own personal spirit body. You
say, 'I never heard that.' Well, do you think you're in
this church to hear things you've heard for the last fifty
years? You can't argue with the Word, can you? It's all
in the Word."[14]

The video tape of the sermon records no laughter from his
congregation.

The video tape of the following week's broadcast sermon
contains no retraction or apology, although it does include the
infamous "I am a God-man" chant-along.

If Christians are to forgive Hinn's heresy, he needs to
report exactly what he said, admit what was heresy, take full
responsibility, and exhibit godly repentance from his ad-lib
theology.

Biographical Problems

Once Hinn has come clean on his doctrine, he needs to
own up to the falsehoods in his biography.

In the previous chapters of this book, claims that Hinn's
father was mayor of Jaffa, Israel, that he was divinely healed
of stuttering at age 21, and that he once preached at an
all-girls Catholic school in Jerusalem resulting in the conversion of the entire student body and faculty have all been
disproved. Other of Hinn's biographical anecdotes, including
his own conversion story, have been documented with several
inconsistencies and contradictions.

Hinn's response to many of these discrepancies has been
to backtrack, blame others for errors, or say he has evidence
supporting the claims but not produce it on request. In doing
so, Hinn often has heaped one falsehood upon another.

Haven't We Been Down this New Road Before?

In fact, Hinn's pledge to reform is itself an inconsistent
veneer. Hinn has promised — and failed — to clean up his act
before.

In a 1987 sermon, after almost a decade of studying the Word-Faith doctrine until it permeated his own teaching and preaching, he said:

> "Like I said earlier, if I hear prosperity one more time, I'm gonna throw up. ... There's too much today being preached that's not gospel. And I was preaching it myself, because I honestly believed that these men whom I respect must be hearing from God and if they're saying it, well it must be God. To then discover that the Scripture states completely the opposite."[15]

A few years later, by 1990, he returned to the "little gods" and "prosperity" teachings. In his series, *Our Position in Christ*, he insisted:

> "Kenneth Hagin has a teaching — a lot of people have problems with it — yet it is absolute truth. Kenneth Copeland has a teaching — many Christians have put holes in it — but it's divine truth. Hagin and Copeland say, 'You are God. Ye are God.'"[16]

Also during a funds appeal message that same year for Trinity Broadcasting Network's "Praise-A-Thon" he protested:

> "And I'm sick and tired of hearing about streets of gold. I don't need gold in heaven, I've got to have it now!"[17]

And later in the same message he asserted:

> "Poverty is a demon. God had to show me a vision of a demon literally to prove this to me. All at the same time when Oral Roberts came to tell me what he told me about believing God for my harvest. All at the same time, I had a vision in my bedroom. I was asleep and woke up and right in front of my face I saw a devil. You say, 'You saw it?' Yes, sir, I did. If you have troubles with it, that's your problem. And that thing was mocking me in my bedroom. And the Lord spoke and said to me, 'That is the demon of poverty.' Brother, when you see demons in your room you really hear

God's voice quick and loud. And the Lord said, 'That's the demon of poverty.' I didn't think there was such a thing, Paul. And the Lord said, 'Now, rebuke it.' I sat up in bed and I said, 'I rebuke you.' The Lord stopped me and said, 'That's not the way you rebuke. You rebuke with My Word.' And suddenly out of my mouth, Scriptures began flying out about the blessings of God. That demon vanished out of my sight and from that day till now, there's been blessings on my life."[18]

The following year he was back on his reformation bandwagon. He told *Christianity Today* magazine that he had "repudiated many of his earlier, controversial statements and said the entire direction of his ministry is in the midst of fundamental reform."[19] The periodical added that Hinn "acknowledged that he has made theologically erroneous statements, and that his attitude toward those who have challenged him has left a lot to be desired."[20]

Hinn also told the magazine's journalist:

"I really no longer believe the faith message. I don't think it adds up. God has already begun showing me some of the things on prosperity. And I'm not about to get up and say, 'God showed me,' because my days of doing that are over. I just believe you begin preaching what you feel and believe without having to say, 'God showed me.' Because then you gonna look like an idiot, you know if you get back two years later and say, 'God showed me something different.'"[21]

Just a year later, *Christianity Today* disclosed:

"Not long after telling CT that the 'faith message' (as articulated by such teachers as Kenneth Copeland) does not 'add up,' Hinn said that speaking out against Copeland was tantamount to 'attacking the very presence of God.'"[22]

Further condemning the prosperity message, Hinn told *Charisma* that:

"The teaching on prosperity has gone too far. It has become a business. It is no longer give so you will bless

somebody. It has become to get. It has become selfish,
worldly. It promotes greed when we tell people that if
they give $10, they'll get back $1,000."[23]

Yet, in spite of the above admission to *Charisma*, Hinn
repeatedly returned to the Word-Faith "give to get" theology
— even making his "sowing and reaping" proclamations
under the auspices of divine revelation. A classic example was
in the fall of 1999 when he again told TBN supporters:

> "This is the time to give. Look, I'm telling you this
> from the Spirit of God who's telling me to tell you this.
> ... I'm telling you this by the Spirit. You hold back from
> God now because of fear and it'll [sic] going to grip
> your life. You won't be able to be free then. You give
> now like you've never given and give laughing at the
> devil. ... Get to the phone. God wants to bless you. He
> wants to prosper you. He wants to heal you. The wave
> of prosperity, the wave of prosperity has begun. I'm
> prophesying this to you. The wave of prosperity is on
> its way. ... Only those who sow will reap. Those that do
> not sow cannot reap. ... God is telling me to tell you,
> don't miss this door now. It's open for you. Get to the
> phones, make that pledge."[24]

Also during the time Hinn was making his "reformations," he continued to routinely verbally assault his critics
and threaten them and their children with divine judgment.

Early in 1993, the television news show *Inside Edition*
broadcast an exposé of his ministry and lifestyle. During an
interview he granted the show, he promised to make
substantial changes in the way he runs his ministry.[25]

As a result of the investigative news report on his life and
healing ministry, Hinn appeared on a TBN *Praise the Lord*
broadcast to employ damage control. There, too, he promised
changes. One of the changes, he told viewers, would be that
neither he nor his ministry staff would make claims that
individuals have been healed. He announced:

> "From now on, starting [in] Cincinnati, we will not say,
> 'She's healed.' Let the person speak for themselves. Let

them say it. We will not say, 'They're healed.' We will
say, 'They say they're healed,' or something like this.
Because how do we know that they are healed? They're
telling us they're healed. So we can't speak for the
people."[26]

Back On the Same Old Road Again

It would appear that even this attempt at reformation
quickly unraveled. Observers at a June 1993 rally in Chicago
heard Hinn announce, "a second ago, someone was healed of
cancer," "a bone condition is being healed," and "a tumor is
disappearing from someone's body," among other things.[27]
Observers at a Kansas City rally heard the same kinds of
pronouncements.[28] He also told the Kansas City audience
that while he was praying the previous day in his hotel room,
Jesus appeared to him.

In the summer 1993 issue of Benny Hinn Media
Ministries' *Celebrate Jesus* magazine, an advertisement appears
for the "Sermon Notes of Pastor Benny Hinn." For a $120.00
annual subscription, the reader will receive one message each
month. The ad contends: "The notes of dynamic messages by
Pastor Benny Hinn on a variety of subjects. Presented in a
useful format for pastors, ministers, and Christian workers.
Nuggets gleaned from years of personal study, ministry
experience, and divine revelation."[29]

The August *Charisma* magazine interview is replete with
Hinn's use of the charismatic anthem, "the Lord spoke to
me." Review a sampling of his comments: "God is shaking
me," "He is showing me," "The Lord has been showing me,"
"I sensed the Lord saying," "The presence of God was so
strong," "The Lord spoke to me," and "The Holy Spirit
reminded me."[30]

All of these statements come in the wake of Hinn's
statement: "There have been times in the past when I have
been mistaken about what I thought was a revelation. I
thought I was hearing from the Lord, but I was wrong."[31]

Moreover, Hinn attempts to attenuate present-day revelation, placing it in a class by itself, when he claims: "The Bible

is the only authoritative source of divine revelation. I believe God speaks today — through the inner voice of the Holy Spirit, through dreams and visions, through prophecy and other supernatural means."[32] Yet, if God speaks today, how is it any less authoritative? If God is truly presently speaking through dreams, visions, and prophecy, how can the Christian attribute a lesser magnitude or worth upon His modern-day Words?

Hinn has also claimed:

> "I am re-examining my entire theology. Every bit of it is being re-examined. I'm rereading this Bible as though I've never read it before."[33]

Yet, Hinn's followers were able to, for $120 annually, subscribe to "nuggets gleaned from years of personal study, ministry experience, and *divine revelation*."

Word-Faith Teaching and
Revelation Knowledge Still There

Hinn has not dropped the concept of speaking out and creating reality by faith-filled words, a foundation of Word-Faith doctrine. He has simply nuanced and redefined positive confession. He now says that if we speak by the Holy Spirit, we can confess and make things happen. He still appeals to Genesis 1 and says we can, like God, speak creative words if we do it in faith through the Spirit of God.

Hinn told *Charisma*:

> "This goes hand in hand with Genesis 1 where the Spirit of God brooded over the face of the deep *before* the Lord spoke the creative word. More and more, I see the importance of the Spirit's involvement before we can speak out in faith."[34]

At his San Antonio Miracle Crusade in March 1994, Hinn delivered a message titled "Who Is This Jesus?" in which he demonstrated a continuing habit of claiming revelation knowledge by asserting a unique insight into Scripture directly imparted from the Holy Spirit:

"And this One who is, one day saw a blind man. And He did this: He collected some mud and spit upon it and made clay and stuck it on the man's eyes. ... I thought to myself, 'Why did Jesus do that?' Why did He just not lay His hands and be healed? Why did He have to make mud and spit on it and stick it on the man's eyes? *And the Holy Spirit gave me a marvelous answer.* You remember when God made man and He squeezed mud into shape and He breathed on that? And he became a living soul. The reason Jesus put mud on a guy's eyes was not because the man was blind. It's because he had no eyes and He just gave him brand new ones. [Hinn repeats the popping sound.] He is the source of creation."[35]

Hinn told his faithful that the Holy Spirit gave him this insight — an understanding of the account never before realized. It is certainly one not supported by any biblical commentary, Greek lexicon, word study or, most importantly, the scriptural text itself. The Holy Spirit inspired the Apostle John to record in the biblical text the events of a man born blind, not a man born without eyes (John 9:2-11).

Equally disturbing is that Hinn's declaration that the Holy Spirit told him Jesus created new eyes, dishonors Paul's command in Colossians 3:9 by bearing false witness against the Holy Spirit, and borders on violating the Third Commandment: "Thou shalt not take the name of the Lord thy God in vain." *Adam Clarke's Commentary on the Bible* states: "This precept not only forbids all false oaths, but all common swearing where the name of God is used, or where He is appealed to as a Witness of the truth."[36] This latter directive would certainly encompass Hinn's "The Holy Spirit gave me a marvelous answer" declaration. (An additional treatment of Hinn's exegesis of the John 9:2-11 passage is found in Chapter 15.)

Hinn has clearly demonstrated time and again the difficulty he has in giving up old habits. His promises to travel a "new road" always seem to lead him back to where he started. It is a road filled with the potholes of heresy, confusion, and myth. God issues a very strong warning for myth makers:

"In their greed these teachers will exploit you with stories they have made up. Their condemnation has long been hanging over them, and their destruction has not been sleeping" (2 Peter 2:3).

Hinn continues to travel down the same old road. His detours onto the road of reformation have been shown to be but brief deviations onto the route of the mainstream. The sign on his ministry door does not read: "Closed for Renovation," but "Open for Business as Usual."

Benny Hinn and the Assemblies of God

In 1994, Benny Hinn sought credentials as an ordained minister with the Assemblies of God denomination. In June of that year, he took the first step in the process by meeting with the presbyters of the Peninsular Florida District. His application was approved by his home state district and forwarded to the denomination's Executive Presbytery for final approval. The Executive Presbytery is the General Council Credentialing Committee.

Because of an outcry within the denomination, the Executive Presbytery said in August that it had placed Hinn's application on hold indefinitely. The office of Thomas Trask, General Superintendent of the Assemblies of God, stated, "...at this juncture, we are not able to say when it will be reviewed again."[1]

However, only a few weeks later, a news release from the Assemblies of God Headquarters said,

> "The Credentials Committee of the General Council of the Assemblies of God has approved the recommendation of the Peninsular Florida District that Benny Hinn, well-known evangelist and pastor, be granted ordination with the church."[2]

Hinn met personally with the General Council Credentials Committee and assured them "he had repudiated his earlier identification with the so-called health and wealth gospel, and that he had received correction offered him when he was wrong."[3] Yet despite his appeal to his theological reforms, he continues to have trouble with the charge made in Colossians 3:9 that Christians should "Lie not to one another." Hinn's declarations at the Assemblies of God Theological Seminary's "Signs and Wonders Conference" in March 1995, clearly exhibited his difficultly with the Apostle Paul's command.

A plenary session during the four-day conference was granted to Hinn to respond to complaints leveled against him and to pacify naysayers. Yet a careful review of the proclamations of Hinn continue to reveal one who exploits with stories he made up (2 Peter 2:3) and who boasts about himself and flatters others for his own advantage (Jude 16).

His responses to Assemblies of God leadership and pastors once again display his ability to talk his way around almost any objection or contradiction in his doctrine or practice. He is a master at disarming criticism, even from an astute cynic.

Consider a few of Hinn's conflicting statements he made to the Assemblies constituency during the conference.

I'll Huff and I'll Puff...

After a television news magazine segment, several major newspaper reports, and a major Hollywood motion picture focused public attention on the quirky and flamboyant stage mannerisms of Hinn, Christian leaders expressed concern about his abnormal methods. One such peculiarity was his alleged ability to "slay people in the Spirit" by blowing on them. The faith healer conceded to the Assemblies group that such action "hurts the cause of the Gospel" and was done in "ignorance." Here's what Hinn told the assembly:

> "When I would pray for the sick years ago they'd say, 'He's pushing them down.' So I was in South Africa and I saw a man blow on somebody and the man fell. And I thought, 'Boy, that's a good idea!' How can they accuse you of pushing anybody down if you blow on them? So the reason I began to blow is because they were accusing me of pushing. But it looks like I got myself in deeper trouble than before. And let me also tell you this: when you do things that are distracting

from the purpose, it hurts the cause of the Gospel. And
I did it in ignorance, I really did."[4]

How could anyone not agree with such a noble admission?
Yet, Hinn's confession loses all sincerity and impact when one
recalls what he told the readers of his 1991 publication, *The
Anointing*:

"Some have asked me what I'm trying to do when I
throw or blow at them. *I only have one answer: 'God told
me to do it, and I know better than not to obey.'*"[5]

It now appears that Hinn "only has two answers," one for
inquirers with little influence, and one for critics with clout.
Nonetheless, Hinn has either lied to the readership of his
book or he is now lying to the leadership of the Assemblies. If
his actions are God-ordained, as he contended in his
publication, then no amount of criticism by any individual or
denomination should cause him to discontinue such conduct.
Moreover, his declaration maintained that he knows "better
than not to obey" God. Yet, it now appears that in order to
stay within the graces of the Assemblies hierarchy his
statement should be revised to read: "Man told me *not* to do
it, and I know better than not to obey."

He Ain't Got No Body

Hinn also tried to downplay problematic areas of his
theology, even attempting to deny that he ever taught some of
the aberrational teachings for which he became notorious.
One such pronouncement was the notion that the Holy Spirit
possesses a body. Hinn told the gathering:

"I mean *I did not believe*, nor do I still believe, *that the
Holy Spirit has a body*. We are His body. God is a
Spirit."[6]

In spite of his efforts to disavow the unorthodox teaching
that the Holy Spirit has a body, the fact remains that Hinn
did "believe" and teach just such a concept. In fact, this
teaching was one which caused his publisher, Thomas Nelson,

to have to work and rework his writings. The original manuscript of *Good Morning, Holy Spirit*, which Hinn submitted to the publisher, announced:

> "I believe the Holy Ghost has a spirit body. Not with actual flesh and blood, but — like the angels — a spirit being with form, shape, and the ability to move."[7]

Realizing the implication of such an unorthodox pronouncement, editors at the publishing firm adjusted Hinn's comments to read:

> "I believe the Holy Ghost is spirit body, not with actual flesh and blood but a spirit being with form, yet without limitation."[8]

Yet despite their efforts to bring Hinn's remarks in line with Christian theology, the statement was still in conflict with orthodoxy. Subsequent editions of the best-selling book were then made to say:

> "I also believe the Holy Ghost can make His presence known through bodily forms, and yet remain without limitation and fully omnipresent."[9]

Conflicting further with Hinn's current declaration were other comments contained in the original manuscript of *Good Morning, Holy Spirit*. Hinn wrote:

> "What I am about to share with you regarding the Godhead gave me an entirely new picture of the Father, the Son, and the Holy Spirit. I found that God is a real person — He has a body, a soul and a spirit. It's true of Jesus. And it is also true of the Holy Ghost. Three separate persons, each with a body, soul, and spirit."[10]

A major overhaul of Hinn's remarks had to be done by Thomas Nelson's editors and the statement was made to read:

> "What I am about to share with you regarding the Godhead gave me an entirely new picture of the Father, the Son and the Holy Spirit. I found that God is eternal spirit yet with nonmaterial form."[11]

Additionally problematic is Hinn's implication to the Assemblies' fold that Christians make up the "body" of the Spirit. Believers are referred to as the "body of Christ," never as the "body of the Holy Spirit."

I Started a Joke

Next Hinn endeavored to dismiss the theological *faux pas* which has caused him his greatest degree of censure, the teaching that each member of the Godhead "is a triune being by himself." In October 1990, Hinn told the congregation at his Orlando Christian Center, "If I can shock you and maybe I should, there's nine of them."

In reference to this unorthodox sermon, Hinn informed the gathering in Springfield that his 1990 comments were made in jest:

> "Now sometimes, you know, I've said things from my pulpit. *One of them was just a plain joke and they made it to be a thing that they thought I actually believed it.* And I'll tell you about it. I was preaching to my church one day and I had read in one book that God the Father, God the Son, and God the Holy Spirit all have a separate body. Stupid me, [I] taught that thing in church. And I could feel the tension of the congregation. ... I thought, 'Oh, dear Lord,' you know, 'How do I get out of this?' Well, I closed my eyes and kept, you know, kept going. I thought it would just go away. And I got much deeper into it. And this book that I read also said that God the Father, God the Son, and God the Holy Spirit all have, you know, all three have spirit, soul and body each. And I taught that and boy it got even more tense. 'Oh, Lord, help me get out of this real quick.' So I thought the best way's [to] joke about it. And that was the biggest mistake. I was trying to break the tension, *I said, 'There must be nine of 'em.' And nobody laughed. Nobody laughed.* And do you know the critics took that thing and said, 'Benny Hinn believes in nine Gods.' I mean can you believe they thought I believed that? But naturally they heard me say it and they thought I did."[12]

Hinn's explanation is flawed in at least two critical points. First, he implies that his comment, "There *must be* nine of 'em," was more indecision than declaration. A review of the video tape of the October 13, 1990 broadcast shows Hinn declaring, "If I can shock you and maybe I should, *there are* nine of them." The tape reveals no uncertainty or doubt on the part of Hinn, but rather a boastful and arrogant preacher whose declarations are not to be challenged. Moreover, no tension or apprehension from the congregation is evident.

Hinn next maintained to his Springfield audience that his comment was just a "plain joke." It was not. Again a review of the video of the ill-famed sermon reveals that the Orlando pastor attributed his declaration to nothing less than a divinely inspired utterance:

> "I feel revelation knowledge already coming on me. ... Holy Spirit take over in the name of Jesus. ... You say, 'I never heard of that.' Well do you think you're in this church to hear things you've heard for the last fifty years?"[13]

Hinn's efforts at subterfuge, making his heretical remarks a "joke," have been utilized on other occasions. In 1992, following criticism from apologetic ministries, Hinn appeared on the *Praise the Lord* show in an attempt to answer his detractors. The "nine of them" statement was addressed:

> "I was teaching on the Trinity and ... I said, you know, the Father as a person, I said, *most likely* is a triune being within Himself. The Father as a person. The Son as a person on earth had a spirit, soul, body which we know from the Word. So well now, *it could be* that the Holy Spirit as a person too has spirit, soul, body. And I thought, well, I don't really think that adds up with the Word of God. *And so I said there must be nine of them. I laughed. Everybody else laughed with me.* Didn't think anything of it."[14]

Just a few months following his TBN appearance, he gave *Charisma* magazine readers the same story:

"In Finis Dake's book *God's Plan for Man*, he teaches that each member of the Trinity has His own spirit, soul and body. One Sunday when I was speaking on the Trinity, I repeated that teaching. As soon as I did, I could feel tension in the congregation because the people sense when you say things that aren't right. So I tried to clear the air. *Jokingly*, I said, '*There must be nine of them.*' Well, *the people laughed* and I thought, *Boy that was a dumb thing to say.* Then I forgot about it."[15]

It has been said, "To be a good liar, one must have a good memory." The chronicles of Hinn's life, ministry, and teaching are replete with confusion, misspeaks, and altered details. His effort to explain away his heretical view of the Trinity to the Assemblies of God leadership is no exception. In 1992 and 1993, Hinn stated that his pronouncement was met with laughter from his congregation. In the current version of the narrative of the event, Hinn now correctly maintains there was no laughter from his congregation.

To Be or Not To Be

Hinn further divulged to the Assemblies pastors and leadership that since his recognition as an Assemblies minister, plans are being made to move his congregation, the Orlando Christian Center, into the Assemblies of God denomination. Hinn stated:

"Well, the church, we are making plans to bring it into the Assemblies. I have met with Brother Don Lunsford already. And the first really step is we want to bring our pastors in and then tell the congregation to vote. And so the process really has begun. You know, it's a slow process, but it's definitely becoming Assemblies. If I'm Assemblies, why shouldn't they be Assemblies?"[16]

Yet OCC administrator Gene Polino, in the May 1995 *Charisma* magazine, takes issue with Hinn's blueprint. The periodical cites Polino as stating that no such agenda for Hinn's church exists:

"Orlando Christian Center has no plans to join the Assemblies of God. Evangelist Benny Hinn, pastor of the 6,000-member nondenominational church, was ordained by the Assemblies of God last September, causing speculation that his church might join the denomination. According to church administrator Gene Polino, there has been no action taken to change the current status of the church."[17]

A Bridge Over Troubled Waters

Hinn closed his "Signs and Wonders" discourse to the gathering with the prayer:

"May we not be distracted by doctrines and by influential men and women, by things which we think are of you."[18]

How opposite Hinn's petition is from the divinely inspired mandates from the apostle Paul to Timothy: "Watch your life and doctrine closely. Persevere in them..." (1 Timothy 4:16) and "What you have heard from me keep as the pattern of sound teaching (doctrine) with faith and love in Christ Jesus" (2 Timothy 1:13). Hinn falsely asserts that doctrines are "things which we *think* are of [God]" and which can "distract" us from true Christian living and ministry!

Only those who teach false doctrine, not in agreement with the sound instruction of our Lord Jesus and to godly teaching, would want to make such a request. Paul's last words recorded in Scripture are abundant with instruction on the importance of *being* "distracted by doctrines" (see 1 & 2 Timothy and Titus). Doctrine does divide. Consider these important examples: the deity of Jesus Christ divides the Church from Jehovah's Witnesses, and the Virgin Birth divides the Church from Mormonism. Scripture never instructs believers to disparage doctrine.

Yet Hinn's prayer seemed to have influence on the Assemblies of God leadership. At the conclusion of Hinn's dissertation, the president of the Assemblies' seminary, Dr. Del Tarr, invoked the need to build bridges:

"I have a witness in my heart that when the church seeks the Christian example of building bridges it is doing perhaps the work that is closest to the Master's heart. ... Few things are more painful than bridge building. And the incredible thing is we will build big bridges, but it is the small bridges that we hardly ever want to build. ... People can build a big bridge to the Episcopalians, a big bridge to the Lutherans, but we don't want to build a bridge to Oral Roberts. We don't want to build a bridge to somebody else who believes almost like we believe. And we can't deny these people are part of the Body of Christ. Why do we not want to build small bridges?"[19]

With the inclusion of Hinn as one of its own, the Assemblies of God had begun to build those bridges. But sadly, the bridges being built to heterodoxy were at the expense of orthodoxy. The Assemblies of God needs to realize the unholy consequences that will result as they tear down their bridges to orthodoxy in order to retrieve components to construct their bridges to aberrational and heretical teachers and groups.

A Revolving Door in Springfield

Hinn's ambition to be accountable and submissive to the authority and leadership of the Assemblies, and his stated desire to move his congregation into that denomination, were shortlived. In October 1996, just two years after his hotly-contested ordination into the church, he quietly resigned his credentials with the Assemblies of God.

Following the acceptance of his resignation, apologist Larry Thomas commented that Hinn "indicated to district officials in Florida that he was pressured to resign by officials at the denominational headquarters in Springfield. The Springfield officials have denied this, but then again they denied that Benny Hinn would be anything but a blessing to the movement."[20]

The Assemblies of God has had a heritage of standing against erroneous and man-made doctrines. That legacy appeared to erode by succumbing to "Christian" idols such as Hinn, with aberrational doctrine and practice. Perhaps the tide has begun to recede, or just maybe other phenomena within the denomination, including the "Pensacola Revival" at the Brownsville Assembly of God, have taken precedent.[21]

Power, Drugs, Politics, and a "Holy Ghost Enema"

Gilbert Chesterton declared: "It is this silent swerving from accuracy by an inch that is the uncanny element in everything."[1]

Faith healer Benny Hinn has been swerving from truth and accuracy for years and continues to do so not by inches but by miles. It is nothing short of amazing that no matter what Hinn says, teaches or practices — even if it is outrageously unbiblical and outlandish — his adoring fans blindly follow and attack anyone who points out his heresies and untruths. And for a man who claims to be in so close communication with the Divine, his life and ministry is unabashedly remiss. One scandal after another have repeatedly plagued him and his church and healing organization.

More Than Just Holy Ghost Power

A series of investigative reports by a Florida television station uncovered that Hinn's perceived powers extend beyond the supernatural and into the Orange County (Florida) sheriff's office.

For several months in 1996, Hinn was plagued by members of a small Volusia County church who demonstrated in front of his World Outreach Center (in Orange County) and near his plush home in a gated community (in Seminole County). The protesters were expressing a number of concerns, including their conviction that Hinn's prosperity gospel is greed.

However, according to the television news report, "Apparently some paid security workers at Hinn's church don't like this display of freedom of speech. Workers who just happen to be Orange County sheriff's deputies."[2] As a result of the Orlando-based ABC affiliate's exposé — which included allegations of civil rights violations — the sheriff's department took immediate action and began an investigation of its own.

A Family Plot?

One deputy who came under investigation for harassment of the protesters was Hinn's younger brother, Christopher. He was a part-time Orange County reserve deputy. As a reserve deputy, he was an unpaid volunteer who was to act only under a superior's direction. However, in June 1996, the younger Hinn presented himself to the demonstrators as one with more authority than he had.

During one confrontation, captured on video, he told the group, "I'm an undercover cop, I want you to take that camera off." When one of the demonstrators asked, "Are you a county deputy?" he said, "I'm telling you, I'm a law enforcement officer. Take the camera off." Then, when asked, "Are you an employee of Benny Hinn?" he retorted, "No sir, I am a sheriff."[3]

Responding to the incident, Christopher told WFTV reporter Jane Watrel, "I was not acting as law enforcement officer, nor was I on duty. I was in [sic] my own personal time. I asked them kindly not to videotape us while we're having a discussion since I was with another offic— uh, deputy." When Watrel asked who authorized his actions, Christopher answered, "I was acting alone."[4]

However, that TV station contended the younger Hinn overstepped his authority a week later when he used an unmarked sheriff's car to pull over protesters who had used a video camera at his brother's church. Accompanying Christopher at the scene was "[Benny] Hinn follower," Robin Johnson, a full-time Orange County deputy. Christopher told them to erase the videotape and watched as the demonstrators did so.

When challenged, Christopher told Watrel: "First of all, I did not — uh, force them off the road. They voluntarily pulled themselves [over], when they see [sic] me approaching." When asked if these people had broken a law, Christopher responded, "No. The problem as far as I had, uh I had spoke to the same gentleman, a week before, not to photograph us as law enforcement officers."[5]

Further compounding the case is the fact that the incident took place in Seminole County, where Christopher Hinn has no jurisdiction as an Orange County reserve deputy.

Civil rights attorney Keith Mitnick told the television news program, "Law enforcement can cross county lines when they're in hot pursuit of a felon or something along that line. But in a circumstance like this, it'd be hard to justify crossing county lines in using a badge as a position of authority."[6]

While Orange County sheriff Kevin Beary apparently knew nothing of the event, the news report indicated that "at least two high-ranking members of his administration did." An interoffice memo, cited by Watrel, said, "Reserve I Corporal Christopher Hinn, Deputy Robin Johnson, Commander II Roger Clark, Commander I Rusty Smallwood and possibly others" will be the subject of an internal inquiry in the department. Clark and Smallwood were said to be members of the sheriff's "inner circle." Watrel further reported that her "sources say Smallwood, Clark, and Johnson are not only followers of [Benny] Hinn, but knew about the harassment and intimidation of protesters and didn't brief Sheriff Beary about the possible civil rights violations."[7]

As a result of the report, Christopher Hinn was suspended as a reserve deputy and was ordered to turn in his gun and badge until the investigation was completed. Also, the sheriff has temporarily prohibited any off-duty deputy work at Benny Hinn's church. The church was reportedly employing between 2 and 20 off-duty Orange County deputies each week.

Hinn's organization asserts that the intensified security is necessary because of "serious death threats" made against the faith healer. The news report said that "Investigators are considering the demonstrators as suspects." However, members of the group claimed no knowledge of the death threats, nor any part in such menacing activities. They said their only desire is to exercise their right to protest against spiritual abuses manifested by Hinn and others.

Loyalty to Hinn Proved Costly

Following a six-month internal investigation, which produced a 200-page report, two commanders were fired. The investigation further led to the suspension of three other officers, while clearing four other deputies of any wrongdoing. Christopher voluntarily resigned from his reserve deputy position.

The two members of Sheriff Beary's "inner circle" who were fired are Smallwood and Clark. They were fired for falsifying off-duty records while working at the World Outreach Center, lying to investigators, and abusing their positions as commanders. Smallwood also was charged with destroying records he kept on the protesters. The officers would travel with Hinn to his out-of-town healing crusades while still on the county payroll. Smallwood also admitted that he would make an additional $4,000-$5,000 a night selling tapes of his music at Hinn's crusades.[8]

Sanctified Manipulation?

The final report said both Benny Hinn and the deputies tried to extend their influence across county lines by intimidating Seminole County Sheriff Don Eslinger. According to the report, Smallwood claimed Hinn said, "Sheriff Eslinger needed to assist him or he and other ministers would denounce him on television."

In an interview with television news reporter Jane Watrel, Hinn said,"I myself was not — and I want to repeat — was not aware of the arrest till afterwards." Concerning the allegations of threats against Sheriff Eslinger, Hinn said: "I had heard that before, that something like this had been said to the sheriff and I got very upset. No, no, no, no, no! I did not say that, nor would I ever say that to a sheriff. My goodness gracious, look, I am a pastor with a reputation here in this city. I'm not that stupid to be saying anything like that."[9] Eslinger confirmed that Hinn personally had not made any threats to him.

Donation and Tax Dollars Hard at Work

The firings and suspensions did not bring closure to the issue for either Hinn or the county. The protesters had charged that their civil rights were violated when they were arrested without cause outside Hinn's church, and filed a legal suit. In October 1998, Hinn and his church, along with the Orange County Sheriff's Office, agreed to pay $610,000 to 10 religious protesters who brought suit.[10]

The case became known as "Church-gate" among the media in Orlando. The trespassing charges made against the demonstrators were never prosecuted. Commander Steve Jones, a spokesman for the Sheriff's Department, told *The Orlando Sentinel*, "Settling their lawsuit against the Sheriff's Office was cheaper than going to court." He also stated, "The agreement is not an admission that the agency was at fault."[11] According to the newspaper, the portion of the settlement agreed to by the Sheriff's Office was $310,000, which includes $10,000 to cover the legal costs of the plaintiffs. Additional money, according to Jones, would come from Hinn's church.

Despite the agreement, not all the protesters were favorable to the settlement. Pastor Ricky L. Johnston issued a November 3 statement to the court and to all attorneys involved that said, "Some things are not about money." He condemned the nine other plaintiffs from the Wholeness in Christ Ministry, saying that, "Benny Hinn bought each of you for a dollar." He further stated that Hinn "got his money, by preying upon the Hopeless, the Sick and Destitute."[12]

Drugs and Delusions

Just weeks later, another scandal hounded Hinn and his ministry. In December, revelations of the heroin-overdose deaths of two of Hinn's employees were disclosed. The deaths, which occurred in late 1997, finally came to light in a report in *The Orlando Sentinel* newspaper. For over a year, knowledge of the deaths was concealed by law-enforcement and Hinn's church officials.

The newspaper disclosed, "A longtime aide to Orlando minister Benny Hinn died of chronic heroin abuse last December, a month after coming under suspicion of supplying a fatal heroin overdose to another church worker."[13] David Delgado, who served the televangelist for a decade, was found dead in New York City after returning from Hinn's crusade in Jordan. According to the newspaper, Delgado, 45, began as a "catcher" (one who keeps those being "slain in the Spirit" from hitting the stage floor) at Hinn's healing campaigns and escalated to become a friend and personal assistant to the faith healer. He would help organize details such as Hinn's "schedule, meals and grooming."[14]

According to Orange County sheriff's records, at the time of his death, Delgado was under suspicion for the heroin-related death of Sydney Williams. Williams, who at one time took care of Hinn's son, Joshua, and later drove a truck for the ministry, died November 15, 1997 at his Florida home after injecting himself with a massive dose of heroin. Delgado was being investigated in the death because Williams appeared to have been drugged following a visit to Delgado's home.[15]

Officials at Hinn's ministry stressed that they had begun random drug testing of employees as a result of the deaths. The ministry declined any knowledge of drug use by Delgado and Williams and issued a statement that, "Benny Hinn Ministries has given many people the opportunity for employment who have rebuilt broken lives through Biblical principles, healing and a new way of life." Church spokesman David Brokaw told the newspaper, "We will not tolerate and will not condone illegal drug use by employees of the ministry. When we find out about it we will act immediately."[16]

Hinn addressed the death of Delgado in his 1999 autobiography. But his description appears more damage control and whitewash, than fact. Hinn contends that "Dave was converted from a life of drug addiction and became a personal assistant to me."[17] He then writes:

> "Later in his life, after becoming deathly ill with hepatitis, he died prematurely. His death was a mystery to his family, our staff, and myself. Although reports of a drug relapse came to our attention following his death, knowing David as I did — and how deeply he loved God — I can only leave the circumstance of his passing in the hands of the Lord."[18]

While Hinn asserts Delgado's death "a mystery," Delgado's widow, Mary, revealed that her husband knew he was dying from cirrhosis of the liver, which can be a side effect of heroin abuse.[19]

Hinn's shaded narration of Delgado's death is also inconsistent with a lofty claim of deliverance from drug addiction. During a miracle crusade, Hinn drew attention to Delgado and told followers that Delgado was one of his "right-hand men," and announced:

> "This guy at one time was on drugs. ... He was a — he used to sell drugs. His father is a preacher. He rebelled against God. He used to attend Kathryn Kuhlman services in New York City. She used to come and minister to Teen Challenge when he was there with Dave Wilkerson. And Kathryn one day said there's somebody that God wants to set free from drugs. And David said, 'Huh uh, I'm not going.' But a few years ago, standing in our church he said, 'Lord, I love drugs. Unless you take that thing out of me, I'm going to die.' *And God took the desire right out of him.*"[20]

Safeguarding Financial Secrets

Then, exactly one week after reporting the drug overdose revelations, the Orlando newspaper reported that Hinn had "gone to court to block his former security chief from disclosing financial secrets that an adviser testified could destroy the television ministry."[21]

Mario Licciardello (brother to popular Christian singer Carman) found himself slapped with a federal court gag order to keep from making known information about the financial practices of Hinn's ministry. The newspaper reported that "Licciardello is demanding money to keep him from revealing what he knows about allegations of theft and corruption at Hinn's World Outreach Center."[22]

Hinn employed Licciardello in 1997 to conduct an internal investigation of possible wrongdoing and corruption concerning the handling of offering money received by the ministry in the mail and at its international healing crusades. Church officials said the investigator was hired to ensure proper and adequate security measures for the handling of donations.

During the investigation, Licciardello secured sworn statements from nearly three dozen current and former church employees. Hinn's organization is insisting upon the return of the transcribed copies of those testimonies, in addition to any written account of the conversations Licciardello had with Hinn, and any documents detailing the personal lives of former employees which were compiled by the church.

The conflict between Licciardello and Hinn's ministry began in September when, following a routine security check of the Oklahoma investigator, it was discovered from obsolete court papers that Licciardello was arrested and convicted in 1967 in New Jersey for burglary and theft. He thought the conviction had been deleted from his record, having received a pardon for the crime, the report stated. As a result of the disclosure, Licciardello complained that church officials tried to destroy "his reputation by conducting an illegal check of his background" and that he planned to reveal to the "secular media" the findings of his investigation into Hinn's business dealings.[23]

Hinn's church officials maintain that, "There was no theft and no corruption." In a subsequent *Sentinel* article, Hinn's organization tried to squelch details that originated from within. The report stated: "Lawyers for evangelist Benny Hinn were mistaken when they wrote in court papers that an investigation of corruption in the ministry resulted in the firings of several 'high-level employees,' a Hinn spokesman said."[24] Two of the ministry's higher echelon, chief operating officer Gene Polino and head of international crusades Charles McCuen, left the organization in 1997. Attorney Stephen Beik said the resignation of these men had nothing to do with the Licciardello inquiry. "It was a joint decision that it was time for them to move on," Beik told the newspaper.[25]

As legal strategies intensified on both sides, Hinn and his organization received a reprieve when Licciardello succumbed to a heart attack on May 3, 2000, near his home in Tulsa.

The Preacher's Wife

But perhaps the most embarrassing development for Hinn came when a sacrilegious video clip, filmed at the World Outreach Church (Hinn's church), hit the airwaves. The footage was broadcast on Comedy Central's *The Daily Show* and featured Hinn's wife Suzanne displaying her own version of the "anointing." She bellows to the congregation at WOC that, "If your engine's not revving up — you need a Holy Ghost enema right up your rear end."[26]

Additionally during her outrageous diatribe, she went on to lambaste the congregation saying:

> "Be God-pleasers. Don't be people-pleasers. Because if you're a people-pleaser, you're a butt-kisser. If you're a people-pleaser, you're a butt-kisser. And there's no other word for it."

The comedy program's "God Stuff" segment concluded with Mrs. Hinn frantically darting back and forth behind the pulpit, shrieking and finally taking an unladylike belly flop on the platform.

Hinn and his organization, obviously embarrassed by the unsavory conduct of his wife, directed lawyers to issue a letter to Comedy Central, its producers, and associate companies, including Time Warner Entertainment and Viacom, Inc. The correspondence charged commercial exploitation of Mrs. Hinn's comments from stolen videotape. In addition, the letter suggested that if the network was involved in any way

with the theft or misappropriation of the heretofore unre-
leased tape, it would be held liable. Hinn's lawyers further
demanded that Comedy Central reveal how it obtained the
footage.

If Hinn possesses the gift of "revelation knowledge" and is
repeatedly in direct communication with the Divine, why
does he need lawyers to demand such information?

Comedy Central and its lawyers were not intimidated by
Hinn's threats.

A Foreign Fiasco, Too

It seems that with each appearance on the *Praise the Lord*
show, Hinn provides for his critics a liberal dose of distortion
of facts and/or specimens of his irresponsible scriptural
interpretations. A May 1999 broadcast was no exception.[27]

On the program, Hinn spotlighted his "miracle crusade"
in Papua New Guinea, held a few weeks earlier. The "spin
doctors" of Hinn and Co. presented glamorized video
segments of the meetings and Hinn's alleged influence in the
country. However, what TBN viewers were not shown or told
was that it was not Hinn's "anointing" that ruled in Papua
New Guinea, but Murphy's Law. It was not miracles but
mishaps that ruled the day. Hinn's efforts there were a public
relations disaster from start to finish.

Papua New Guinea is a Pacific island nation of about 4.5
million people, 96.8% of whom profess Christianity. There are
600,000 Pentecostals alone.[28] The Roman Catholic population is over a million strong and is a potent religious and
political force. It is one of the most heavily religious places on
earth. With all these demographics working in Hinn's favor, it
is no wonder he was able to pull in 300,000 people for the
meeting. He was, for the most part, preaching to a largely
Pentecostal "choir." All those who attended the New Guinea
meetings became unwitting partners in this charade, becoming
free "extras" for what amounted to a slick promotional film
that tried to foster the illusion that Hinn had won an entire
heathen nation to Christ. During the *Praise the Lord* show, the
people of Papua New Guinea were referred to by Hinn and

Jan Crouch as "headhunters." Hinn's promotional piece called them "witch doctors and headhunters."[29]

Paul Crouch, Trinity Broadcasting Network's chief executive, was trying to establish a TBN affiliate in Papua New Guinea. A letter from Crouch to New Guinea's Prime Minister apparently tried to capitalize upon what appeared to be Hinn's influence with the chief political leader of the country. Hinn promised that because of his intervention through the Prime Minister, TBN would be moving into Papua New Guinea.

Raging Romans

Hinn's Papua saga all started with advertisements for the crusade, which enraged the Roman Catholic establishment. Hinn had a photograph published in the local newspapers of himself with Pope John Paul II. It was supposed to give him credibility and acceptability, but backfired with a vengeance.

The *Post-Courier* of Papua announced, "Hinn's crusade gets Catholic rebuff." The newspaper's report disclosed:

> "The Catholic Church has questioned the benefits and genuineness of the Benny Hinn crusade to be held in Port Moresby over the next two nights. The church said this in a statement issued yesterday when objecting to the use of a photograph of Pastor Hinn's meeting with the Pope to promote the crusade. President of the Catholic Bishop's Conference of PNG and Solomon Islands, Bishop Stephen Reichert, said the advertisement implied that the Holy Father (Pope) and the Catholic Church gave uncritical support for this and similar crusades. ... 'We see the use of Pope John Paul's picture in the advertisement for the Benny Hinn Crusade as an unscrupulous misrepresentation that is meant to mislead those who see it.' ... Fr. Ambane said in a statement that people should be wary of televangelists who line their already rich pockets under the guise of faith healing. He said Pastor Hinn had come under strong criticism, doubt and skepticism by those he tried

unsuccessfully to heal, theologians and by the international media."[30]

The news article went on to fault Hinn for being a "multi-millionaire" who lives in a "luxurious mansion," suggesting he was a con artist who was in collusion with certain politicians there for mutual gain.

Hinn was off to a bad start, but it got worse.

No Miraculous Foresight

Hinn says he has a gift of "revelation knowledge" and can speak "words of knowledge." His faithful believe he can somehow discern their ailments, call them out and pronounce healings. Although this is more like fortune-telling than truth, it is always used on those who blindly believe in Hinn's powers. It is an illusion based on the laws of probability that anyone can perform. There are no supernatural powers involved.[31]

Apparently Hinn's supernatural radar was off considerably in angering the Catholic Church and stirring their ire even more by showcasing his meetings with Bill Skate, Prime Minister of Papua New Guinea. Skate was, for months before Hinn's crusade, under attack by members of his parliament and the hierarchy of the Catholic Church for poor management, corruption, and unethical and immoral behavior. His administration, from the very start, was rife with scandals. An international news report disclosed:

> "Just four months after national elections in Papua New Guinea resulted in the installation of Bill Skate as head of an unstable coalition, a corruption scandal has left the government in disarray."[32]

Hinn presumably was oblivious to the sour political climate of the country, knowledge of which could have been easily obtained from published news reports by the self-proclaimed conduit of supernatural information. Such information would have perhaps kept Hinn from making the bold pronouncement that "God has put you [Skate] in that position because you are a righteous man. And I am volunteering as your ambassador at large, spiritually speaking, to keep promoting your country."[33]

Skating on Thin Ice

Skate was a poor poster boy for Hinn in spite of his political position. *Tete-a-tetes* with corrupt politicians are not the best advertisement for a Christian minister. The local headlines could have read "Skate on thin ice." It was, perhaps, thinner than Hinn and Skate realized.

The *Post-Courier* newspaper reported on January 4, 1999, that the Catholic Archbishop of Papua New Guinea had called for Skate's ouster to "rescue the country and its people from suffering and disaster."[34]

Skate, the man whom Hinn was using as a photo opportunity, was a corrupt politician who in turn thought he was using Hinn to bolster his image as a moral kind of guy. Hinn would have been just as well off buddying up to a mobster.

Despite the political unrest prior to and in the wake of his crusade, Hinn apparently decided to pitch his New Guinea Crusade on TBN to prove to his supporters and partners all that God was doing through him. Perhaps Hinn reasoned that there was no use in dumping a perfectly good publicity newsreel — especially when the presentation stemmed from a small and otherwise remote island in the Pacific. Patronizing and fawning, Jan and Paul Crouch surely agreed with Hinn as they gushed all over him at the amazing demonstration of his abilities, great powers, and political influence.

Hinn's ministry web site advertised that "Prime Minister Bill Skate, a Christian, personally invited Pastor Benny Hinn to come and speak to the nation."[35]

It was during this time that Skate was under investigation by his own cabinet for corruption and was in a struggle for his political life. He had been firing opponents and hiring accomplices to try to hold onto his faltering position. This political battle was being reported daily by the news media.

Yet those with a handle on New Guinea's political climate and Skate's legacy were not beguiled by Hinn. A reporter who specializes in Pacific politics said:

> "I take it you saw the way Hinn made sure to build up
> Skate at his rally in PNG? Sickening and utterly
> transparent. The pair needed each other — Skate
> because he desperately required some sort of religious
> backing to deflect the criticism from the churches, and
> Hinn because he can use his relay station in PNG to
> extort more money from gullible Americans on the
> theory that he is saving a whole country from
> cannibalism and headhunting and turning the poor
> ignorant savages to Jesus. Never mind that PNG has
> been almost totally Christian for the last hundred or so
> years and the place is overrun with churches, that won't
> get widows digging into their pensions in Indiana to
> send to Benny Hinn to 'convert the natives'."[36]

But Skate's effort at a public relations coup failed.

Exit Stage Right

Just two months after Hinn's crusade, on July 7, Skate
resigned as Prime Minister to pre-empt his expected ouster by
a no-confidence motion of his cabinet. He stated that his
resignation was to stabilize Papua New Guinea's politics. If
Hinn accomplished nothing else, he helped to hasten the
demise of Bill Skate. Unwittingly, Hinn and Skate focused the
opponents and set up Skate's last outrage. Many in Papua
New Guinea would say that this is the only blessing that came
out of Hinn's visit.

Everything around the New Guinea Crusade and its
aftermath conspired against Hinn. As the Pacific politics
reporter further deduced, "Now that Skate is gone, it looks as
if Hinn and Crouch have lost their chance."[37] Even before
Skate's departure, influential parties were calling "for PNG
not to grant U.S. televangelists broadcast license."[38]

An Australian radio news article reported:

> "Church leaders in Papua New Guinea have reacted
> angrily to comments by a leading American evangelist
> that the country needs a Christian television station
> because Papua New Guineans are cannibals and head

hunters. Prime Minister Bill Skate has indicated approval for American evangelists Paul Crouch and Benny Hinn to set up a Christian television station in PNG. But, the general secretary of the Catholic Bishops conference of Papua New Guinea and Solomon Islands, Father Henk Kronenberg, says the comments are un-Christian and a disgrace."39

Go West Young Man, Go West

In 1999, Hinn bid farewell to Orlando making a personal move to Southern California. Hinn said that while he and his family were relocating west, his ministry would stay in Orlando. However, just weeks after the initial announcement, Hinn changed his plans because "God has spoken." The ministry operation, he said, would move to the Dallas area.

Final closure came to Hinn's career as pastor of the World Outreach Church when the Rev. Clint Brown and his Faith World Church merged with Hinn's church. Brown and Faith World received WOC's facilities and 30 acres of property and assumed its $5.7 million debt. Both Hinn and Brown say they "loathe" the suggestion that Hinn "sold" his congregation.

Hinn's ambitions for Dallas included not only his ministry operations, but a plan to build a $30-million "World Healing Center." During his October 1999 Dallas Miracle Crusade, Hinn announced to the 17,000 faithful in attendance his plans for the center and solicited funds for its construction. However, more than two and one-half years later, *The Dallas Morning News* questioned Hinn's honesty for raising funds for the project that never happened.40

According to the newspaper's report, the facility was to "include acres of lush gardens, a Gothic cathedral and virtual reality chapels featuring faith healers of the past."41 Hinn told his followers at the 1999 crusade that $5 million was needed by 2000, and that another $25 million had to be raised over the next two years. At the meeting, Hinn distributed donor cards to finance the project. The preprinted donation amounts on the cards started at $1,500. Shortly thereafter, the undertaking vanished from Hinn's agenda of divinely inspired endeavors.

Apparently, the project never really made serious headway. In the summer of 1999, Cirrus Group, a Dallas real estate developer working for Hinn, agreed to purchase an 8.2-acre plot of land in Las Colinas-Irving, Texas. The firm put up $40,000 to $50,000 to hold the property for 60 days. Eventually the earnest money was forfeited, the Dallas newspaper reported.

Hinn's response to the derailed project is typical. His ministry stated, "Pastor Hinn felt God had revealed to him in prayer back in February 2000 that the timing was not right for the construction of the healing center portion of the development project in Texas, and he should wait."[42] But God was not solely responsible for the delay. Hinn's spokesman, David Brokaw, told the *Fort Worth Star-Telegram* that the ministry's donors wanted a larger parcel of land.

Although the "World Healing Center" would not be an immediate reality, a $3 million "parsonage" for Hinn would be. Construction of a 7,200-square-foot mansion began in 2000 in a gated community overlooking the Pacific Ocean in Dana Point, Calif. According to *The Dallas Morning News*, the "two-story home will have seven bedrooms, seven bathrooms, three fireplaces, a library, a meditation room with a balcony and a five-car underground garage."[43]

The newspaper disclosed that the "owner of the property is listed as Cove Holding Ltd., a partnership formed six days before the Dana Point home site was purchased for $450,000 in August 1997. Mr. Hinn is president of Cove Holding, which lists its address as his attorney's office in Irving, [Texas]."[44] Cove Holding, said to be a tax-exempt, religious title-holding company, claims its board of directors wanted to build the residence as an investment. It also maintained that Hinn does not personally own the property, neither was he involved in the decision to build it.

Hinn's domestic and foreign scandals and fiascoes are drugs, dollars, religion, politics, and theatrics in a continuing sad but comedic opera. His world is not only confusing but it is a disastrous world as well. It is a dark and bizarre world, filled with untruth and make-believe. It is sad that so many gullible people hang on the words of such a confused man.

10 ──────────────────────

False Hope
and Empty Miracles

Without question, Benny Hinn has achieved the distinction of *Faith Healer Extraordinaire.* He has become a modern-day phenomenon like none other. In the past decade, he has called and they come — by the tens of thousands, and now by the hundreds of thousands. Across the country and across the world, arenas and stadiums are filled to capacity for his miracle crusades.

It is difficult to determine if Hinn really believes his own claims of the miraculous, or if he knows he is just performing illusions for gullible followers. From nearly the inception of his "healing ministry," his miracles have raised questions and been challenged.

The Call for Evidence

As his traveling miracle crusades moved to a heightened degree in the early 1990s, so too came an intensity of scrutiny. *The Orlando Sentinel* reporter Mike Thomas repeatedly sought from Hinn's organization documented, verifiable cases of healing performed by Hinn. In his article, which appeared in the *Florida Magazine,* Thomas wrote:

> "Hinn says that about 1,000 people are miraculously cured of a variety of ailments at each crusade. He says he is a conduit for the Holy Spirit. Sometimes, while preaching, he will stop and listen as the Spirit tells him something to pass on. ... But despite all the thousands of miracles claimed by Hinn, the church seems hard pressed to come up with any that would convince a

serious skeptic. Medical literature is filled with examples of cancer going into sudden remission. The
American Medical Journal in 1981 reported on a
woman cured of lupus erythematosus, a typically
deadly disease of the immune system, after seeing a
Philippine witch doctor. If God cures through Hinn, he
does not cure ailments such as permanent paralysis,
brain damage, retardation, physical deformities, missing
eyes or other obvious ailments. When pressed for truly
convincing miracles, Susan Smith [who documents
miracles for Hinn's church] cited a woman in Orlando
who was cured of blindness caused by diabetes. But she
would not give the woman's name. She later admitted
that the woman's vision may still be cloudy. 'She still
has diabetes, strangely. I wish she would get off insulin.
That's what makes them blind. She was just re-
hospitalized. I don't understand everything, the whys
and why nots.' For another miracle, Smith cited an
Oregon woman who was cured of 'environmental
illness.' When contacted by telephone the woman said
that her illness was caused by the mercury fillings in
her teeth and that her chiropractor would vouch for the
cure. Smith also said there was a documented AIDS
cure, but when pressed for details, she later said the
final tests weren't in yet."[1]

Even more disturbing than the failure to present documented healings is the fact that a few years earlier during a
1986 Oklahoma City crusade, an 85-year-old woman, Ella
Peppard, died from complications suffered after someone who
was slain in the spirit by Hinn fell on her, fracturing her hip.[2]
Thomas comments on the incident:

"The ushers quickly pulled her off the stage and sat her
in a pew where she cried out in pain for 20 minutes.
She later died from complications related to the injury.
The woman's family alleged the ushers refused to call
an ambulance because an ambulance would not look
good at a miracle service. A lawsuit was settled out of
court. Hinn says he never knew the woman was injured
or he would have sought medical help."[3]

Charisma & Christian Life reported that a "$5 million lawsuit" was filed by relatives of Peppard. The magazine also detailed Hinn's knowledge that the woman was injured:

> "The suit also claims an usher tried to seek medical help for Peppard, but Hinn told him, 'Leave her alone, God will heal her.' The woman died two weeks later from complications resulting from the fall, the suit claims."[4]

"Really, there was no definite healing..."

Another sad example of Hinn's empty miracles is Ernestine Rodriguez of Santa Fe, New Mexico, purportedly healed of brain cancer during his December 1992 Houston crusade. Hinn took her and repeatedly "slayed her in the Spirit," proclaiming, "Satan, you've lost this one and you'll never get her back!" The spectacle was shown on Hinn's nationwide broadcasts.[5]

What Hinn didn't know was that producers from the television program *Inside Edition* were present when medical tests were performed on Rodriguez three weeks later.[6] The tests showed the cancer still there.

During his interview with *Inside Edition* reporter Steve Wilson, Hinn argued, "I'm told by my staff this lady had this — it's gone. ... It's not my job to call their doctor." When Wilson further questioned Hinn about the actress the news program hired to pretend to be healed of polio (and was proclaimed by the faith healer to be healed), Hinn said, "That was one we missed."

Faced with mounting charges against him, Hinn responded on the March 4, 1993, broadcast of the *Praise the Lord* show.[7] Instead of expressing repentance for his undocumented proclamation of healings and his declaration to Rodriguez that, "Satan, you've lost this one and you'll never get her back," he said, "Really, there was no definite healing, which we found out afterwards." Hinn then evaded any responsibility, saying:

> "There are cases where someone may receive something and not keep it or something goes wrong that I'm not

even sure fully I understand yet. I do know this: Healing is received by and must be kept by faith. There's been the cases where they've lost their healings."[8]

He then launched into a plug for his newly released book, *Lord, I Need a Miracle*, saying: "And that's why I really wrote, one of the reasons why I wrote this book."

A few weeks earlier, Hinn promised extraordinary abilities for his *Miracle* book. "People will be healed just reading this book," he told the faithful at his Philadelphia Miracle Crusade in February 1993, as the book was released. Ironically, for so monumental a work and in a relatively short period, publication of the volume was halted. In 1995, Hinn told the leadership and ministers of the Assemblies of God:

> "One of the books has been removed off the shelf. Actually shredded. My third book, *Lord, I Need a M—a—Lord*, I—uh the—uh healing book. Half of it was on faith. So I called the publisher, I said, 'I don't want that on the shelves.' They took it and shredded the book."[9]

Shredding books was not the only adjustment. Hinn apparently had to hedge daily telecasts of his *This Is Your Day* program in response to media scrutiny. Blame for healings that didn't pan out could no longer be aimed at Hinn, but was deflected toward his followers. His daily broadcasts during the mid-1990s concluded with the disclaimer:

> "The testimonies of healing and changed lives included in this program are personal accounts of individuals as shared with the ministry during the crusades."

However, at the very same time the disclaimer was being shown at the conclusion of his broadcasts, Hinn was telling readers that he knows whom God is healing and from what:

> "The Holy Spirit makes this knowledge available to His servants through the 'word of knowledge,' which is an insight into the condition of a person's life. In my case, not only does He reveal to me certain sicknesses, He

also tells me what to do and sometimes reveals to me
what He's doing in the service. That's how I know whom
He's healing and from what."[10]

A commitment to reform comes easy for Hinn. What is
not so easy for him is the change itself. The television news
program *Inside Edition* continued to monitor Hinn. A subsequent report, broadcast 15 months after its initial investigation, found his promise to have mended his ways to be
exaggerated.[11]

In one scene, Hinn claimed to have healed a mother and
her two young children of AIDS. "Father, a perfect healing,"
he said. However, it was learned that Hinn's organization
never verified the "healing" prior to his ministry running and
rerunning the spot on national television. When confronted,
Hinn admitted: "If she's not healed then we have a problem.
Do you know something about it that I don't know?" *Inside
Edition* producers did know something Hinn apparently did
not know or care to know. The woman and her children had
not been healed of AIDS. In fact, one of the children shown
was not even hers.

Upon being told this, Hinn again tried to justify himself:

> "All I know is what she said. I was praying she'd get a
> [miracle]. And I put it on showing me praying for
> someone with AIDS to give someone hope with
> AIDS."[12]

Other Dubious Healings

Crusade highlights from a series of meetings in Toronto,
Ontario, features a 21-year-old woman from Windsor, Ontario. She said that during Hinn's Lansing, Michigan, crusade
she had been healed of juvenile arthritis, an ailment she had
for 10 years.

The woman told the audience that she had undergone five
operations and had been taking the medication methotrexate
for some time. She reported that during the Lansing crusade
her "knees felt warm" and that she no longer had symptoms
of the arthritis. Hinn acted as though a healing had occurred.

What Hinn does not realize — or is not telling — is that juvenile arthritis often resolves itself and is outgrown. That is why it is called "juvenile" arthritis. *The American Medical Association, Home Medical Encyclopedia* says, "In most children the arthritis disappears after several years."[13]

Similarly, *The Merck Manual of Diagnosis and Therapy* reports concerning juvenile arthritis, "complete remissions are seen in 75% to 80% of patients."[14] Moreover, the woman admitted she had been taking methotrexate. *The Arthritis Helpbook* by Doctors Kate Lorig and James Fries says of methotrexate: "This drug is remarkably effective in many cases of rheumatoid arthritis and has become the preferred drug for many patients."[15] Further, Dana Sobel and Arthur Klein report the startling effects of methotrexate in their book, *Arthritis: What Works*, stating that studies prove that the drug gave dramatic results in over 50% of those taking it.[16]

Another example was the testimony of a man who said he was healed of colon cancer at a rally. Hinn cited the case when responding to a request by Hank Hanegraaff of the Christian Research Institute (CRI) for three verifiable miracles. However, when CRI hired a medical consultant to investigate, it was found that, "A careful examination of the medical records supplied by Hinn reveals that the malignant tumor had been surgically removed (along with the appendix and eight lymph nodes), rather than miraculously healed."[17] The other two case studies were equally questionable.[18]

Foreign Attention

Hinn's methods have also received condemnation outside the United States. In Switzerland, *Udfordringen*, a Christian newspaper, reported:

> "The American Evangelist Benny Hinn has received strong criticism from the Evangelical Alliance; following a healing service in Zurich. Thus it is reported by the newsletter 'Idea' which is published by the German Evangelical Alliance. The organiszers [sic] of the

healing service are being criticised [sic], for not having informed much about the evangelist's approach (the way of doing things). The criticism has made alive a debate regarding Hinn amongst the Christians in Switzerland. Further, a similar meeting that was held in Basel last year is being brought to light where Hinn prophesied over a man who had Cancer and said that this person had yet many years to live. But the man died just two days after the meeting. Hinn's meetings are called 'well-organised [sic] shows' and Hinn is accused for his sole interest in money. 300,000 Swiss-francs were collected in Basel. Though people were encouraged (requested, challenged) to write their prayer requests on the rear of the money envelopes the empty envelopes were instead thrown away."[19]

General Hospital: The Soap Opera Continues

One very notable example of Hinn's persistence in fabricating the miraculous is found in *Welcome, Holy Spirit*. It is purportedly a fulfillment of prophecies by Demos Shakarian and Kathryn Kuhlman. Shakarian prophesied that someone would walk through a hospital and instantaneously heal patients. Kuhlman's prophecy was an aspiration that all would be healed in one of her own services. These "prophecies" provoked Hinn to think and record: "I wondered, would God raise masses of people from their beds of affliction?"[20]

In 1976, Hinn went to Sault Ste. Marie, Ontario, for a crusade at the invitation of Pastor Fred Spring at Elim Pentecostal Tabernacle. Hinn said the meetings drew overflow crowds ("God moved mightily in that city") and were covered by the secular media.[21]

Joan Dorse, who handles the archives of Sault Ste. Marie's only newspaper, *The Sault Star*, checked the records and found one small article about Hinn. However, that article appeared in 1977, during his third crusade in the city. Apparently the media were not paying much attention to his earlier campaigns. The events Hinn describes are neither recorded nor documented.

Hinn continues:

> "I received a special invitation from the Reverend
> Mother of a Catholic Hospital in the area. She wanted
> me to conduct a service for the patients — along with
> three other Pentecostal preachers and seven Catholic
> priests. The chapel of the large hospital seated about
> 150."[22]

Hinn describes the chapel as being filled with chronically
ill, bed and wheelchair patients, and doctors and nurses
watching "from the balcony," with some being turned away
because of limited space.[23]

The hospital described is General Hospital, 941 Queen St.
E. in Sault Ste. Marie. The only other hospital in town,
Plummer Hospital, does not have a chapel that fits the
description.

General Hospital has 182 beds. The picture being painted
is that many of those patients were at that meeting, if the
150-seat chapel was so full "that many could not attend
because of the limited space."[24]

Hinn recounts that he took control that day, and with
anointing bottles in hand, ministers and priests were told to
anoint and pray for everyone present. Hinn says one priest
kept knocking down patients as he anointed them. Hinn adds
that patients all over the chapel were being healed instantly.[25]

At this point, according to Hinn, even Mother Superior
got caught up in the excitement:

> "After the service in the chapel, the Reverend Mother
> asked, 'Oh this is wonderful. Would you mind coming
> now and laying hands on all the patients in the rooms?'
> ... More than fifty doctors, nurses, Pentecostal preach-
> ers, priests and nuns joined this 'Miracle Invasion'
> team as we headed for those hospital rooms."[26]

Hinn recounts that as they walked down the hall "you
could feel God's Spirit all over the building. Within a few
minutes the hospital looked like it had been hit by an
earthquake. People were under the power of the Holy Spirit
up and down the hallways as well as in the rooms."[27]

Even the visitor's lounge could not escape the power:

> "We entered the lounge ... One by one, they fell under the power. In fact, as we began to pray for one gentleman who was smoking, he fell under the power with a lit cigarette still in his mouth."[28]

The full account in *Welcome, Holy Spirit,* is much more embellished and tops anything in the book of Acts or in the annals of Church history. Something of this magnitude probably never would have been forgotten at Sault Ste. Marie (1977 population: 80,219) or General Hospital. How did it ever escape the attention of the news media? As described by Hinn, this could have been the most incredible happening Canada had ever experienced. Many people could verify it. Yet there is neither anyone at the hospital who remembers it as Hinn tells it, nor records to confirm facts clouded by faulty memories. The real story is neither extraordinary nor miraculous.

An inquiry to the hospital received the response, "Benny *who?*" Director of Community Relations for Sault Ste. Marie General Hospital, Lois C. Krause, instantly denied all that Hinn claimed. She said that it could not have happened in the way Hinn's book describes. She laughed after reading a copy of the story. No miracles occurred in the hospital, as Hinn claims, she said, adding that "no patients left that day" due to miraculous occurrences.

Some older staff members did recall Hinn's name, but did not remember anything as extraordinary as his book describes. They did not deny the possibility that chapel meetings were held, but did not recall the meeting as recounted in *Welcome, Holy Spirit.*

Mother Superior Mary Francis, of the Gray Sisters of the Immaculate Conception order, also disputed Hinn's account. She affirmed that she did not invite Hinn, but reluctantly allowed his chapel service in deference to the Pastoral Care Department, which initiated the service.

The hospital then released a statement, which included the following remarks:

"No such events have ever occurred at General Hospital. His pronouncement can neither be verified through the medical records nor by testimony from past or present personnel of this hospital. Mr. Hinn's claims are outlandish and unwarranted."[29]

Broken Promises and Bogus Miracles

Renowned illusionist André Kole has taken a serious look at the modern day practice of faith healing. His study found faith healers who employ illusion techniques while leaving their audiences and followers to think they are witnessing miraculous healings. In 1992, he engaged in a face-to-face meeting with Hinn. A report of his interview with Hinn is contained in a chapter he wrote about faith healers in Richard Mayhue's *The Healing Promise*. Kole's synopsis reveals Hinn's failure to make good his word:

> "Benny faithfully promised time after time to work with me to prove to me and the world that divine, organic healing miracles are taking place every day and by the hundreds in his Miracle Crusades. He faithfully promised to start sending me documented examples immediately. At one point I said, 'Benny, I don't mean to be unkind, but I think I should mention that for 35 years every Christian faith healer I have contacted has made the same promises you have, and I never heard from them again.' Benny replied, 'You will hear from me. I'll supply you with those names right away. I will get them to you. I'll have my secretary immediately send them to you. We'll start feeding them to you by next week, by Monday.' After a month had gone by, I contacted Benny to remind him of his promises to me and requested documentation for several of the cases he had presented on his television shows, but there was no response then or any time since."[30]

In 1997, CNN explored "The Miracles and the Money" of Hinn on its newly inaugurated news program *Impact*. In the segment on healing, investigative journalist John Camp explored two very compelling examples of people who came to a Hinn crusade — hoping and believing for their miracle.

They were there with complete faith and confidence that God would work a miracle through Hinn.

The stories depicted by CNN are just two more examples of similar heartbreaking stories which are told time and again. The only things that change are the names and afflictions of the victims. CNN's news report revealed:

> "Thirty-five-year-old Laura Twilley, her body ravaged by cancer and chemotherapy, has been told by doctors she only has a few weeks to live. In desperation, she's turned to Benny Hinn. Like many others in the pre-show crowd, she experiences what she calls a miracle."[31]

Camp then reported: "Four weeks after the crusade, Mrs. Twilley died, leaving behind her husband and three little girls."[32] The other case study cited by CNN, that of Shandez Tyson, met with no greater success. Tyson, a 17-year-old student paralyzed during a high school football game, returned to his home in the same physical condition.[33]

A few years following the CNN report, another cable network, HBO, also made an investigation into the realm of faith healing. The report entitled, "A Question of Miracles," premiered on Easter Sunday 2001, and examined the claims of "two high-profile leaders of Charismatic Christianity." One of those investigated was Hinn. "Production Notes" for the documentary special demonstrated Hinn's continued blatant inability when it comes to providing evidence for his many "healing miracles":

> "Preaching in Portland, Ore., Benny Hinn performs 76 'miracles' on stage before an adoring ecstatic crowd. In order to make an independent assessment of the results, the filmmakers ask for the names of the healed. Thirteen weeks later, the ministry produces five. None of these turn out have experienced lasting healing. Among the devotees who sought a miracle from Hinn that evening was 10-year-old immigrant Ashnil Prakash, afflicted with two brain tumors. Although his impoverished parents pledge thousands of dollars to

Hinn, Prakash dies seven weeks after the Portland event."

It's Just Not Getting Any Better

Four people, including two young children, died while attending healing evangelist Benny Hinn's crusade in Nairobi, Kenya, in May 2000. The report from the Reuters News Service said police told a local newspaper, the *Kenya Times*, that "the four had been released from a hospital to be cured at Benny Hinn's 'Miracle Crusade.'"[34]

In addition to the four deaths, it was reported that "Ten other people suffered serious injuries including broken jaws after falling from trees they climbed to get a view of the American preacher."[35]

An earlier news article, which appeared in the *Daily Nation*, identified one of the deceased as Clondin Adhiambo, "an ailing four-month-old baby." The infant was taken to Hinn's meeting by her mother. The newspaper reported that, according to police, "the baby's condition worsened at the prayer venue and she was taken to MP Shah Hospital where she was pronounced dead on arrival."[36]

The Reuters story noted that faith healing in Kenya has become a well-received enterprise. "Preachers promising miracle cures from ailments ranging from AIDS to blindness have become increasingly popular in recent years in Kenya, a country where health care is out of the reach of many ordinary people and living standards have been gradually falling for years," the report stated.[37]

Before the Kenya services, Hinn took publicity of his crusades to a new level. On several television broadcasts, he suggested that Jesus Christ would personally and physically appear at the Kenya meetings. However, such purported appearances apparently are not unheard of among Kenyans. The *Kenya Times* reported in 1988 that about 6,000 worshipers at a Muslim village in Nairobi believed they saw Jesus Christ in broad daylight.[38]

The newspaper described that a tall, white-robed, barefoot and bearded figure appeared at the Church of Bethlehem during a miracle prayer meeting conducted by spiritual healer Mary Sinaida Akatsa. The man believed to be Jesus left the meeting by car, but the driver later claimed he was instructed to stop the car at a bus terminal where the man got out "walked a few paces beside the road and simply vanished into thin air." The *Times* article also identified the person claiming to be Jesus Christ as the Lord Maitreya. New Age guru Benjamin Creme stated that "Maitreya's appearance was in keeping with the crowd's expectations, as Jesus Christ, hence his bearded face and biblical robes."[39]

Despite Hinn's hype of the crusade in early May, media coverage of the event was sparse. The limited coverage by the secular media appears to be a strategy orchestrated by Hinn's ministry to control and filter crusade details. A reporter for the *Daily Nation News* told PFO that "there was minimal coverage as the local press were prevented from entering the crusade compounds."[40]

A freelance news writer in the United States said that while Hinn's organization permitted her to attend the Philadelphia Miracle Crusade (which was held a few weeks after the Kenya meetings), no cameras were allowed. The reporter was further instructed that she was forbidden to speak directly to anyone presented onstage as healed. Any details of those claiming to be healed were to come solely from Hinn's crusade representatives.

This strategy has long been part and parcel of Hinn's subterfuge. In 1996, news writer Mark O'Keefe remarked:

> "Reporters trying to get near the stage to find out more are sternly told by a gantlet [sic] of ushers, backed up by the faith healer's bodyguards, to stay back."[41]

Once the myth of healing powers is created in one man — and confirmation perimeters tightly controlled — we set ourselves up for the acceptance of a "superman" and are vulnerable to exploitation.

Quentin Schultze, in his book, *Televangelism and American Culture*, discusses the problem of personality cults, which Hinn appears to be promoting. He says:

"Televangelism is primarily the televangelists themselves. ... Charismatic personalities often attract uncritical believers who submit to the authority of their leader. ... Televangelists share some of the same charismatic qualities of other celebrities, including show business personalities. ... Protestantism still yearns sometimes for its own pope-like celebrities. ... Televangelism is an important seedbed for the growth of American personality cults. ... Today, people with money are godlike. ... Mass media enabled evangelical leaders to become major celebrities with national followings. ... These men became modern-day saints whose own lives seemingly displayed the special work of God. ... The tube gives authority to the voices and images of certain individuals, making them celebrities. ... He is not only a preacher, but the source of truth and knowledge. He is not only a person, but the special person that represents God to his people. The televangelist becomes the mediator of not only the message, but the relationship with God. ... Personality cults are always evidence of the human need to have someone to follow."[42]

If pastors are to be "above reproach" (1 Timothy 3:2), and Church leaders are to "have a good reputation with those outside the church" (1 Timothy 3:7), then Hinn fails the test. He has fabricated healings and miraculous story after story for self-promotion and self-aggrandizement.

The Miracle Worker

They come looking for a miracle. Some come searching for themselves personally, others for a loved one, and still others just to witness the miraculous. Benny Hinn's miracle crusades draw not just common folk, but have become a stage for celebrities as well. Hollywood actress Dyan Cannon, who frequents Hinn's miracle crusades, is one example.

A Heavyweight Healing?

In late April 1994, heavyweight boxing champion Evander Holyfield lost his championship belt to Michael Moorer in a 12-round decision. Reports say that during the 36-minute fight, Holyfield appeared to age 10 years. Four days after the fight, he retired from boxing. He was diagnosed with a congenital heart defect, which prevented sufficient oxygen from being pumped to muscles and tissue. Holyfield's "stiff heart" condition is not life-threatening — "It was not like he was sitting on a time bomb," cardiologist Dr. Douglas Morris said — but it precluded him from continuing his boxing career.[1]

Then in June, Holyfield traveled from his home in Georgia to attend Hinn's Philadelphia Miracle Crusade. "There are a lot of people who feel I went to the crusade to be healed," Holyfield said. "But I didn't go to the crusade to be healed. I went to the crusade to get closer with the Lord. And I got anointed and I got closer to the Lord and got healed as well."[2]

"The Lord is telling me right now He is repairing Holyfield's heart completely," Hinn shouted to the 9,000 cheering faithful during the first evening of the crusade, according to the *Philadelphia Inquirer*.[3] And so Hinn abandoned his earlier promise to "Let the person speak for themselves." During the subsequent services in the crusade, Hinn used Holyfield as a trophy, having him sit on the stage with his other VIPs.

And then, less than one week after Hinn claimed the Lord repaired the boxer's heart "completely," he and Holyfield headlined a segment of TBN's *Praise the Lord* show. Host Paul Crouch initiated the discussion concerning Holyfield's claim of "healing":

> **Paul Crouch:** Let me ask you one final question here. Have you been back to your doctor? Do you really have evidence yet that there is a change in your physical body?
>
> **Evander Holyfield:** I went to the doctor yesterday and I got out this morning. And the only thing the doctor could say is that I'm better. And I have recovered and so I can fight if I choose to fight, but I'm only going to move if it's God will.
>
> **PC:** I see. Okay. So at this point, you're not 100% sure then that you're going to jump back in the ring. ... Is that where we're at now?
>
> **EH:** You're right. It's God's will if I'm going to fight. I'm not doing anything these days to glorify myself, but to glorify the Lord.[4]

It appears that Holyfield has been caught in the web of deceit of Hinn's traveling healing show. Not only was he showcased at Hinn's crusade, but segments of the crusade with the boxer were featured on the TBN broadcast. Hinn's conquest even gained the attention of *Time* magazine and other publications.

Holyfield now has had to cover for Hinn's "revelations" of healing. While he said, "I feel good ... I'm healed," he has told his doctors not to release specific results from his physical tests. The *Atlanta Journal-Constitution* reported that Dr. Douglas Morris, following his examination of Holyfield, avoided a direct response to a question about the "healing." When asked if he sanctioned the boxer's physical condition to fight again, he stated: "I don't know that. I'm not at liberty to say." When pressed further about the results of Holyfield's examination, he conceded that the improvement wasn't unusual considering that his heart hasn't been subject to nearly as much stress as before and during the April title fight.[5]

Holyfield appears to have succumbed to the "faith-healer admiration syndrome," an exercise in group dynamics. Not wanting to make a faith healer look bad is nothing new. Wayne A. Robinson, a former vice president of the Oral Roberts Association, addresses this phenomenon in his book, *Oral*:

> "But there's a principle at work that's often missed by the casual observer: Not only do people want to be as he says they can become; they also want to do it *for Oral*. If they're in a wheelchair they desperately want to walk yes—but they also want *to please Oral*."[6]

Robinson further relates the story of a blind woman who attended one of Roberts' crusades. After prayer, Roberts asked, "Tell us what's happening inside you." The woman replied, "There — there was a light." The next day the newspaper featured an eight-column spread with the woman's picture and headline boasting, "'There Was a Light,' Says Blind Woman." However, when Robinson interviewed the woman he inquired, "What happened to you up there on the platform?" "Nothing," she responded. When asked as to why she said what she did, she responded: "I didn't want to disappoint him."[7]

Hinn's followers may not be aware of this phenomenon. Boxing administrators, however, were not as convinced of Holyfield's "completely repaired heart" as were those who attended Hinn's meetings or those viewing the *Praise the Lord* show. Boxing officials issued a statement days after the purported healing that they would need medical proof that Holyfield was cured of his heart problem before letting him back into the ring.

Further, it appears that "God's will" as to whether the former boxing champ will "choose to fight" again will depend solely upon boxing authorities. "I'm better" and "I have recovered" won't cut it in the ring.

Holyfield's assertion that, "I have recovered and so I can fight if I choose to fight," may be but wishful thinking or a "positive confession" on his part. Perhaps he may be able to "fight" in a back alley somewhere, but according to the *Atlanta Journal-Constitution*, "Leaders of the top two U.S. sanctioning bodies said Monday [June 20, 1994] that Holyfield couldn't box in their states without undergoing more in-depth, pre-fight heart tests than the usual EKG."[8]

Moreover, Hinn has found his way into Holyfield's bank account. A source from Hinn's Philadelphia Miracle Crusade told PFO that donations to cover crusade expenditures were low after the initial Thursday evening service. On Friday morning, because of the poor offering the previous night, the evangelist asked people to donate $1,000 to help with expenses. Holyfield raised his hand. Hinn then solicited the boxer for $100,000, and when he agreed, Hinn publicly requested the full $265,000 to completely underwrite the cost of the crusade. Holyfield agreed to donate the total amount. Hinn then prayed that God would return the blessing, and that the boxer would earn $200 million.

Hinn asked the Lord for "another bonus" to be given to Holyfield. "Give him a wife," he petitioned, "because he's got five children that need a mother." And then the evangelist said his future wife would be found among those attending the Friday morning service of the Philadelphia crusade.

Then in late 1994, boxing officials lifted the ban on the former heavyweight champion's return to boxing. Hinn basked in the glory of that announcement.

During the December 6, 1994 installment of TBN's *Praise the Lord* show, Hinn said:

> "Oh, by the way, I've got to tell about Evander. It was on the news, you people probably saw it but, he went to the Mayo Clinic and they gave him a clean bill of health. Isn't that great? ... So he's getting back into boxing. ... [Holyfield had been ordered] not to fight. Of course, he had something wrong with his heart. But in

Philly [Hinn's Philadelphia Miracle Crusade], God did touch him and I have it on video when I said, 'The Lord is telling me He's healing his heart completely.' And now we have the confirmation and he's going back into boxing."⁹

But a medical mixup, not divine intervention, has allowed Holyfield to return to the ring. The lifting of the ban had nothing to do with Hinn's "revelation," nor the boxer's "miraculous" encounter with the controversial faith healer. According to the December 3, 1994, *Atlanta Journal-Constitution*:

"Dr. Christopher Vaughns, Holyfield's internist, said last week that 'circumstances may have misled cardiologists' to conclude Holyfield had a non-compliant left ventricle. Those circumstances had to do with his treatment immediately following the fight in Las Vegas, including excessive fluids for dehydration and pain medication."¹⁰

Therefore, the medical attention and treatment Holyfield received, in addition to inadequate information being forwarded to cardiologists, led to an "inaccurate diagnosis." There was no heart problem to be repaired.

The December 28, 1994, *Atlanta Journal-Constitution* added:

"But a five-physician panel confirmed Tuesday what Holyfield had learned in recent months — that he was misdiagnosed by cardiologist Dr. Douglas Morris of Emory Crawford-Long Hospital, in large part because Morris had not been fully apprised of Holyfield's treatment in Las Vegas following the fight. Holyfield was given excessive drugs and fluids during his 30-hour stay at Las Vegas' Valley Hospital, testimony showed, and, for reasons still unknown, that information was never forwarded to Morris."¹¹

The doctors now confirm what Holyfield says he knew all along. "Holyfield now believes circumstances unbeknownst to doctors at Emory may have led to the non-compliant-ventricle diagnosis. He is confident he never had a heart problem."[12]

In addition, Holyfield "now denies ever intimating he was 'healed' by self-proclaimed faith-healer Benny Hinn. He merely insists he never had the heart ailment that was diagnosed."[13]

Additionally, sports writer Terence Moore of the paper said:

> "Holyfield told me in the aftermath that he never thought the faith healer had an effect on his heart. ... Says Holyfield, 'There really wasn't anything for him (the faith healer) to heal. That's because I don't believe I had a problem with my heart to begin with.'"[14]

Holyfield maintained:

> "I'm not upset, I'm just thankful everything is OK. ... Truth prevailed. Doctors are human. I'm not going to bash doctors. I believe in doctors. All I wanted was true answers."[15]

A Not-so *Holy*field

For the four-time heavyweight boxing champion, "everything" is okay. Holyfield's name and achievements will be indelibly recorded in boxing history books. However, revelations of his current lifestyle should cause Christians to restrain from making him a superstar or role model.

At his Philadelphia Miracle Crusade, Hinn had prayed for the then ex-boxing champion, asking that God would "Give him a wife, because he's got five children that need a mother." Hinn "prophesied" that his future wife would be found among those attending the Friday morning service of the Philadelphia crusade. Attending that service was a Chicago-based physician and licensed minister, Janice Itson. Itson did volunteer work at Hinn's crusades. Holyfield met her there and soon afterward began calling her on the phone. The couple were married October 4, 1996, in a private courtroom ceremony in Atlanta.

Holyfield married his first wife, Paulette, in 1985, a year after the birth of their first child. The couple broke up in

1991 with "infidelity" being named as a factor in the divorce.

Faithfulness to his present wife Janice has not risen significantly, either. According to a report in the *Atlanta Journal-Constitution*, prior to the birth of his first child with Janice, Holyfield confirmed "that he has fathered two children out of wedlock in the past year with previous girlfriends." In all, the boxing champ has nine children: one with his current wife, Janice; three with his first wife, Paulette; and five others born out of wedlock to four other women. In October 1998, a paternity suit between Holyfield and Tamie Dewan Evans "was filed, settled and sealed in one day in Fayette County [Ga.] Superior Court."[16]

The Atlanta newspaper also stated that Holyfield and Janice "have been in and out of counseling" since their marriage began. *People* magazine portrayed to its readers a veneer of marital bliss of the couple: "A fervent born-again Christian, Holyfield can see God's fingerprints on every part of his life, especially his marriage to Janice ... What they are sure of is their marriage. 'I always thought I wouldn't want to be married again until after I stopped boxing,' says Holyfield. 'But the way God wanted it turned out right.'"[17]

The *Atlanta Journal-Constitution* also reported that Holyfield "told Janice of his infidelity and the impending births and suggested they get divorced 'quietly' to spare her any humiliation." She declined and the couple has continued to attend counseling. She was against Holyfield speaking publicly on his infidelities and issued a statement through her husband's attorney: "Tell them Evander's wife has forgiven him, and that's all that should matter."[18]

Several months later it was announced that Holyfield and his second wife agreed to an out-of-court divorce settlement in March 2000. The agreement, which ended the couple's 3½-year marriage and full year of divorce proceedings, precluded what could have been a very messy split, including the incarceration of Holyfield's pastor, the Reverend Creflo Dollar, for refusing to give a deposition in the case.

According to the *Atlanta Journal-Constitution*, Holyfield claimed "that a prenuptial agreement existed, an allegation denied by Janice Holyfield."[19] The issue was never settled, the newspaper reported. In May 1999, Mrs. Holyfield sought that the divorce case be dismissed claiming that she and her husband had marital relations after he had filed for divorce, thereby constituting a reconciliation. Holyfield "said he couldn't remember when they had sex," the newspaper further reported. Fayette County Superior Court Judge Ben Miller, who presided over the divorce, denied Mrs. Holyfield's request, saying that Holyfield would only re-file his petition for divorce.

Holyfield also sought a paternity test on Elijah, the couple's child. John Mayoue, lawyer for Mrs. Holyfield, said he was "appalled" at the boxer's request, given his "track record of fidelity." The *Atlanta Journal-Constitution* reported that, "The tests showed the boxer was the father."[20]

The divorce proceedings caught even more of the news media's attention when Mayoue alleged that Holyfield gave $7 million to his pastor, the Reverend Creflo Dollar, and his World Changers Ministries. *Charisma* magazine quoted the Atlanta newspaper as stating, "The boxer reportedly gave more than half the sum to the church in the 60 days before his filing for divorce in March 1999."[21] Mrs. Holyfield's attorneys wanted Dollar to account for the millions of dollars Holyfield gave to the church and to Dollar personally.

Dollar promised he would go to jail before he would respond to questions in a court deposition. He cited constitutional provisions for the separation of church and state, pastor-parishioner privilege, and his personal opposition to divorce as the reasons for his refusal. Judge Miller found the minister in contempt of court. Dollar appealed the judge's ruling. On March 9, the Georgia Supreme Court dismissed Dollar's appeals. However, the oral agreement between the Holyfields the following day put to rest the possibility of arresting Dollar.

A Broadway Healing?

Holyfield is not the only celebrity to succumb to Hinn's anointing and be promoted as one of the faith healer's spiritual tokens. However, his efforts to lend credibility to his miracle powers only give him further opportunity to show his lack of discernment.

Appearing on a TBN *Praise the Lord* broadcast, Hinn highlighted video segments from his July 1994 Miracle Crusade in Indianapolis, where he says he healed Broadway and movie star Ben Vereen from a series of injuries and ailments related to two traffic accidents.[22] It was claimed that the actor had been given only a 1-2 percent chance of survival, but he did survive.

Hinn wanted the viewing audience to be convinced of the Vereen healing. Throughout the *Praise the Lord* broadcast, viewers were told: "Ben Vereen was literally healed," "You're going to literally see this dear man, Ben Vereen, receive his healing. You're gonna see it before your very eyes tonight," and "God willing, we will be showing tonight the Ben Vereen healing."[23]

Hinn also said:

> "By the way, I must say, we almost had a surprise for you tonight because he [Ben Vereen] was to be here with me tonight. But he has a little cold and just because he really couldn't. ... He just called and said, 'Look, I've got a cold, I don't feel right.'"[24]

Why one would cancel a television appearance because of a "little cold" after having been delivered in Indianapolis from the brink of death — not to mention being on the program with "one of the great healing evangelists of our time"[25] — is not explained. But neither Hinn nor the other TBN lot seemed to realize the inconsistency or incongruity of it all.

Even more toxic to Hinn's miraculous claim was when Vereen appeared on *The Suzanne Somers Show* a few weeks later and attributed his "healing" to his doctors and therapists and to a pastor who gave him the spiritual persistence to pull through. He did not mention Hinn.[26]

The pastor, the Reverend Johnnie Coleman, instructed Vereen to look to the supernatural for his healing. Coleman told Vereen:

> "People can be healed by a greater power — by God
> power. ... Your voice is not your voice, that's God's
> voice and nothing can ever happen to God's voice ...
> those are not your legs. God will dance, God will sing,
> God will do anything through you that He wants to
> do."[27]

Vereen said of her spiritual guidance, "At some point you
realize that you can't do it. You get into a higher power
consciousness."[28] These statements sound more New Age
than Christian. Perhaps this is because Vereen's true spiritual
mentor is no Christian. She is a former Unity School of
Christianity minister and credited with being one of the first
Afro-American New Thought ministers. She leads a church in
Chicago that, while not presently affiliated with Unity, has
beliefs that are largely harmonious. Followers of Unity believe
that Jesus is only the "wayshower," not the way, as the Bible
declares. Unity also espouses the unbiblical teaching of
reincarnation.[29]

According to *The Encyclopedia of American Religions*:

> "In 1953 she [Coleman] learned that she had an
> incurable disease. She moved to Kansas City and
> enrolled in the Unity School of Christianity. In a few
> months she was healed and she stayed at Unity to
> become the first black person ordained as a Unity
> minister (1956). Moving to Chicago, she founded the
> Christ Unity Temple, which first met in the Y.M.C.A.
> building on South Cottage. She became a prominent
> Unity minister and was the first black to be elected
> president of the Association of Unity Churches. How-
> ever, in 1974 she withdrew from the association and
> renamed her congregation Christ Universal Temple."[30]

The encyclopedia further states:

> "The beliefs of the foundation are largely in harmony
> with that of Unity School of Christianity, the break
> being largely a matter of social policy, not doctrine."[31]

Strangely, during the Indianapolis crusade segment featured on the *Praise the Lord* show, Hinn called attention to

Coleman's presence and asked the audience to "Give her a big 'God bless you'" as they applauded. "Pastor Coleman, bless you, sweetheart," he said on the tape.[32]

Hinn's blessing of Coleman is wholly foreign to the divine instruction recorded by the Apostle John:

> "Any one who goes too far and does not abide in the teaching of Christ, does not have God; the one who abides in the teaching, he has both the Father and the Son. If any one comes to you and does not bring this teaching, do not receive him into your house, and do not give him a greeting; for the one who gives him a greeting participates in his evil deeds" (2 John 9-11).

A Bigger Star Set to Appear

Perhaps even those with the celebrity status and clout of a Holyfield or Vereen became too mundane for Hinn. As his healing campaign moved forward into the new millennium, an even more dramatic and astounding dignitary was scheduled to appear on stage with Hinn.

Hinn's friend and colleague, Ruth Ward Heflin,[33] who acquired a trivial amount of fame with claims that "gold dust" would appear at her revival meetings, gained a further measure of notoriety with a "prophecy" regarding Hinn's ministry. In the months just prior to her death, Heflin got word to him that a monumental encounter at one of his crusades was about to occur.

Hinn, on his *This Is Your Day* broadcast, told followers:

> "Ruth prophesied over me back in the '70s and everything she said has happened. She's just sent me a word through my wife and said the Lord spoke to her audibly and said that He is going to appear *physically* in one of our crusades in the next few months. ... She said the Lord spoke to her audibly and said, 'Tell Benny I'm going to appear physically on the platform in his meetings.'"[34]

Hinn alluded to Heflin's prophecy at various times while promoting his upcoming healing crusades, most notably his June 2000 meetings in Kenya. Despite Heflin's audible word from the Lord and Hinn's fanfare of the prophecy, Jesus never "physically" appeared at his meetings "in the next few months."

All of the nonsense, hype, and public relations by Hinn makes Christianity look irresponsible and mindless. As author and skeptic Henry Gordon staidly comments:

> "The huge throngs that attend these faith healing performances are part of a ritual that's been going on for thousands of years. It's a crying out for the need of magical solutions to life's many problems. On stage is the shaman or witch doctor — only now he's impeccably dressed in modern clothes, his hair carefully coiffed, his jewelry updated from the ancient rattles and beads."[35]

Distorting facts and reality is lying. Hinn continues to do so, which makes one wonder if he no longer knows what truth is. In both Middle Eastern culture and Word Faith doctrine, one can speak untruths to create facts. Hinn is a product of both. In the Western world, it will not work for very long. Reality and truth will always catch up. And when they do, the Gospel is scorned and ministers are labeled shamans and witch doctors.

Back to the Dark Ages

In the years following his significant theological *faux pas* of the early 1990s, Benny Hinn, along with his editors and publishers, labored hard to present the pastor and faith healer as one well within the perimeters of orthodox teaching.

For example, a reading of his 1993 book, *The Blood*, shows that he has heeded the criticism of his earlier works. While the book's illustrations of the supernatural are as questionable and subjective as any in his previous works, its theological content, albeit borderline, gives an appearance of moving toward the mainstream of Christianity. If *The Blood* had been his first effort, it may well have passed without much note.

However, for Hinn, old habits die hard — there always had to be new or neglected biblical insight heretofore missed by the Church. As such, Hinn's subsequent teachings, while perhaps less controversial, still proved to be questionable at best. Hinn continued to introduce convoluted theories and presented them as indisputable Bible doctrine. They were theological steps backward into the Middle Ages and Roman Catholicism.

Hinn has displayed and even admitted a Roman Catholic mind set. During a September 1991 interview with Randy Frame of *Christianity Today*, Hinn said: "My upbringing, of course, was Catholic in that I attended Catholic school in Jaffa, Israel. And so my mentality basically is a Catholic mentality."[1] His background as a Jaffa-born "Christian" Arab (formally Greek Orthodox), may cause him to manifest a pre-Reformational mind set. Well-taught believers will find the assertions and implications of his teaching distressing and distasteful.

The Blood: Reviving a Medieval Fetish

How should we view the blood of Christ and to what extent will saying the word "blood" help us as Christians? Have we missed something in not constantly calling out the word "blood"? Does the Bible offer us protection over our house and from demons when we say "blood"? Hinn's book, entitled *The Blood* (i.e., the blood of Christ), is an enigma and somewhat contradictory. His is just one of several books which seek to put a mystical aura around the blood of Christ. Its teachings are by no means new. Some of its ideas have been around for centuries.

Hinn was quoted in *Charisma* magazine as saying:

> "But we have an invincible weapon in our warfare against the forces of evil: the blood of Jesus Christ. ... Satan and his demons are helpless against the blood."[2]

In the book itself he writes, "the blood does not have 'magical' power by itself. The power comes from the Lord Jesus Himself."[3] And then later maintains, "But there is no magic formula or phrase that activates the power of the blood."[4]

Yet, the book's abundant illustrations and admonitions contradict his statements. For example, he maintains, "Demons recognize the power of the blood of Jesus. If demons know it, then how much more should we know it?"[5] He further writes of delivering a woman from demonic bondage by saying, "I apply the blood of Jesus Christ!"[6] and of delivering another demon-tormented man by calling out, "The blood of Jesus is against you."[7]

Other statements include: "Immediately I said, 'Lord, cover me with your blood. Please protect me'";[8] an instruction to ask God to "cover your family with the blood," for their protection;[9] and the claim that Job applied the blood regularly.[10] Hinn writes that he asks God to cover him with the blood every time he prays,[11] and that he covers his children with the blood daily.[12]

Answers from Where?

Hinn told *Charisma,* "the Lord is once again bringing the blood of Jesus Christ to the attention of the church."[13] In *The Blood,* he writes: "When I asked the Holy Spirit to give me an understanding of the blood covenant, I had dozens of questions. But He gave me the answers from the Word."[14]

Hinn's volume even claims to equal the Bible. During the close of his February 7, 1994, Orlando Christian Center broadcast on the Trinity Broadcasting Network, an advertisement for the book asserted: "Inspired by the Holy Spirit and thoroughly researched, *The Blood* will enlighten, instruct, and guide you into a deeper knowledge of your personal relationship with the Savior."

However, a study of this topic reveals that Hinn's answers came not from the Holy Spirit or God's Word, but largely from a Canadian Pentecostal preacher who was prominent two decades ago. It appears that what Hinn is calling attention to is an old error discarded during the Reformation: the blood/ritual, blood/relic teaching.

Hinn's Influences

Within Hinn's Catholic "upbringing" lies the first clue to where Hinn got his teaching. The doctrine of Christ's blood having a power all its own dates to the old superstitious relic system of the medieval Roman Catholic Church. Philip Schaff writes that at the height of the relic frenzy in Europe, the Roman church was circulating a bowl of what purportedly was Christ's blood.[15]

Roman doctrine revered Christ's blood beyond the realm of many modern imaginations. Louis Bourdaloue, the French Jesuit and mystic (1632-1704), suggested, "...we ought to go to the foot of the cross and catch the blood as it flows."[16]

Benjamin B. Warfield, the former Princeton theologian, writes that the blood fetish became such a craze in the Middle Ages that so-called miraculous blood — purported to be the blood of numerous saints — was turning up in churches across Europe.[17]

The concept of the "blood" as having a power of its own was prevalent into the Reformation period. The *Westminster Dictionary of Christian Theology* says:

> "Since the Council of Trent referred to the body and blood of Christ as *partes Christi Domini*, it was subsequently argued that the blood shed during the passion was united with the body at the resurrection, save for those few particles which were now holy relics (i.e. the blood that adhered to the spear, the scourging pillar, etc.). Such blood, it is argued, is worthy of worship, and the Roman Catholic Church has appointed feasts of the Most Precious Blood."[18]

Some of this crept into the beliefs of the Moravians during the mid-1700s. Arnold Dallimore wrote:

> "...the lack of Biblical study and preaching was countered by the invention of elaborate forms and ritual. Most of the practices were without the least Scriptural basis. They included the burning of incense, the marching around graves, the display of gaudy paintings and the use of grandiose music, and these procedures were usually marked by the same irreverence that characterized the honouring of 'the blood and wounds'."[19]

Dallimore further cites Count Zinzendorf, who pushed the blood concept to an irreverent extreme, stating:

> "I am ... a poor sinner washed in the blood of the slaughtered Lamb in which I live, and to swim and bathe in Jesus' blood is my element."[20]

The people even spoke of themselves as "little fish swimming in the bed of blood."[21]

The blood/magic idea filtered into the Charismatic/Pentecostal wing via metaphysician and Word-Faith exponent E.W. Kenyon (1867-1948). Kenyon wrote:

> "...when Christ carried His blood into the Holy of Holies, and the Supreme Court of the Universe accepted it, Redemption was a completed thing."[22]

He goes on to write:

> "Perhaps no one sentence from the lips of the Master
> has been more misunderstood than the one that He
> uttered on the cross — 'It is finished.' Most of us have
> believed that He meant He had finished His Redemp-
> tive work, but that is not true."[23]

Kenyon taught that the words "It is finished" only meant
that Jesus had fulfilled the Abrahamic covenant. Kenyon goes
on to state:

> "...His Substitutionary work that began when He was
> made sin on the cross and was consummated when He
> carried His blood into the Heavenly Holy of Holies and
> it was accepted there for us."[24]

Kenyon was, in effect, saying that Jesus was limited to
physical things. He could heal the sick, feed the multitudes,
raise the dead, and turn water into wine, but He could not
re-create anyone. He could not give eternal life because it was
not available until after He had put sin away, until He had
satisfied the claims of justice, conquered Satan, arose from the
dead, and carried His blood into the heavenly Holy of Holies.

Trance-evangelist Maria Woodworth-Etter, who preached
just after the turn of the century, was said to wave her hands
in sprinkling motions, "sprinkling the blood" on her followers. This usually brought pandemonium.

This idea of the independent power of literal blood may
have been mainstreamed by Radio Bible Class' M.R. DeHaan
in 1943, when he wrote, "Perhaps there is a golden chalice in
heaven where every drop of the precious blood is still in
existence, just as pure, just as potent, just as fresh as two
thousand years ago."[25] Radio Bible Class now disavows the
idea and no longer sells or distributes *The Chemistry of the
Blood* because of this and other items of medical misinforma-
tion it contains.

From the 1950s through the 1970s, H.A. Maxwell Whyte,
a Canadian Pentecostal minister, promoted some unorthodox
ideas on the blood. For example, he wrote:

"Stretch your imagination for a moment. Wouldn't it be wonderful if Jesus Blood could be kept in the blood banks of our hospitals? Do you not see that everyone who could obtain a transfusion of Christ's Blood would actually be receiving God's eternal life in pure Blood?"[26]

Whyte, like Kenyon, also taught that Christ's blood had to be carried to heaven.[27] Further, according to Whyte, "speaking the blood" could keep the death angel away from cattle and dogs;[28] that "applying the blood" could keep away germs;[29] that "pleading the blood" could stop impending auto accidents;[30] that "pleading the blood" over a paycheck could result in a cash bonus;[31] and that "pleading the blood" over a broken car would repair the engine.[32]

The Link is Confirmed

Hinn says he attended Whyte's church and that Whyte was a mentor.[33] Whyte's widow confirmed that Hinn attended her late husband's church as a teen and received his water baptism and spirit baptism under Whyte.

Hinn regurgitates Whyte's and Kenyon's teaching that Jesus had to carry His blood to heaven:

"Remember that the Lord purchased man's redemption by His atoning death and resurrection, then ascended to His Father and there presented the blood which was the evidence of redemption. ... When the Father accepted the blood, I believe Christ Jesus received from the Father the gift of the Holy Spirit to pour out upon those who believed in Him."[34]

Colossians 2:14-15 shows us that Jesus secured redemption and spoiled principalities *on the cross*, not later.

One must be careful with interpretations. Take, for example, the imagery and poetry of hymns. There is "power in the blood," but it is the power of Jesus Christ and the power of His merits secured by His death and resurrection. On the other hand, there is no literal fountain into which people dive and swim in blood.

Holes in the Blood/Magic Theory

The fundamental error in the blood/magic theory is the assumption that references in the Bible to blood only refer to a red fluid or at least only a red fluid when it refers to the blood of Jesus. This is a gross error that misses the oriental concept of blood or blood poured out as a reference to death. Millard Erickson rightly observes, "References to Christ's blood are not to His actual physical blood *per sé* but to His death as a sacrificial provision for our sins."[35]

In what sense could Revelation 1:5 — "He washed us from our sins by His own blood" — be literal? No Christian ever was dipped, smeared, or wiped with red fluid to obtain salvation. The verse is metaphorical and portrays spiritual reality of forgiveness and salvation.

Joseph Thayer points out the vast meaning of the word "blood." He says it can refer to blood "simply and generally," or it can denote "generation and origin" as well. It also can mean "blood shed," "bloody death," and the "pledge of redemption."[36]

R.K. Harrison writes:

> "Because of its fundamental importance for individual existence, blood was frequently used as a synonym for life itself. ... The OT, therefore, indicates that atonement for human sin was obtained by the death of an acceptable substitute, rather than by its life, and this emphasis, which is basic to the Old Covenant, is carried over into the NT with specific reference to the work of Jesus Christ in the New Covenant. ... The sacrificial blood is associated with the death of the Savior (Heb 9:14), and the author of Hebrews makes it plain that the blood is associated with death rather than life (12:24). It seems evident, therefore, that sacrifices were efficacious through the death of the victim, and the blood indicates life given up in death, not life set free."[37]

J.C. Macaulay cites the observations of W.H. Griffith Thomas who commented, "Is there any charm or virtue in that red fluid which we call blood, that it can put away sin?

No, the material substance itself is nothing, it is what the blood represents and symbolizes, death and life." Macaulay then states that, "Blood shed means life poured out. Sacrificial blood is life poured out, yielded up, for redemptive purposes."[38]

Leon Morris agrees:

"Blood points not to life set free, but to life given up in death."[39]

James Atkinson affirms the same truth:

"The word 'blood' in the OT, apart from the everyday physiological meaning, is generally associated with the idea of death, violent death in particular. ... In fact, the phrase, 'the blood of Christ', like the word, 'the cross', is nothing but a pregnant phrase for the death of Christ in its salvation meaning."[40]

If we still have to have literal blood today, then we would have to have a literal wooden cross. Remember that Paul said he would "glory in the cross" (Galatians 6:14).

We are said to be saved by: Christ's blood (Hebrews 9:12), Christ's death (Hebrews 9:15), the offering of Christ's body (Hebrews 10:10), Christ's sacrifice (Hebrews 10:12), Christ's offering (Hebrews 10:14), and Christ's flesh (Hebrews 10:20). If one must ascribe such power to the blood, then one also must do so to the flesh and anything else mentioned in such fashion.

The term "Christ's blood" points not to itself but to the grand theme of Atonement. His blood is the ground of our Atonement. *The New Bible Dictionary* points out:

"...the sacrifices are still understood to be efficacious by virtue of the death of the victim. 'The blood of Christ' accordingly is to be understood of the atoning death of the Saviour."[41]

The *Holman Bible Dictionary* agrees:

"The term 'blood of Christ' designates in the New Testament the atoning death of Christ."[42]

It is important to note that Paul does not mention "the blood" as part of the armor of God in Ephesians 6, while Hinn calls it "an invincible weapon in our warfare." Those who opt for a crass literalism and want a literal relic, a fetish, a bowl of red fluid, may be closer to paganism than Christianity. They have a superstitious view of blood, they misunderstand biblical words and concepts and create a subtle diversion from the person of Jesus. They lead unsuspecting believers astray, making them think they need to rely on vain repetitions, such as "pleading the blood," to secure spiritual safety.

Bad Company

Blood/magic doctrine turns up among some suspicious doctrinal company. Trevor Ravenscroft took the idea a step further with his "spear of Longinus." Ravenscroft said that the spear which pierced the side of Jesus was so empowered by Christ's blood that, when it ended up in Germany, it was the reason for Hitler's power in Europe. This teaching originated from two mediumistic women who claimed to receive messages from the dead.[43]

In 1980, Ray Stedman's Discovery Foundation helped finance a book by Arthur Custance, titled *The Seed of the Woman*. Custance, who believes in soul sleep and annihilationism, teaches in this book that Jesus rose in a flesh-and-blood body and that He transported that mutilated, bruised, wounded body to heaven, leaving the blood there and assuming another body to come back and make post-Resurrection appearances.[44]

Trouble in the Endnotes

There are two additional concerns. Hinn, or his ghost writers, use footnotes to appeal to some well-respected, mainstream authors. We should not suppose that writers such as R.A. Torrey, Billy Graham, A.W. Tozer, Andrew Murray and others would, for a minute, endorse the blood/magic or blood/relic ideas of Benny Hinn. The misquoting or misusing of authors is something one would expect from The Watchtower Society, not a minister of the Gospel.

On the other hand, some may see footnotes citing Maxwell Whyte, Derek Prince, and David Alsobrook, and assume that these authors are biblical and safe. Hinn's citations of these men, especially Whyte, may be, for some of his readership, a springboard to full-blown heresy.

While "the blood" is a term used in Scripture to denote the death and merits of Christ, Hinn's teachings on the subject must be rejected. Christians need to understand biblical terms both linguistically and contextually. Because of teachers such as Hinn, many sincere but misinformed Christians are trying to "plead the blood." While this may produce euphoric feelings and a sense of spiritual well-being, it lacks scriptural support. Additionally, it sets the pleader up for disappointment by creating false expectations.

Reversing the Reformation?

In 1994, Hinn moved forward with *Miracles: Yesterday, Today & Forever*, a three-hour video which not only promoted him as the greatest faith healer of all time, it also set him up as a kind of Charismatic priest or pope.

What gets lost in Hinn's brazen and self-serving video are crucial biblical doctrines. He is presented as a modern-day "Holy of Holies" and a "point of contact" for the power and anointing of God, much as Roman Catholic priests were presented in teaching of medieval times that believers needed intermediaries through whom to approach God.

The three-hour video features footage of Hinn's assemblies interwoven with past footage from services conducted by Oral Roberts. Both provide commentary.

In the presentation, Hinn says:

> "In Oral's case, the presence of God would come on his hand. ... Oral had to touch them, he felt it on his hand. I don't feel anything on my hand. Instead I felt it all through my being. ...my whole body goes numb. ... It's as though I get plugged into some electric plug or something."[45]

Many come to Hinn to be touched for healing, to be "slain in the Spirit" by his touch, or to just get a blessing. On his television broadcasts he invites viewers to stretch forth their hands toward his.

Medieval Catholic priests were believed to have power to absolve sins and turn communion bread into Christ's literal flesh through a miracle called transubstantiation. The priests of that day mediated the grace of God. The Reformers challenged that teaching by insisting that all believers can directly contact God through his Son, Jesus Christ. They cited 1 Timothy 2:5, which says, "There is one mediator between God and men, the man Christ Jesus," and 1 Peter 2:9, which says, "But you are a chosen race, a royal priesthood, a holy nation, a people for God's own purpose."[46]

Albert Barnes, commenting on 1 Peter 2:5, notes that the whole body of Christians are priests and that every believer should be engaged in offering acceptable sacrifice to God. He further instructs:

> "The business is not intrusted to a particular class to be known as priests; there is not a particular portion to whom the name is to be particularly given; but *every* Christian is in fact a priest, and is engaged in offering an acceptable sacrifice to God."[47]

Gerhard Kittel's *Theological Dictionary of the New Testament* agrees:

> "...the whole new people of God is a priestly fellowship."[48]

Commenting on the priesthood of all believers, B.K. Kuiper asserts:

> "Closely related to this aspect of reform was the stress on the priesthood of all believers. This meant that men went directly to God; they did not gain salvation through the Church, but became members of the Church when they became believers. The Roman Catholic Church used the name priest for clergyman, which meant that they stood, as in Old Testament times, between man and God. The reformers spoke of

all men as priests, personally speaking to God, without the mediation of the Church."[49]

This vital doctrine is laid out in the *Dictionary of Christianity in America* in the following way:

> "**Priesthood of Believers.** A Protestant principle whereby each believer has immediate access to God through the one mediator, Jesus Christ. One of the great principles of the sixteenth-century Protestant Reformation, as expounded by Martin Luther, was the priesthood of all believers. Joined with justification by faith alone and the authority of Scripture alone, it cut through the tangles of medieval Catholicism that tended to place barriers between the individual Christian and God. The implications of the principle were that no priest was necessary."[50]

The *Dictionary* further comments:

> "The general effects of this Protestant principle were at least threefold. First, it meant that lay-people prayed directly to God through Jesus Christ, thus increasing lay involvement in private and public worship. Second, it meant that God communicated directly to the individual Christian through his Word, the Bible, thus encouraging the production of vernacular versions of Scripture and the pursuit of lay Bible study. Third, it meant a new sense of Christian liberty for the ordinary Christian, who felt no longer bound by the authority of extrabiblical traditions or by ecclesiastical hierarchies."[51]

This principle was insisted upon by the Reformers and went hand in hand with the understanding that there are not two levels of Christians, those that are "spiritual" and those that are just ordinary. The Reformers knew that ordinary versus "spiritual" would only establish another pseudo-priesthood with the "spiritual" ones being sought for mediation.[52]

A doctrine closely related to the priesthood of believers is the doctrine of access, which says believers have access to the presence of God. Prayer is possible because of access. Ephesians 2:18 says, "For through Him we both have *access* through one Spirit to the Father." Ephesians 3:12 says, "In whom we have boldness and confident *access* through faith in Him."

W.E. Vine says:

> "...associated [with] the thought of freedom to enter ... This access involves the acceptance which we have in Christ with God, and the privilege of His favour towards us."[53]

This doctrine of access is beautifully described by Henry Gariepy as he comments on Hebrews 6 and 7 and notes its connection to the believer's priesthood:

> "...Christ went as the High Priest and opened a direct access to God for us. No longer is there required a human intermediary. The veil was rent in two. The middle wall of partition was broken down. Christ conferred the sacred privilege of the priesthood on all believers."[54]

It appears that Hinn's message obscures these biblical truths. As one prominent Pentecostal leader wrote concerning Hinn, "This man is an instrument in the hands of the Holy Spirit to bring people into the presence of God."[55] One of Hinn's superstar supporters, four-time heavyweight champion Evander Holyfield, also unwittingly acknowledged that the presence and words of the faith healer are tantamount to hearing from God. During a broadcast of Trinity Broadcasting Network's *Praise the Lord* show, on which Holyfield was a guest, the former boxing champ said:

> "So this young lady would come over every day and share the Word with me. And this young lady would tell me, 'Well, God said this, God said that.' And I was kind of curious and kind of wondering what she said. It only just made me want to be able to get in the presence of the Lord to hear for myself. And I asked her, 'What can I do, where the Lord can speak to me

instead of just speaking to you all the time?' And with that she spoke about coming to the Benny Hinn service."[56]

The idea that Hinn is a kind of Charismatic pope contradicts all that the Reformers strove to teach.

Hinn doesn't derive his authority from anything in the Bible, so he must go to others, such as Oral Roberts. The Hinn video has Oral Roberts passing his "mantle" to Hinn.

As stated earlier, Hinn claims a whole-body anointing, although he previously had said that he only felt it in his hand. Roberts' son, Richard, claimed the same kind of anointing in 1982 when he tried to launch his own "healing" career. The younger Roberts later settled for a daily broadcast with a safer "word of knowledge" ministry.[57]

Roberts' Endorsement

Students of Oral Roberts' life know his tendency to endorse "healers" and religious figures to enhance himself, and enter political alliances when he deemed them advantageous.[58]

In the *Miracles* video, Roberts says, "The Lord has chosen to manifest the word of knowledge more in him [Hinn] than he did in me. ... I saw Kathryn Kuhlman, who I thought was unparalleled," implying that Hinn is greater than Kuhlman. Roberts then reaffirms that God's power was in his right hand, however Hinn's anointing "fills the building. It's a total atmosphere change. ... I think a higher level has come."[59]

David E. Harrell, Jr., is considered Oral Roberts' authorized biographer. In writing his 622-page tome, Harrell had complete access to Roberts, as well as his family and friends. Apart from financial records, Harrell was given carté blanch to the Roberts organization to be able to write his book, *Oral Roberts — An American Life*.

Tracing Roberts' life in this very informative book (remember — written by a friend, a confidant, and an admirer) we find that early on (ca. 1940s) the faith healer learned the nuances and struggles of "political" alliances. Harrell gives us this insight:

"Oral admitted with some remorse that he had been completely caught up in the 'politics' of the 'kingdom of God.' It was a thinly veiled and tough political world in which dexterous revivalists and tenacious organizers struggled for position within their tiny universe. Shut off from positions in mainstream Christianity, those in power doggedly defended their status against young interlopers. The ministerial rank was freely given, but denominational standing was won in battle. Pentecostal superintendents and bishops were Christian warlords jealously protecting their small and ever-vulnerable financial and spiritual fiefdoms. In short, in the midst of the ecstasy and free flow of the spirit there was an undercurrent of peasant cunning and political common sense."[60]

In 1949, Roberts found it necessary to make friends with and endorse arch-heretic William Branham. Branham opposed the doctrine of the Trinity and believed himself to be the "angel" of the Church of Laodicea.[61] Roberts was Branham's nearest rival on the healing circuit, and Harrell details the "working agreement" they had together. They especially gave one another joint endorsements that Harrell calls "patly religious politics."[62] They, as well, published one another's schedules of meetings. It can be established that Branham was influenced by Franklin Hall and the heretical Latter Rain Movement, which we will mention later. Roberts was certainly affected by Latter Rain teaching in at least a few areas, as is Hinn.

Roberts' biggest and most helpful alliance was with Billy Graham in the 1960s. Harrell notes that Graham's appearance with Roberts "was a giant step toward mainstream American Christianity, calling the attention of the outside world to the new image of Oral Roberts."[63]

In the 1970s, Harrell points out that Kathryn Kuhlman "signed on as 'head cheerleader'" for Roberts and his university. In 1972, she was granted the first honorary doctorate from Oral Roberts University.[64]

In the 1980s, Roberts gave all kinds of support and promotion to Word-Faith teacher Kenneth Hagin. Hagin took part in the dedication of the City of Faith. It seems that Roberts is not much interested in theology or proper belief. Both Kenneth Hagin and Kenneth Copeland have been featured speakers for Roberts.[65] Harrell makes the telling statement that Roberts' "friendships were functional and superficial."[66] He also notes that Roberts' ties with Hagin gave him a "whole new constituency that loved and honored him."[67]

Roberts' association to Ken Copeland rubbed off on son Richard. Harrell says that, "Kenneth Copeland presented him a four-engine Viscount airplane as a gift."[68]

Roberts' "passing the baton" to Hinn may be good theater and boost careers, but it is hardly impressive because it perpetuates the bondage of a Charismatic priesthood and flies in the face of the biblical doctrine of the priesthood of all believers. Roberts has a penchant for endorsing questionable people.

Besides Hinn's apparent attempt to establish a Charismatic priesthood headed by himself, his video promoted a heresy spawned by the Latter Rain Movement of the 1940s. Latter Rain taught that the power and gifts of God could be transferred through human mediators. This established a priesthood of Latter Rain shepherds and spawned many abuses of the Shepherding Movement. Latter Rain also taught the possibility of sinless perfection and the possibility of immortality in the flesh.

The Assemblies of God has denounced the prophets and practices of the Latter Rain Movement.[69] In particular, the Assemblies of God denounced Impartation, a practice clearly visible at Hinn meetings. Dr. W.E. Nunnally, Associate Professor of Early Judaism and Christian Origins at Central Bible College in Springfield, Mo., explains Impartation and its ramifications. He cites Hinn's impartation and says:

> "A case in point is his belief in and practice of the heretical 'Latter Rain' doctrine known popularly as 'Impartation' (i.e., the belief that certain 'special' people have a 'special' ability to 'impart' the Baptism of the Holy Spirit, the gift of tongues as well as other

gifts, and special enduments of power to others; cf. *Dictionary of Pentecostal and Charismatic Movements*, pp. 532-534). 'Impartation' services, testimonies, and advertisements have been regularly featured in recent months on his broadcasts. It should be remembered that this and other 'Latter Rain' doctrines were officially condemned by the General Council of 1949 (cf. *Minutes*, 1949, p. 26)."[70]

Lewis Sperry Chafer reminds us:

"As the Old Testament high priest is a type of Christ, so the Old Testament priest is a type of the believer. The priest of both Testaments is (1) born to his office, (2) properly inducted into service by a full bath, (3) serving under divine appointment. Israel had a priesthood in one family only; all the Church is a priesthood. The New Testament priest offers no efficacious sacrifices, but is unceasingly responsible in matters of worship, sacrifice, and intercession (Rom. 12:1-2, etc.). A distinction must be observed between the priestly office of the believer which all share alike and equally, on the one hand, and gifts for service which differ among Christians though to each believer some gift is given, on the other (1 Cor. 12:4)."[71]

The apostle Paul warned of personality cults when he said "each one of you is saying, 'I am of Paul,' and 'I of Apollos,' and 'I of Cephas.'" Today we could easily paraphrase since some are saying: "I am of Benny," or "I am of Jimmy," or "I am of Morris," or "I am of Rodney." Yet Paul answers, "Has Christ been divided? Paul was not crucified for you" (1 Corinthians 1:12-13). Because Jesus is there for all of us all the time, we can see the error of factions and the emptiness of personality cults.

True pastors are not mediators, or "points of contact," or manipulators of physical states. They are teachers, coaches, friends, examples, instructors, shepherds, and encouragers to the body of Christ. They do not pretend to function as priests in any sense. They are to be humble examples. Peter advises pastors:

"Shepherd the flock of God among you, not under compulsion, but voluntarily, according to the will of God; and not for sordid gain, but with eagerness; nor yet as lording it over those allotted to your charge, but proving to be examples to the flock" (1 Peter 5:2-3).

The words of Loraine Boettner are so true and so needed today:

"...since the merely human priesthood was but a shadow of that which was to come it was but temporary. Just as we put out our artificial lights when the sun rises, and as the blossom falls away when the fruit appears, so the entire ceremonial and sacrificial system of the Old Testament has fulfilled its function and ceased to be when Christ's work was completed. This being the nature of the Christian priesthood, it is clearly evident that all those today who, in the Roman Catholic or any other church, pretend to function as priests mediating between God and man are simply usurpers of divine authority."[72]

An Adam Before Adam

Other of Hinn's theological abnormalities do not necessarily derive from the Middle Ages or Roman Catholicism. He also teaches a convoluted creation account from Genesis 1 which originated in the early 1800s.

During various broadcasts of *Praise the Lord*, Hinn has taught the TBN audience on demons and their strongholds.[73] Much of what he unfolds on these programs is a rehash of his 1984 book, *War in the Heavenlies*. He proposes the creation of Genesis 1:1 occurred billions of years ago, thereby placing a long gap between it and Genesis 1:2. This idea and teaching departs drastically from historical orthodox interpretations of creation.

Hinn's "gap theory" idea (as have many other heresies and quirky doctrines) has been fostered straight out of the dangerous and heretical *Dake Annotated Study Bible*.[74] "I found out some things that to this day most Christians have no clue about," he boasted.[75]

The view of creation Hinn presented has been referred to as the "Ruin/Reconstruction theory," or more simply, the "gap theory." Briefly, it proposes that God created everything in Genesis 1:1, including dinosaurs, land animals, and multitudes of people (a pre-Adamic race). It was during this juncture that Satan fell and became the god of this world. Women from this pre-Adamic race had sexual relations with fallen angels, producing grotesque and monstrous offspring. Chaos followed and the world entered into God's judgment.

God then sent a flood, called "Lucifer's flood," to annihilate the former world and we today walk on the graveyard of fossils from this former ruined creation. In Genesis 1:3, God began a new work or restoration of creation to substitute for the original one. So it would be generation in Genesis 1:1, then degeneration in verse 2, and regeneration in verse 3 and following. According to Hinn (and others who subscribe to this theory), the fossil evidence in the earth has no relationship with any creatures today because they are the remains of the pre-Adamic creation.

A New Theory

Some, like Arthur Custance in his book, *Without Form and Void*, suggest that ancient sources support this gap. As already stated, it is referred to as the Ruin/Reconstruction theory. It has also been called the Ruin/Re-creation theory. Studies of ancient Jewish and Christian sources reveal that, in a very few cases, some ancient writings may possibly refer to a time gap, *however, none suggest a pre-Adamic race, a Lucifer's flood, or another prior creation.*[76]

As noted above, the Ruin/Reconstruction theory is less than 200 years old. The impetus for the gap theory was Georges Cuvier (1769-1832), who proposed many, many floods before Genesis 1 to account for the fossil evidence. It presupposed a prior creation sometime before Genesis 1:1.

The person responsible for the gap theory as we know it today was Scottish theologian Thomas Chalmers (1780-1847). Chalmers missed the implications, impact, and effect of Noah's flood as a way to account for geological deposits, and wanted to harmonize Scripture and "science." He took the theory of evolution far too seriously.

John Davis looks at the motive behind the gap theory:

> "While the motive of gap theorists — the harmonization of the Bible with current geological theory — is commendable, the validity of their argument is extremely doubtful."[77]

Weston W. Fields concludes:

> "The Gap Theory was not generated by compelling exegetical considerations. On the contrary, it arose in recent times, and its popularity has been maintained for one and only one reason — the fixation of science-intimidated minds upon harmonizations, a practice not only futile if all the pronouncements of science are accepted uncritically, but something highly dangerous as well."[78]

Bernard Ramm addresses the historical background of Chalmers and his advancement of the gap invention:

> *"Creation-ruination-re-creation theory — or restitution theory, or gap theory.* ... its great popularity dates from the work of Chalmers. ... If it was Chalmers who first vigorously advocated it in modern times, it was the work of G.H. Pember (*Earth's Earliest Ages*, first edition, 1876; frequently republished) which canonized it. The gap theory was adopted by Scofield in his *Reference Bible* and so accumulated to itself all the veneration and publicity of that edition of the Bible."[79]

Later editions of the *Scofield Reference Bible* dropped the footnote to the gap theory. However, Finis Dake would then popularize the theory for the Pentecostal world.

There is a paucity of ancient sources that may be construed to believe in a gap between Genesis 1:1 and 1:2, and it must again be stated that these works would not have postulated any ruin, reconstruction, and worldwide work of Satan ending in Lucifer's flood. There are no real philosophical or historical roots for the Ruin/Reconstruction ideas. Its origins are in the 19th century.

The theory also has no linguistic support, as Fields points out:

> "There does not seem to be one shred of evidence in favor of the Gap Theory left remaining. Its fanciful cosmogony, Satanology, and allowance for billions of years, all, indeed, appeal to the imagination; but the facts of grammar have consigned the Gap Theory to the graveyard of exegetical misconceptions. We must forever rid ourselves of harmonizations with science which are based on its intimidating power. We must embrace a presuppositional method of apologetics which will deliver us from such an ever-present and powerful danger."[80]

After 222 pages of exhaustive investigation of the historical, biblical, and linguistic deficiencies of this theory, Fields then concludes:

> "It is our inescapable conclusion that the only interpretation of Genesis 1:1, 2, which accounts for all the facts of grammar and all the facts of analogous Scripture is one which makes 1:1 refer to *creatio ex nihilo* of the heavens and the earth on the first day of creation, 1:2 refer to the state of the earth as it was first created and as it existed on the first day; and the remainder of Genesis 1 refer to an original filling and forming of the heavens and the earth but a few thousand years ago."[81]

There are a number of Scriptures which clearly militate against Hinn's view. For example, Exodus 20:11 declares: "For in six days the Lord made the heavens and the earth, the sea and all that is in them and rested on the seventh day." Exodus 31:17 repeats the above, showing that the creation of the heavens and the earth (Genesis 1:1) is clearly connected with the seven-day creation, not separate from it.

Seven Weighty Objections

Creation apologist Henry Morris, in his book, *Studies in the Bible and Science*, provides a lengthy refutation of what he calls the "Ruin-and-Reconstruction Theory." We summarize:

"1. It is explicitly contradicted by the explanatory clause of the fourth Commandment: 'For in six days the Lord made heaven and earth, the sea, and all that in them is, and rested the seventh day' (Exodus 20:11). ... 2. The Bible teaches plainly that sin and death entered this earth only as a result of Adam's sin. (See I Corinthians 15:21; Romans 8:20-22; Romans 5:12.) ... 3. No worldwide geologic catastrophe such as the theory requires is found in the historical geology which the theory attempts to adopt. Many fossils, attributed by the theory to pre-Adamic ages, including human fossils, are practically identical with modern plants and animals. ... 4. No passage of Scripture anywhere plainly and unequivocally teaches the ruin theory. The few passages that have been offered as possibly implying a ruin and reconstruction of the earth before Adam can easily be shown to yield other and preferable interpretations. ... 5. None of the standard translations of Genesis 1:2 renders the verse as: 'The earth *became* waste and void' as the theory requires. ... 6. The Hebrew words for 'create' (*bara*) and for 'make' (*asah*) are very often used quite interchangeably in Scripture, at least when God is the one referred to as creating or making. ... Finally, the summary verse (Genesis 2:3) clearly says that *all* of God's works, both of 'creating' and 'making,' were completed with the six days, after which God 'rested.' 7. The chief proof-text for the theory, Isaiah 45:18, which says that 'God created the earth not in vain (Heb. *tohu*, same word as 'without form' in Genesis 1:2), can easily be understood without any reference to a hypothetical ruin of the primeval earth. ... God created the earth not without a purpose — to be forever empty and formless — but rather He formed it with the intent that it would be inhabited."[82]

False Distinctions

Hinn and his fellow gap theorists also try to make an artificial distinction between the word "created" (*bara* in Hebrew — Genesis 1:1, "God created") and the word "made" (*asa* or *asah* in Hebrew). The word "made" is used for God's other creative acts on the other days of creation. However, this false distinction cannot be supported because the words *bara* and *asa* are synonymous and interchangeable.[83]

John Davis also affirms that the Hebrew language allows for no gap in the first two verses of Genesis. He writes that "Hebrew grammar will not allow for a chronological gap between verses 1 and 2."[84]

Is "Was" — Was?

The gap theory is premised on translating Genesis 1:2 not as "the earth *was* without form and void" but as "the earth *became* without form and void." Can the word *was* be properly changed and translated as *became?* After a painstaking search into the Hebrew text, Weston Fields states that it is a grotesque error to do so. He emphasizes: "We must conclude that the traditional translation of *hayeta* as 'was' is the *only* legitimate one."[85]

The respected Hebrew linguists, Keil and Delitzsch, arrive at essentially the same conclusion:

> "'*And the earth was* (not became) *waste and void.*' The alliterative nouns *tohu vabohu*, the etymology of which is lost, signify waste and empty (barren), but not laying waste and desolating. ... The coming earth was at first waste and desolate, a formless, lifeless mass, ... the theosophic speculation of those who 'make a gap between the first two verses, and fill it with a wild horde of evil spirits and their demoniacal works, is an arbitrary interpolation' (*Ziegler*)."[86]

John Davis concurs and says it is reckless exegesis to suggest that *was* can be translated *became:*

> "The fact is, the verb is used as a simple copulative in circumstantial clauses: Jonah 'went unto Nineveh. ... *Now* Nineveh *was* an exceeding great city. ...' (Jonah 3:3); 'He shewed me Joshua. ... *Now* Joshua *was* clothed with filthy garments. ...' (Zech. 3:1-3)."[87]

So as Davis' commentary indicates, Ninevah did not become a great city nor did Joshua's clothes become filthy, but were already.

Hinn also makes a false case for the English word "replenish" in Genesis 1:28 ("Be fruitful and multiply and *replenish* the earth"). On the face of it, *replenish* would mean to "fill again" or to "supply again." The problem is that the Hebrew word only meant to "fill." Literally the command is to "fill" the earth. Again we refer to Davis:

> "The argument based on the English rendering, 'replenish the earth,' is extremely weak. The Hebrew verb simply means 'fill,' not '*re*fill.' The gap theory postulates a pre-Adamic population that was violently destroyed, but this is neither described nor alluded to in the Bible. Such a theory lends itself too easily to uncontrolled subjectivism and imagination. Almost anything can be postulated for this mysterious gap of indefinite duration."[88]

The Septuagint, as well as all other modern translations, translates Genesis 1:28 with the word "fill."

What is more appalling about Hinn's gap theory teaching is that when one examines the preface of his book, *War in the Heavenlies,* it is claimed to be "direct revelations from God's Word and great insight of the scriptures."[89] Hinn's outdated, unbiblical borrowing from Dake and others is neither direct revelation nor great insight. Hinn is not skating on thin ice here, but is unsuccessfully trying to walk on water.

On the May 12, 1999, TBN broadcast, Hinn proceeded step-by-step through his book, all to the amazement of the Crouches. So enthralled by Hinn's marvelous scriptural insight, Jan asks, "Have you written a book on this?" Of course, the answer should be a resounding, "Yes!" But Hinn responds without missing a beat, "No, I never have written a book." Paul then bids: "You must write." Hinn's response to the Crouches and their viewing audience is patently a lie. It is mind-boggling to try to understand why Hinn answered as he did unless he is planning to reissue *War in the Heavenlies* to try to sell it as a new book.

Another reason for the untruth may possibly be that the 1984 volume includes some even more damaging statements. At that time, Hinn wrote of his spiritistic practices. He reveals himself as an occult practitioner. He has never repented of these things.

Confessions of Occultism

Hinn's regurgitation of his gap theory on TBN may do him more harm than good. For one thing, it will cause researchers and critics to revisit his *War in the Heavenlies*. The stumbling block occurs within the publication as Hinn boasts of practicing an occult art called astral projection or astral travel. Throughout Hinn's prominence as a Charismatic superstar, his legacy includes claimed anointings at grave sites of dead faith healers and of visions of the dead. So his prior admission of astral travel is not surprising. The occult kingdom is on the move and Hinn is helping to advance it.

Hinn boasted in the book:

> "...the most unusual thing happened. In an instant, I was out of my body. I assure you I was out of my body. ... I was out of my body. John says also 'I was in the spirit' which means he was out of the body. I came out of my body in a split moment. I know exactly what it feels like when you die. Believe me, you will feel nothing. ... Michael now looks at this angel and asks him to take care of me, and leaves the room. As he said that, I was straight back in my body. The Lord gave me that mighty experience. I was now back in my body, ... I had this experience, please believe me. I did not see the angels nor hear the angels until I was out of the body."[90]

On the May 12, 1999, *Praise the Lord* show, Hinn repeated the above with a few variations.

Kurt Koch describes this occultic practice:

> "*Astral Traveling (Astroprojection)* Spiritists who practice the excursion of the soul send their souls on journeys around this world only. Strong mediums who have mastered astral traveling claim that they can send their soul to the moon or the planets to discover things there. Some are even so bold that they claim to have

penetrated the sphere of God. This is completely absurd.''[91]

Craig Hawkins describes the tools of the trade for the occultists, which include out-of-body experiences:

> "Irrespective of the view held of what magic is and how and why it works, magic is very important to many witches. In fact, the working of magic, diverse divination techniques, and other 'occultic technologies,' are part and parcel of their religion. *Altered states of consciousness (e.g., trance states)*, astrology, *astral projection (out-of-body experiences)*, divination, incantations, the making of potions, mediumship (channeling), necromancy, raising psychic power, sex magic, spell casting, and spiritism are all tools of their craft.''[92]

Apostle John or Occultist John?

It is one thing for Hinn to applaud himself for an occult pursuit. However, when he tries to justify his unbiblical behavior by attributing occult and demonic phenomena to the Apostle John, it becomes appalling. Does John's statement "I was in the Spirit" mean the Apostle John was out of his body as Hinn alleges? No careful exegete of God's Word would agree. How could "in the Spirit" equate to "out of the body"?

The verse from Revelation 1:10, "I was in the Spirit on the Lord's day," is straightforward. It has always been translated by commentators and exegetes as a term for spiritual ecstasy and is connected with divine revelation.[93] It is something the Scripture writers (given direct divine revelation) experienced *in their bodies*. It is a purification and elevation of the mind. We only experience this today in a faint, secondary, and derivative way as we meditate on Scripture and are strengthened and blessed by its promises. It is not in any way even remotely related to an occultic experience.

John Walvoord gives us the meaning of the phrase, "in the Spirit":

> "John's statement in verse 10 that he was in the Spirit refers to his experience of being carried beyond normal

sense into a state where God could reveal supernaturally the contents of this book.''[94]

Linguist Gerhard Kittel explores the meaning of "in the Spirit" (Greek = *en pneumati*):

> "The reference here is obviously to an extraordinary event: the state *en pneumati* is differentiated from the usual state, 1:10; ... The *pneuma* is the power which gives visions the ordinary man cannot have.''[95]

Nowhere does Kittel suggest in this state of direct divine revelation given to the Scripture writers that they left their bodies. Therefore, it is obvious that John did not go anywhere since he states that he heard behind him a loud voice (verse 10). His faculties were still working.

Paying careful attention to the language, William Henrikson offers this:

> "He is in direct spiritual contact with his Saviour. He is alone ... with God! ... He is wide awake and every avenue of his soul is wide open to the direct communication coming from God.''[96]

Alexander Maclaren describes "in the Spirit" as "a state of elevated consciousness and communion.''[97]

A Better Mousetrap? Maybe Not!

Hinn may have thought himself on more solid biblical ground when he appealed Paul's experience of being caught up into heaven in 2 Corinthians 12. However, his citation is no better for the following reasons:

1. Hinn is not Paul. Paul was the recipient of unique and solitary visions, revelations, and experiences, as he affirms in 2 Corinthians 12:1. Being knocked off a horse at conversion, blinded, and later encountering a serpent without harm were other unique events that made Paul one of a kind. Paul called us to emulate his *faith*, not his exploits (2 Timothy 3:10-11), to follow his ways, not his wonders (Philippians 4:9).

2. This dramatic, unique vision and revelation of heaven as told by Paul to the Corinthians was not to be discussed in

detail, nor rejoiced in (2 Corinthians 12:5). It had no informational value as far as details.

3. The purpose of this one-time experience of a heavenly visit was to further verify Paul as an *apostle* (2 Corinthians 12:11-12). Though Hinn may try to claim he does what the apostles did, he has not claimed to be an apostle — yet.

4. Paul minimized the heavenly experience and told his hearers that it was dangerous in that it could engender pride (2 Corinthians 12:7). It was more negative than positive.

5. Paul talked of the extreme value of suffering over even a heavenly experience (2 Corinthians 12:10), truth which Hinn would deny.

6. Since God was the direct author of this experience for purposes of divine revelation, it is totally unlike anything Satan would do either in quality or intent.

7. The self-serving nature of Hinn's claim to astral projection is obvious. He is "super-healer," a cut above the rest, one who can go out of his body and interact with angels.

8. Though we will never know for sure and cannot be dogmatic, it is possible that Paul actually died and that the 2 Corinthians 12 experience is connected to a real death experience (possibly in Acts 14:19). Paradise mentioned in 2 Corinthians 12:4 is shown in Luke 23:43 to be a place where the righteous dead go. If this is true and the suggestion correct, Paul would have had an experience similar to Lazarus or others who were raised from the dead.

In any event, Paul's experience cannot be connected to anything demonic, nor could it be used to justify claims of astral projection. Astral projection, in the end, may only be in the mind and imagination of the practitioner, or a demonic hoax. Historically, it has been connected with Gnosticism, Shamanism, Theosophy, and Witchcraft.[98]

In light of the above, it is not difficult to discern that Hinn made up the space travel story and fabricated his out-of-body experience as he has so many other stories, not even realizing he has implicated himself in spiritism. As has become his legacy, it was all for effect and drama because Hinn always combines religion and show biz.

Because of his blood teaching, an attempt to reverse the reformation, the promotion of an outdated, defunct theory as "revelation," and the promotion of occultism, Hinn's world is not only confusing, but it is a disastrous world as well. It is a dark world, filled with untruth and make-believe. It is sad that so many gullible people hang on the words of such a confused man.

Hinn is going backward. He is trying to push the Church away from Scripture and back to the ignorance and confusion of 200-year-old theories and into the dark ages of 500 years ago. Christians must not embrace Hinn and his teachings. When they do, they revert to mysticism, superstition, humanism, occultism, and personality cults.

The Deadly Move into Necromancy

The Disney Corp. in Orlando, Fla., is always coming up with new theme parks and new attractions with which to captivate and draw in tourists. Disney has to get not only new customers, but repeat customers in order to survive. The world of televangelism appears almost the same.

To keep the gears of the ministry well-lubricated with the donations and gifts of the faithful, it seems that nearly every month there has to be a new attraction, a new "prophecy," a new "word from the Lord," or some new sovereign act of God. These claims and revelations serve to hold onto a floating, thrill seeking, quickly dissatisfied Charismatic population.

Easily Dissatisfied

The superstars of televangelism over-promise to an audience they know is fickle and has a short attention and commitment span. What is popular this month may not be next month. What's hot and what's not depends on the creativity of the man and his organization. Rising fortunes and empires can begin to dwindle if new "power" centers or new spiritual "power brokers" offer a new and more exciting ride, attraction, or innovation. *Charisma* magazine and the Trinity Broadcasting Network are the main marketplaces for the wild, weird, and bizarre world of Charismania.

So what does Benny Hinn have to offer? As repeatedly documented in several of the previous chapters of this book, the Orlando-based faith healer has spawned many a new vision, a new testimony, a new claim, a new gimmick, a new cure-all, and a new twist on an old "deliverance" scheme over the past several years.

In all, the world of televangelism has become as unrestrained as professional wrestling, with Hinn being crowned as the current "reigning champ." False prophecies, heretical doctrines, spurious healings, an exorbitant lifestyle, and fabricated personal historical accounts have not been able to dethrone Hinn as the leading guru of Charismatics.

In the mid-1990s, Hinn sought donations from those attending his crusades and from the viewers of his daily telecasts, to go head-to-head on cable and television networks featuring psychic hotlines. The donations he received would permit his evangelistic efforts to reduce the spread and success of occultism being broadcast into homes. Yet today, these psychic hotlines are bigger and more intense than ever, and Hinn has become a fellow traveler in the world of the occult.

Kathryn Kuhlman Returns

Hinn has long been infatuated with the late faith healer, Kathryn Kuhlman. His books and sermons are replete with the impact she supposedly made on his life and ministry. Now, Hinn has her as a female spirit guide. And with this claim, he is introducing a deadly spiritist virus to his followers.

Hinn has claimed that he was shown the future of his ministry from Kuhlman and Jesus in what he described as a "vision of the night." This revelation undoubtedly will electrify the bulk of his following. But perhaps some may now view Hinn as having crossed the line into dark and dangerous territory. This may be a ride that sounds the alarm and wakes them up to Hinn's pragmatic unorthodoxy and false teaching.

His account of this alleged vision was delivered to those attending his "Partner Conference" in Atlanta, and to those viewing the June 11, 1997 installment of his daily *This Is Your Day* program.

On the broadcast, he stated:

"Ladies and gentlemen, I'm going to tell you something right now. The Lord showed me a vision about — goodness it's almost been a year now. And I — I — I — I can tell you I sense now the time has come when this vision is gonna be fulfilled. I had a vision of the night. What I saw, myself walk into a room. I've shared this before but just in case you — you've not heard it, I want you to hear it. I saw myself walk into a room and there stood Kathryn Kuhlman. And I've not seen Kathryn in a dream or a vision [in] years. Uh, when she died, the day she died, the morning she died, I had a dream what I — what I saw in a — in a — in a — in a casket with a white dress. And when I woke up in — in the morning I knew she had died, and it was on the news that same morning. And so it's been many years. And there she was standing in this room and she said to me — of course this was a dream, but really more of a vision. A lot of times dreams are really visions of the night, and the Bible calls them that. When — when God gives to you in the fashion it really came with me. When I was a little boy, I saw the Lord in this dream. It was really so real, it was really a vision because when — when he appeared to me, my body became electric, just like electricity went through me, and when I awoke, that electricity was still on my body."[1]

Hinn goes on recounting his "vision":

"Well, anyway, in this one, in this vision that — that I saw — saw Miss Kuhlman. And she said, 'Follow me.' That's all she said. And I followed her to a second room. In that second room stood the Lord. When the Lord, uh — when — when I saw the Lord, Kathryn disappeared. She was just gone [Hinn snaps fingers]. And now the Lord looked at me and said, 'Follow me.' And I followed him to a third room. In the third room sat a gentleman — I still remember his face. I can tell you, I still remember the man's face. And the man sat in this wheelchair in that third room. There was a big hole in his neck. A tube down his throat. He was crippled on that wheelchair. And he had tubes down his body. Totally crippled, totally para — totally, of course, paralyzed. The Lord laid his hands on this man and as he did the tubes disappeared, the hole closed, he was completely healed and got up off the wheelchair. It was a creative miracle. Now I'm standing watching the Lord in this vision heal this man. And now as the man was healed, the Lord looked at me with piercing eyes — I'll not forget that one, I'll tell you. Looked at me with piercing eyes and said, 'Do it!' And the [Hinn snaps fingers] — and the dream and the vision came to an end."2

Hinn next interprets the "vision" for his faithful:

"When I woke, when I got up, when I came out of the vision, I was trembling and perspiring from head to toes. I know exactly what that vision means. It was Kathryn Kuhlman who took me, who introduced me to the Holy Spirit. That is the meaning of that first room when she said, 'Follow me.' But when Kathryn was gone, Jesus was there. Kathryn did her job and was gone and the Lord said, 'Follow me' into a third room. And there was this man. I believe I'm about to enter that third room. [Audience applause.] I'm telling you I feel it. I sense it. I believe that room speaks of a dimension, a new dimension in the Spirit. I believe I've been in that second room now for the last seven years. What is amazing to me, what's amazing to me is God works or has worked in my life in seven year cycles. I'm now in the seventh year — beginning the eighth of the ministry of these crusades. 1990 we started — March. This is what? '97. And just now I feel another platform, another dimension, another level is really coming. Well, saints, you're going to be a part of it. God — God has sent you as partners to be a part of it. So how many are ready to see greater things for the glory of God?"3

Hinn's description is somewhat confusing and at one point he says the apparition "was a dream," and, if left at that, would be less of a concern. However, he qualifies the nature of the "dream" by claiming it was "really more of a vision." In fact, he uses the word "vision" ten times to describe the experience. Moreover, he is using this event as a mystical prescription from the other side. This apparition, Hinn says, declares and describes what is to become the new by-product of his ministry. It moves him to a claimed oracle from Jesus of new "creative miracles" — a higher level of signs and wonders. He is using it to solicit support from his followers, and as such, must be considered and examined in a serious and biblical manner.

Hinn's "Mount of Transfiguration"

A few months earlier, Hinn lured the audience at his Honolulu Crusade with his revelations of not only Kuhlman, but the Old Testament prophet Elijah.[4] "I have not just seen angels, I've seen saints," he announced. His narrative in this area is even more brazenly spiritistic:

> "You may have a problem with this, but I honestly don't really care. I've walked in that [supernatural] world. I've seen things you will never be able to understand, unless you've been in it. *I've had individuals appear to me in my room.* Not only angels. I've seen sights in prayer, incredible sights!"[5]

What were the "incredible sights" Hinn had "seen"? He detailed one powerful encounter for his faithful:

> "Can I tell you something? I've never shared this. Never! I was in prayer one day and a man appeared in front of me. It happened for two — for two days in a row. Ev — twice one day and the next day. The same man appeared. I've never told this, never. ... This is recently, I'm not talking about a long time ago. He was about six feet two. Old man. Had a beard. ... Glistening white beard. His face was somewhat thin, but very bold! Eyes — crystal blue. He had on a white garment, whiter than my shirt could ever get. On his head was a — like a shawl, like a — like a — like a covering. He looked like a priest. But every part of him glistened like crystal. And I spoke out and I said, 'Lord, who is this man I see?' Now, I know you may think I've lost my mind, but the Lord said, 'Elijah, the prophet.'"[6]

Hinn next brought Kuhlman into the performance:

> "Seven and a half years ago, just before the ministry
> started, before these crusades began, I was in prayer
> when suddenly in front of me I saw a group of people. I
> couldn't even tell you who they were. I recognized only
> one of them. It was Miss Kuhlman. And every one of
> them seemed to be urging me to pray. Now, I know this
> sounds crazy, but it's all right. I don't mind if you call
> me crazy because I liked what I saw."[7]

The purpose of the visitation by Kuhlman and the saintly
host is then explained by Hinn:

> "At least fifty to seventy of them were sitting in a
> group, and they were saying to me, 'Pray! Ask God to
> give you a healing ministry that will touch the world!'
> And suddenly I heard Kathryn's voice, [Hinn snaps
> fingers] and out of the blue, suddenly there — there she
> was, it's crystal clear. And she in her beautiful smile,
> the way she said, 'Ask! We're waiting for you to ask!
> We're praying with you to ask!' And the vision
> disappeared."[8]

Interestingly, video tapes of Hinn's 1997 Honolulu
Crusade are not being made available by Hinn's ministry.[9]
Perhaps someone more theologically astute in the faith
healer's organization realizes the occultic implications of his
revelations.

On Deadly Ground

From the very inception of his ministry, Hinn has had a
penchant and an obsession with the late Kuhlman. Hinn has
publicly stated that Kuhlman's grave carries a supernatural
"anointing." He alleges the same effect from the body and
grave of Aimee Semple McPherson. The theatrical, twice
divorced McPherson, who probably died by suicide, is hardly
a model of Christian anointing.[10]

During a sermon on the Holy Spirit, Hinn offered the
following, eerie, testimonial:

"One of the strangest experiences I had a few years ago [was] visiting Aimee's tomb in California. This Thursday I'm on TBN. Friday I am gonna go and visit Kathryn Kuhlman's tomb. It's close by Aimee's in Forest Lawn Cemetery. I've been there once already and every so often I like to go and pay my respects 'cause this great woman of God has touched my life. And that grave, uh, where she's buried is closed, they built walls around it. You can't get in without a key and I'm one of the very few people who can get in. But I'll never forget when I saw Aimee's tomb. It's incredibly dramatic. She was such a lady that her tomb has seven-foot angels bowing on each side of her tomb with a gold chain around it. As — as incredible as it is that someone would die with angels bowing on each side of her grave, I felt a terrific anointing when I was there. I actually, I—I, hear this, I trembled when I visited Aimee's tomb. I was shaking all over. God's power came all over me. ... I believe the anointing has lingered over Aimee's body. I know this may be shocking to you. ... And I'm going to take David [Palmquist] and Kent [Mattox] and Sheryl [Palmquist] this week. They're gonna come with me. You — you — you gonna feel the anointing at Aimee's tomb. It's incredible. And Kathryn's. It's amazing. I've heard of people healed when they visited that tomb. They were totally healed by God's power. You say, 'What a crazy thing.' Brother, there's things we'll never understand. Are you all hearing me?"[11]

The prophet Isaiah talked about the abomination of seeking an "anointing" and contact with the other world at a grave and called it "rebellious" and "a way that is not good" (65:2), "iniquity" and "blasphemy" (v. 7). He further indicts those: "Who sit among the graves, and spend the night in the tombs" (v. 4). The worst of judgments are pronounced on these vile practices (vs. 13-15).

Jewish teaching was that dead bodies were unclean (for instance, Numbers 19:11), but Hinn thinks otherwise. Hinn apparently has never shaken his Arab roots. Arabic people superstitiously believe in the efficacy of praying at tombs of famous or saintly people. Arabs regularly make pilgrimages to venerated, holy graves.[12] It seems Hinn has never rid himself of the superstitions of his childhood.

He even, knowingly or unknowingly, mirrors in himself and his following the bizarre Convulsionaries of the 18th century, whose focus was tombs and miracles:

> "Groups of visitors to the tomb were gripped by uncontrollable urges to dance or fall into seizures. In these states the 'convulsionnaires', as they came to be called, seemed to lose contact with the external world, even to the point of becoming insensitive to pain. They had religious visions and reported miraculous healings. On one occasion, a skeptic who came to the tomb to mock the proceedings found herself struck with paralysis."[13]

A Grave Deception

Hinn tries to buttress his morbid preoccupation with graves and the dead (in the above) by referring to the Old Testament miracle of Elisha's bones bringing a man to life. In a similar vein, one could refer to manna to insist on getting free food from heaven, but it just won't work. A close examination of the Elisha event shows no comparison or parallel to what Hinn is claiming.

The miraculous event after the death of Elisha is found in 2 Kings 13:20-21. A dead man was thrown into the tomb of Elisha, and upon coming into contact with Elisha's bones, "he revived and stood up on his feet." A careful study of the passage will note clearly four things:

1. This is a miracle of resurrection from the dead — not some nebulous feeling or quivering. There is nothing in the verses in 2 Kings 13 about some subjective or lingering "anointing." Hinn is not raising the dead, and neither are the corpses of Kuhlman or McPherson. The Elisha event is clearly about life from death — resurrection of a body.

2. It is obviously a seal of divine attestation to Elisha's dying prophecy regarding Joash's victory over Syria (2 Kings 13:14-19).

3. Even though Elisha died of sickness (2 Kings 13:14), God's approval was still on his life and death. Certainly this is contrary to faith teachers like Hinn and others. You can be sick, and die of that sickness, and still have God's favor and approval. This event contradicts and proves just the opposite of the health gospel preached by Hinn.

4. Hinn's loose use of the passage opens the way for all kinds of weird excesses. Adam Clarke cites one of the misuses: "This is the *first*, and I believe the *last*, account of a *true miracle* performed by the bones of a dead man; and yet on it and such like the whole system of miraculous working *relics* has been founded by the popish Church."[14] As creation was unique, as manna was unique, as clothes that would not wear out were unique, this was a unique resurrection event. Hinn cannot claim it for validation of his trips to the graveyard.

Vision or Revision?

Hinn's Atlanta claim of a "vision of the night" with Kuhlman and Jesus also demonstrates his blatant misuse of the vocabulary of the Bible. It is a failed attempt to make what he is practicing, somehow, appear to have justification from the Word of God. He is deceptive in this. Even a cursory look at this expression, its context, and biblical meaning demonstrates Hinn's erroneous interpretation.

The word "vision" appears approximately 100 times in the Bible, mostly in Old Testament passages. And, except when referring to false prophets and false visions, the majority of these have to do with *God giving direct revelation of Himself, about Himself and His plan, or prophetic information.* It is revelatory, special, life-giving information. This information was written and inscripturated for us in the Bible. Hinn is trying to impress his followers that his extrabiblical revelation is on a par with the inspired Scriptures.

Never, ever, when used in a positive way (of legitimate information and revelation from God) is the word "vision" ever linked with the occult or the dead. The exact phrase "visions of the night" is found in Genesis 46:2 and has to do with God revealing Himself directly to Jacob. It is not a message from the realm of the dead. Our God is the Living God. It is a message from heaven. Messages from demons and the dark underworld should not be referred to as "visions of the night." This is clear and obvious chicanery on Hinn's part.

The word "vision" in Hebrew is *marah* and literally means to "see." Jacob saw God in some form and fashion (a theophany or Christophany) and heard Him give promises and comfort. To connect this with efforts to raise funds to support one's ministry is Scripture twisting of the most horrible and pernicious kind. Shame on Hinn for this deception and distortion of God's truth. Once again, Hinn has proven that he does not have even an elementary understanding of biblical interpretation.

Hinn's so-called "vision of the night" fits better into the category of Jeremiah 14:14 and 23:16:

> "And the Lord said to me, the prophets prophesy lies in my name. I have not sent them, commanded them, nor spoken to them; they prophesy to you a false vision, divination, a worthless thing, and the deceit of their own heart."

> "Thus says the Lord of hosts: Do not listen to the words of the prophets who prophesy to you. They make you worthless; They speak a vision of their own heart, not from the mouth of the Lord."

Dark Seduction: A Grave Delusion

Perhaps Hinn's "visions" detailed in Atlanta and Hawaii are merely contrived fiction as foretold by the Apostle Peter (2 Peter 2:3). Or the tales may be the result of actual dreams or delusions, and embellished for effect. Yet, a worse case scenario does exist — if he is receiving "visions" of the dead, he is in contact with demons! If the latter is true, then Paul's warning surely is being fulfilled:

> "The Spirit speaks expressly that in the latter times some shall depart from the faith, giving heed to seducing spirits and doctrines of demons, speaking lies

in hypocrisy, having their consciences seared with a hot
iron" (1 Timothy 4:1).

For all the moral failings of Jim Bakker and Jimmy
Swaggart, they did not try to introduce their followers to the
world of spiritism and spiritualistic practices. Hinn has
entered into a dangerous practice called necromancy, which
literally means "Divination by communicating with the
dead."[15] In practicing necromancy, hidden, secret, or clandes-
tine knowledge is brought forth by someone who has died.
Direction is sought from the other side. However, the Bible
reveals that the real source of the information, when obtained,
can be demonic entities or evil spirits *who imitate the dead*. This
practice is at odds in every way with the Bible and the true
worship of God.

A careful reading of Isaiah 8, and research into the
language, shows a medium being manipulated by a demon
spirit. Isaiah's blunt question (v. 19) cries out for an answer:
"And when they say to you seek those who are mediums and
wizards, who whisper and mutter, should not a people seek
their God? Should they seek the dead on behalf of the
living?" The obvious answer is that God's people should *never*
seek the dead on behalf of the living.

Bible commentator Dr. H.A. Ironside's observation on
Isaiah's words is both "prophetic" and chilling:

> "It is a grievous offense in the eyes of God for anyone
> to turn from His revealed Word to those who profess to
> have power to summon the spirits of the departed in
> order to give light and help. Such are either charlatans
> deceiving those who go to them or else possessed by
> impersonating demons misleading all who follow
> them."[16]

Dead End

So there are numerous strong prohibitions against contact-
ing the dead *in any fashion*. Our guidance is to come from
Scripture, not the departed. The ancient pagan cultures that
clashed with Israel practiced this and other occultic abomina-
tions. To consult mediums or familiar spirits was viewed as

apostasy from God. The death penalty was required for the practice of necromancy.[17]

J.R. Dummelow's *A Commentary on the Holy Bible* spells out who the objects of this severe judgment are in Leviticus 19:31 with these words: "That have familiar spirits; necromancers who profess to hold communication with the dead."[18]

King Saul earned the death penalty as a severe judgment from God for the practice of seeking enlightenment and information from the dead. "So Saul died for his unfaithfulness which he committed against the Lord, because he did not keep the word of the Lord, and also because he consulted a medium for guidance" (1 Chronicles 10:13).

Merrill Unger captures the demonic underpinnings of necromancy:

> "But mediumship and spiritism are closely connected with the ventriloquial whispers and mutterings, which the seducing demons employ in their human agents in subtle imitation of the utterances of the dead, in order thoroughly to deceive and win over their ready dupes."[19]

Unger also forcefully reminds us:

> "If it is forbidden in the Scripture for a child of God to resort to a 'familiar spirit,' then it is equally wrong for the departed dead, either godly or wicked, to communicate with the living. By so doing, both infringe upon the law of God."[20]

Indeed, a familiar spirit can be translated as the spirit of a departed family member or friend, because demons convey information as if from someone close or familiar to us.

Gleanings from the Great Vine

The vigilant research of W.E. Vine on "Spirit (of the Dead), Necromancer" is worth reading in its entirety:

> "The word usually represents the troubled spirit (or spirits) of the dead. This meaning appears unquestionably in Isa. 29:4: '...Thy voice shall be, as of one that

hath a familiar spirit, out of the ground, and thy speech shall whisper out of the dust.' Its second meaning, 'necromancer,' refers to a professional who claims to summon forth such spirits when requested (or hired) to do so: 'Regard not them that have familiar spirits, neither seek after wizards' (Lev. 19:31 — first occurrence). These mediums summoned their 'guides' from a hole in the ground. Saul asked the medium (witch) of Endor, 'Divine for me from the hole.'"[21]

Vine then points out God's prohibitions:

"God forbade Israel to seek information by this means, which was so common among the pagans (Lev. 19:31; Deut. 18:11). Perhaps the pagan belief in manipulating one's basic relationship to a god (or gods) explains the relative silence of the Old Testament regarding life after death. Yet God's people believed in life after death, from early times (e.g., Gen. 37:35; Isa. 14:15ff.). ... Necromancers' unusual experiences do not prove that they truly had power to summon the dead. For example, the medium of Endor could not snatch Samuel out of God's hands against His wishes. But in this particular incident, it seems that God rebuked Saul's apostasy, either through a revived Samuel or through a vision of Samuel. Mediums do not have power to summon the spirits of the dead, since this is reprehensible to God and contrary to His will."[22]

The message delivered to Saul for the above practice was a message of judgment and death.

In Jesus' account of the afterlife in Luke 16, a man seeks to go back from the dead to warn others of torment. He is not permitted, and is told, "they have Moses and the prophets; let them hear them" (v. 29). The Word of God is to be our information source for our life and ministry, not occultic pursuits.

Spiritism by Any Other Name

According to Robert Burrows of the Spiritual Counterfeits Project, full blown spiritism hit our country in the mid-1880s, beginning in New York and generated by teenage sisters, Margaret and Katie Fox. At its height, it had ten million followers, including Sir Arthur Conan Doyle, the creator of Sherlock Holmes. Its "central belief is implicit in the spirit contact foundational to it: the dead continue to exist and communication with them is possible."[23]

Spiritism went through ebbs and flows of popularity, and then mutated into its modern form — channeling. Actress Shirley MacLaine is probably the most well-known endorser of channeling.

British apologist Alan Morrison traces the modern revival of necromancy through Jane Roberts:

> "In the present New Age scenario, Channelling began with a vengeance with the contribution of a woman called Jane Roberts (1929-1984). In 1963, she and her husband had begun to experiment with an ouija-board and they were soon contacted by an alleged spirit-entity calling itself *Seth*. Within a short time, she found she could go into a trance during which this spirit-being would speak through her. This led to a series of best-selling books in which a great deal of occult information about every aspect of life — past, present and future — is presented in a readable style. Interestingly, it is common for these spirit-entities which channel through humans to adopt a biblical name. Whether this is the case with Jane Robert's 'Seth' is not immediately apparent. ... Other well-known chanelling [sic] works are Virginia Essene's 'New Teachings for an Awakening Humanity', and Amy Brown Loomis' channelled messages which were alleged to be from Jesus Christ and several of the Apostles. By far the best known and most popular of all the New Age channelled works is the 1200-page book, 'A Course in Miracles'."[24]

Spiritists have "churches" in which they practice seances and other occultic specialties. *They even claim healings and prophesies*, and have joined together under the umbrella of the National Spiritualist Association. The N.S.A. lists as one of its nine principles:

"5. We affirm that communication with the so-called dead is a fact scientifically proven by the phenomena of Spiritualism."[25]

Hinn would fit better with the N.S.A. than anywhere else. J. Stafford Wright reminds us:

"If for a moment we consider what the Bible says about attempting to communicate with the departed, we may be astounded to find that, whenever this is mentioned, it is condemned as something evil. ... The Christian similarly is not to aim at gathering information from the departed, but at hearing the message of Christ. ... It is clear that the Biblical verdict on Spiritualism is completely hostile. One may assume that the reason is because of the deception (conscious or unconscious) that is inherent in it. There may, in fact, be two sources of deception. 1. *The unconscious mind of the medium.* ... The sitter cannot be certain of being in touch with the one who has passed on, for the medium may in fact be interpreting a projected image from the sitter's own mind. 2. A more dangerous deception would arise if we suppose *the intervention of evil spirits.* Spiritualists themselves recognize this possibility."[26]

Hinn's move in the direction of the occult should not be a surprise. The modern-day Pentecostal movement, which began in 1906, has muddled beginnings and a prior history of involvement in spiritism. Azusa Street drew in spiritualists and mediums, and contemporaries of that day were reporting seances, trances, and other outlandish and occultic behavior.[27] Once the door of unrestrained subjective mysticism is opened, Satan and the flesh can have a field day. God's Word is our *only* protection against the demonic.

Endorsing Catholic Occultism

Hinn appeared on the April 23, 1998 installment of *Larry King Live*. King challenged him as to why he does not go from "bed to bed" in hospitals with his healing power. Hinn indicated that he does visit hospitals, and when he prayed for people, there were some who were healed but others who were not. He then offered King this explanation for his mixed results: "But, you see, the gift does not work when you want it to work. The anointing must be there."[28]

The driving force of his ministry then came to light as he told King: "In a crusade — in a meeting when I am ministering, the anointing of God comes on me and that's when things happen."[29] Yet, all of this begs the question: Why would the Holy Spirit limit Himself to work in power in only emotionally charged meetings? Hinn would have us believe that the anointing comes and goes, but mostly comes in arenas and convention centers. Hinn's concept takes issue with Scripture as 1 John 2:27 states: "The anointing which you have received from Him abides in you."

Hinn then endorsed the reputed divine healing power of the Marian shrines at Lourdes and Fatima. He told King and the viewing audience:

> "Look, God has given us, Larry, many sources of healing. Look at Lourdes. People have been healed going to Lourdes and Fatima. There was a pool, even in the Bible, the pool of Bethesda, where the angels stirred the water — people were also healed. So God has given us many avenues of healing. He wants us to be healed."[30]

It is disturbing to see Hinn put these two extrabiblical shrines in the same category as a biblical event. It must also be noted that in the incident in John 5, the man was healed by Jesus (John 5:12-13), and Bethesda is never mentioned again after this chapter. (It is a dry archaeological ruin today.) Further, no one is ever pointed back to it for help or healing. In Acts 3, the man is not pointed to the pool (which was nearby), but to Christ (Acts 3:6). Whatever temporary mercy God had shown at Bethesda, ended with the person of Christ. But the point must be made that there is a universe of distance between what Lourdes and Fatima are promoting, and the Jewish pool of John 5. At the Pool of Bethesda, no one was being encouraged to hold to teachings contrary to God's Word.

The message of both Lourdes and Fatima are messages supposedly from the Virgin Mary, promoting veneration and prayers to her.

The Catholic Almanac, under "Apparitions of the Blessed Virgin Mary," tells us that in Fatima, Portugal, "Mary appeared six times between May 13 and Oct. 13, 1917, to three children in a field called Cova da Iria near Fatima, north of Lisbon. She recommended frequent recitation of the Rosary."[31]

Most are not aware that in the Rosary one prays to Mary these words: "Holy Mary, Mother of God, pray for us sinners, now and at the hour of our death." There is only one Mediator for sinners (1 Timothy 2:5) and only one who can deal with our sins, that is the Lord Jesus (2 Corinthians 5:21).

The *Almanac* goes on to say that Mary urged "works of mortification for the conversion of sinners; called for devotion to herself under the title of her Immaculate Heart."[32] Can our works of mortification convert sinners? Did not Christ command us to preach the Gospel to every creature (Matthew 28:19)? It is not our suffering and sacrifice that brings conversion to others, but the preaching of His suffering and sacrifice and a sinners' hearty response to the Savior. It may cost us in time and effort to evangelize the lost, but ultimately it is the Gospel that is the "power of God unto Salvation." Fatima's message is a total contradiction of the Gospel.

Fatima also calls for making holy communion on the first Saturday of every month, and the *Almanac* informs us that: "Fatima, with its sanctuary and basilica, ranks with Lourdes as the greatest of modern Marian shrines."[33]

So what about Lourdes? Hinn evidently approves of it. Lourdes is just the French version of Fatima. The *Almanac* gives its history: "Mary, identifying herself as the Immaculate Conception, appeared 18 times between Feb. 11 and July 16, 1858, to 14-year-old Bernadette Soubirous at the grotto of Massabielle near Lourdes in southern France. Her message concerned the necessity of prayer and penance for the conversion of men."[34]

It has been a longstanding controversy as to what, if anything, is really happening at these Marian shrines. Certainly there can be improvement of psychosomatic illness simply through expectations. Because of the false beliefs being promoted so blatantly at both of these shrines, we cannot rule out the demonic and the occultic (1 Timothy 4:1-3).

In all of this, Hinn moves toward the worst groups in history.

Back to Basics

How many more dead people will Hinn report "visions" of? Hinn has spun yet another yarn as he has so often, or is being duped by demons. God's Word leaves him no other options. Either choice ushers his followers into deep deception and may well give them leave to seek such encounters from the other side. In either case, Hinn needs to repent before God and seek the forgiveness of the body of Christ. Following that, he needs to step down and enroll in some basic doctrine courses and stop his overt approval of the occult.

In October 1996, Hinn resigned from the Assemblies of God denomination. Following his resignation, he returned to being accountable and answerable to no one but himself. His new attraction and "ride" is a ride that can lead his faithful to darkness and destruction. These followers need to get off quickly and stay off. The truth is out. But will even the truth be able to convince the emotion-intoxicated followers?

14

The Spurious Oracles of Benny Hinn

False prophets are just as plentiful today as they were in the time of Jeremiah, whose words in Jeremiah 23:16 address those who "speak a vision of their own heart, not from the mouth of the Lord." False prophets of today, as in times past, elevate the perception of their spirituality in the eyes of others, seduce the undiscerning with a false sense of hope, and draw disciples to themselves rather than Christ.

Yet, when the predictions of modern seers do not even come close to fulfillment, they offer a number of excuses or rationalizations for the failures, leaving their prognostications nothing more than retractable doublespeak.

Many contemporary prophets simply go on to a new scheme or revelation, forgetting or ignoring the previous ones as though they never uttered them. Few of these prophets offer a trace of repentance or apology following the failure of these "words from the Lord."

When these modern false prophets do acknowledge their past predictions, they often reinterpret the prophecy to make it seem to fit current events, or spiritualize it to some completely new meaning or understanding. Or the "prophet" may attempt to distance himself from his alleged divine utterance by claiming "I am no prophet, I am a mere man and I do make mistakes."

William Branham tried to sidestep the issue of his failed prophecies by saying he "predicted" rather than "prophesied."[1] Semantic games abound in the world of failed prophets.

False prophets who find themselves cornered and unable to ignore, redefine, or spiritualize their predictions, sometimes will resort to the "Touch not the Lord's anointed" line, calling their detractors "quenchers of the Holy Spirit."

Christians need to take a long hard look at Jeremiah's words, "For thus says the Lord of hosts, the God of Israel: Do not let your prophets and your diviners who are in your midst deceive you, nor listen to your dreams that you cause to be dreamed. For they prophesy falsely to you in My name: I have not sent them, says the Lord" (Jeremiah 29:8-9).

Jeremiah's edict is very clear: If anyone claims to prophesy and then gives false prophecies, believers are to reject the prophet. If "prophecies" are found to be false, we know that God is not the author of the revelation.

God also, through Moses, gave a test to determine the source of a prophecy: "If the thing does not happen or come to pass, that is the thing that the Lord has not spoken: the prophet has spoken it presumptuously; you shall not be afraid of him" (Deuteronomy 18:22). God's standard for prophets is "one strike and you're out."

Benny Hinn has also tried his hand at prophecy and proved to be a showman and a master manipulator of emotions, but not a prophet of God.

The Agony of Deceit

One clear example of Hinn's ineptitude as a prophet was even reported by his Charismatic counterparts at *Charisma* magazine. In his article, "What Hollywood Forgot to Show," the magazine's associate editor, Steven Lawson, reveals "the true story behind the box office hit" *Steel Magnolias*. The 1989 motion picture, based upon an off-Broadway play and featuring several of Hollywood's most esteemed actresses, was based upon the life — and death — of Susan Robinson. Robinson (called Shelby in the film and portrayed by Julia Roberts) died at age 31 as a result of complications from diabetes.

Lawson, in presenting "the spiritual side of the young woman" which Hollywood neglected, discloses Hinn's erroneous prophetic handiwork:

> "Susan was sick much of the six years of their marriage. ... The couple attended healing services led by Kenneth Copeland and others. Once Benny Hinn gave a word of knowledge that a woman in the audience wanted to bear children. When Susan went forward, Hinn prophesied that she would have many children. She gave birth to one baby boy."[2]

Robinson's husband, Pat, attempts to exonerate Hinn of his failed and misleading pronouncement by telling the magazine that he "does not question Hinn's prophecy, saying that because of the play and movie, Susan may have many 'spiritual children.'"[3]

Yet Hinn's initial "word of knowledge" and ensuing prophetic word directed specifically to Robinson addressed her physical bearing of children, not "spiritual children." Even more alarming is the potential devastating effects to which false prophecy and false hope can lead. The *Charisma* piece, perhaps unknowingly, spells this out when it states:

> "Giving birth to a baby against recommendations by doctors weakened her body, requiring two kidney transplants and constant insulin treatments."[4]

Tragic consequences can and do result when one is placed in the situation where a message from "God's prophet" is contrary to the cautious advice of doctors and physicians. Many, like Robinson, find themselves in a highly vulnerable and suggestible state when they look to modern-day "prophets" like Hinn.

His Prophetic Word for the 1990s

A cassette tape from a late-evening service on December 31, 1989, at Hinn's former church, the Orlando Christian Center (World Outreach Church), invalidates to the fullest extent his claim to speak for God. On this tape, Hinn presents a dramatic sequence of "prophecies" concerning events which were to occur in the 1990s.[5]

During the New Year's Eve service, Hinn, supposedly under direct divine influence and in a trance-like state, gave his audience a whimsical look into what he said would occur in the upcoming decade. He tried to heighten the dramatic effect of his performance by interspersing speaking in tongues throughout the presentation — all of which was done without an interpreter. *"Ta-Kaa-Pa Kaa-Paa Daa,"* he intoned, in violation of 1 Corinthians 14, which says tongues are forbidden without interpretation. If Hinn was trying to both speak in tongues and supply his own interpretation, he still was on questionable scriptural ground.

He began his prophetic discourse by declaring:

> "Our Lord says this year in Orlando, you're gonna see new ministries arrive. Some are gonna move into Orlando and start new ministries, but I am not in it. I am not in it. They will come here because of the growth and the Lord says to tell you that ... what I do not begin will fall."

Hinn went on to say God would send three ministries that would be based in Orlando. One would "spark the fires of evangelism," another would "spark the great commitment" in the Church that God has been waiting for, and the third one, which has "just been birthed," would "reach the young people of America from Orlando."

To get even more specific — thereby digging himself deeper into his error — Hinn proclaimed this latter ministry-church would "expose Satan's last hidden secrets" and would "even go into the high schools of America and bring God back into the classrooms." This "new breed of fighters," Hinn said, "will even affect the minds in Washington, D.C., concerning Me."

As the 1990s concluded and a new decade (and new century) began, there is nothing that could be construed as reaching the youth of America from Orlando, either when the prophecy was given or any year subsequent. In fact, national statistics report increasing drug use and suicide among young Americans. Cocaine and LSD use are at an all-time high. Orlando itself was not immune from these problems. A front-page story in the July 14, 1996 edition of *The Orlando*

Sentinel said heroin is proving deadlier than ever, causing more teen-age deaths there than in all other Florida cities and towns combined. Other reports listed Florida as the third most dangerous state in the nation.

Furthermore, Washington, D.C., is still Washington, D.C., and secular education continues in a downward spiral. The only thing *from Orlando* that could be said to be reaching out *with nationwide impact* to the young is the Walt Disney Co., with its theme parks, movies, and other entertainment and consumer entities. Recall that Hinn declared: "This year in Orlando" it was going to begin. What happened? Who is wrong, God or Hinn?

Surely, if anything so dramatic and revolutionary would have happened in the early nineties, the Church at large would have heard of it. At the very least, we would have read an enhanced version of the occurrence in an issue of *Charisma* magazine.

Then, further into his message, Hinn predicted two notable deaths within Christian circles would occur within the next few years. "The Lord also says that two of his great giants will die in the mid-nineties. They have held the torch of revival for the last forty years — these two," Hinn purported.

This is a good example of a "shotgun prophecy," especially since a number of the "Christian leaders" are up in age. It is akin to announcing that in the next few years there will be two major airline disasters or earthquakes. Although Hinn does give some details of these deaths, he was, on an identification level, careful to keep the pronouncement vague. He said:

> "One will die suddenly while asleep and the other will die with sickness. And as both giants die, which will be in the mid-nineties, I will shake this world with the last revival. Their deaths will be the closing pages of this move and the new move of God will begin which I have promised."

While it is agreed that it would be troublesome to give the names of the "giants," nonetheless, if the message truly had been from the Lord, one wonders why Hinn could not have provided more precise details, such as a more exact time frame, cause of death, or other such specifics.

Several years later, with time running out for this particular segment of Hinn's prophecy, evidently he had to widen the perimeters of the meaning of "giant." He tried to reestablish and confirm the validity of this revelation by telling viewers of the *Praise the Lord* show:

> "The Lord said this to me. He said in the mid-nineties, two of my giants will go home. And right after that, the greatest revival in the history of man would begin. Well, just recently one mighty giant went home, that's Dr. Sumrall. ... My very precious friend. Now I don't know who's next. I'm not going to predict anyone to go home now. ... But we are now in the mid-nineties. This is — this is — this — this is the time. Saints, put your seat belts on. Something is about to happen."6

Surely, the definition of "giant" is in the eye of the beholder. Pentecostal minister Lester F. Sumrall died of meningitis on April 28, 1996, at age 83. While the former Assembly of God minister was a notable personality in Pentecostal circles, Sumrall did not possess the distinction gained by some of Hinn's other "precious friends" such as Oral Roberts, Paul Crouch, Kathryn Kuhlman or Aimee Semple McPherson. Nor could it be argued that Sumrall was one who could be said to have "held the torch of revival for the last forty years."

In a pinch, perhaps one could equally consider John Wimber, the late leader of the Vineyard movement, as a potential candidate. Wimber, who died Nov. 17, 1997, at age 63, initiated a self-style brand of "power evangelism" evidenced by signs and wonders. Yet the message Wimber preached — that tongues and healing could eliminate "Satan, sin and sickness" — was clearly absent from his own life. Wimber, for years prior to his death, suffered a number of catastrophic ailments. However, like Sumrall, the late Vineyard leader cannot be said to have "held the torch of revival for the last forty years," because his prominence in the "signs and wonders" movement lasted for slightly more than a decade.

Perhaps, based upon the age (and in some cases the failing health) of those prominent for "forty years" in the religious scene, such as evangelist Billy Graham, Oral Roberts, Robert Schuller, and several others, Hinn thought it a safe call that one or more of these aging leaders would pass off the scene before 2000. This, while seeming to be a sure prediction for anyone to make, failed as men like Graham, Roberts, and Schuller lived on into the twenty-first century.

Back at the New Year's Eve service, Hinn's claims continued and grew more incredible:

> "There will be many raised from the dead in that day. Many visitations of angels that will come as young men knocking at your door. You will not recognize them as angels at first, but then you will be burned within your hearts."

Resurrections have yet to become commonplace, or even occasional. Every cemetery in America is intact. Even the isolated claims of alleged resurrections by the likes of Oral Roberts and others are quickly silenced by a scrutinizing media and requests for documentation.

While Hinn himself has repeatedly claimed angelic appearances and could easily turn up someone who claims to have had an angelic visitation, "many visitations" would be somewhat harder to document. Even if Hinn were to appeal to the books and TV programs that have promulgated the angelic phenomenon, he would have to answer for the unscriptural theology and questionable motives of those productions.

It was then that Hinn moved into the most damaging segment of his prophecy. He said:

> "The Lord also tells me to tell you in the mid-nineties, about '94 or '95, *no later than that*, God will destroy the homosexual community of America" (emphasis added).

Hinn's declaration was greeted with a loud applause from his congregation. Perhaps the enthusiastic response caused

Hinn to further bury himself:

> "But He will not destroy it with what many minds have
> thought Him to be. But He will destroy it with fire.
> And many will turn and be saved, and many will rebel
> and be destroyed."

The first sentence probably refers to AIDS. Hinn has been confronted over undocumented claims of healing from AIDS, from which he has retreated quickly.

Given that the homosexual population became more overt and militant during the decade of the 1990s, it is obvious that Hinn has spoken with great presumption.

The irony is that the Disney Corp., also based in Orlando, has given the homosexual community a great boost. This has led to a call by the leadership of the Southern Baptist Convention for people to boycott Disney products, a move endorsed by publisher Stephen Strang, Hinn's good friend.[7] There has been no nationwide destruction of homosexuals, and evidently Hinn did not know that the mid-nineties would have a previously family-oriented organization lending its weight to a group and lifestyle that militates against the family.

In his quest to be a prophet, Hinn left nothing to personal interpretation with these statements. Remember that he repeatedly emphasized that the source of his edict was the Lord, and was specific in what would happen and to whom, and even provided a date by which the event would occur. Those who still consider Hinn anointed of God need to contemplate what the Lord has said concerning would-be prophets in Deuteronomy 18:21-22.

Since the 1994-1995 "no later than that" deadline has come and gone, and with the homosexual community alive, militant, and continuing to make substantial progress in pursuit of its goals, Hinn is shown to be a false prophet. There was no mass, fiery annihilation of homosexuals. Neither could one argue that because of mass conversions or repentance among the homosexual populace, God's judgment has been restrained. It is also sad to think that Hinn's congregation would cheer with applause the destruction of the homosexual people. This proves the adage, "When truth disappears, the vacuum is filled by power."

This type of mindset also provides added motivation for the homosexual agenda. It polarizes and does nothing to show to the needy the love or forgiveness of God, nor does it convey to them the power He can provide to change their lives. If the militant homosexual community ever gets hold of Hinn's prophecy, it might really "fire" them up — in ways Hinn never envisioned.

Hinn next predicted that:

> "The economy of the United States of America is going to fall. ... And what will bring America to its knees, says the Spirit, is the economic collapse. The allies she has depended upon will turn their backs."

The late 1980s and early 1990s witnessed a rising national debt. As such, the financial collapse of America has become a staple in the prognostications of many a doomsday prophet. It is not hard to imagine the source of this part of Hinn's prophecy. However, any serious economist would disagree adamantly that Hinn's fiscal doomsday revelation was an accurate depiction of the nineties, especially with the stock market reaching record highs in the nineties. Moreover, Hinn implies that this financial collapse will occur because America has depended upon her allies, and they "will turn their backs." America's economic strength is not dependent upon her foreign allies. Rather, it could be said that throughout the last century, quite the opposite has been true.

Despite the warnings of financial ruin, Hinn promises that America will again be exalted:

> "I've heard the voice of my saints ... I will look again on this nation — even as I've looked on Israel long ago — and I will restore its greatness. In that greatness, I will be magnified."

The error of "manifest doctrine," the idea that America is the exact parallel of Israel in terms of God's dealings, is a myth and does not have one scintilla of evidence in Scripture.

God's primary dealings are with individuals of "all nations" and the Church, the body of Christ. America has been blessed, but it is not Israel in any sense.

Hinn's predictions went on to focus on the spiritual:

> "Canada will be visited with a mighty revival that will start in the west coast of British Columbia. It will sweep across the west. It will sweep across even Alaska and will come east. But the great move of God that I've planned for America will not begin on the west coast but on the east coast. It will break loose in the next three years, and sweep across the west."

Hinn's specifics have again narrowed and all but negated the possibility of variety of purported fulfillments of his words. He has prophesied himself into the proverbial corner. For example, he cannot claim the so-called "Toronto Blessing" as the fruition of his spiritual-awakening forecast. Toronto is in south-central Canada. Moreover, the roots of this movement are traced not to British Columbia, but to the United States by way of Rodney Howard-Browne and a Saint Louis Vineyard pastor named Randy Clark. Additionally, there was no major revival occurring in western Canada between 1990 through 1993 that would accommodate Hinn's pronouncement in any way. Again, he has seriously missed the standard for a biblical prophet.

Earthquakes are usually a dramatic theme and an attention getter. Hinn picked up on and addressed this theme as he warned his congregation: "The Spirit of God tells me an earthquake will hit the east coast of America and destroy much in the nineties."

Hinn even went so far to claim that, "Not one place will be safe from earthquakes in the nineties. These who have not known earthquakes will know it."

Hinn then turns his efforts to the political scene and combines it with the "rapture" of the Church. And, just in case his audience has forgotten the supposed source of his message, he asserted: "People, I feel the Spirit all over me." In his discourse on world politics, he maintained:

> "The Spirit of God tells me there will be a woman that will arise as a leader in the west. In her day, much evil will take place. She will be very powerful. The Spirit tells me that the Church, once raptured, following the rapture, a woman president will be in the White House. And that woman president will destroy this nation. But My Church will be gone. My saints will be home."[8]

We also learn that, "The Spirit tells me Fidel Castro will die in the nineties. Oh my. Some will try to kill him and they will not succeed. But there will come a change in his physical health and he will not stay in power." Yet, as the nineties drew to a close, Castro lived on and the very state which Hinn called home for over a decade witnessed firsthand the Cuban leader's power as he used Elian Gonzalez, the child refugee from Cuba, as a political pawn.

And as the grand finale to his worldview vision, Hinn said:

> "A world dictator is coming on the scene — my! He's a short man. He's a short man! I see a short man! Who's a perfect incarnation of Satan. ... Never in my life have I had anything happen like what's happening to me now. This man will rule the world. The next few years you will see him. But not long after that you will see Me."

A "few years" from December 31, 1989, have already passed. There is no short man ruling the world and we haven't seen God. Thus, it is painfully obvious that all of the above has to be, at best, human deception and stage antics from the mind of Benny Hinn, or at worst, satanic deception. False prophecies need to be called just that. Graves have not opened, homosexuals have not gone up in flames, and the short man never showed up.

As a teenager, Hinn traveled with a drama group. He was known as a showman.[9] He learned his skill well. His prophecies on December 31, 1989, were all a stage play. It is, as we have seen, false prophecy and a diversion from what is important. Yet Hinn evidently knows that his kind of a show feeds the sensational and fuels his followers' emotions. As in his "healing crusades," he has taken them on yet another adrenalin and endorphin high. These kind of highs become addictive and make one less able to discern. Judging from his congregation's response (heard on the cassette tape), they loved every second of it.

Jesus did not titillate emotions, and we can trust what He taught about the future. At times he totally downplayed speculative pursuits about future knowledge.

David Hagopian and Douglas Wilson point this out:

> "When our Lord stood on the mount, about to ascend to the right hand of the Father, His disciples, sensing His imminent departure, anxiously asked Him when He would restore the kingdom to Israel (Acts 1:6). Instead of indulging their end-times inquiry, He told them that it was of no concern to them *when* God had ordained such things to take place, only *that* they would take place. Far more important than probing the secret will of the Father was the obedience they were to render to His revealed will (v. 7). In particular, He told them to be His witnesses in Jerusalem, Judea, Samaria, and even to the remotest part of the earth (v. 8)."[10]

"Tell Me What I Said"

Hinn then closed his "revelation" in dramatic fashion, asserting that he was so caught up in the Spirit that he was totally unaware of what he had said:

> "I wish somebody would make sure to tell me what I said. Did you tape that, brother? Did you tape that? Ooh! I was totally drunk. I'm still drunk. Lord, if You spoke through me, if what You said is of You, then as I stretch my finger towards the people let Your power fall on every one of them. If what I've said, Master, is of You, let the power flow now. Here it goes in the name of Jesus."

Some shrieked, some fell as "proof" of the divine nature of it all. Hinn was in total control as he led his people into altered states of consciousness.

Hinn acted more like a shaman than a Christian minister. In occultic and pagan societies, a shaman enters a trance-like state and presumes to act as a mediator with the gods or spirits. The shaman may declare cures or tell the future. Postmodern religious practices have now entered the world of the occult.

Noted German theologian and author Kurt Koch writes:

> "Speaking in a trance is a practice of mediums. It only takes place when a medium is present who has mastered this form of spiritism. The medium puts himself into a trance, a kind of deep sleep, and the spirits are then said to be able to speak through the medium to the people present."[11]

What Hinn purported to do belongs in the realm of black magic or a gypsy tea room. Divination, or divining and predicting the future, is soundly condemned in Deuteronomy 18:10, Jeremiah 14:14, and Acts 16:16 (in context). Apart from God's ordained prophets in the Scriptures, there are only false prophets. Even if one engages in the realm of "prophecy" simply as a product of the flesh, doing it is a dangerous practice.

It seems almost ironic that in the mid-1990s, Hinn loudly assaulted mediums by declaring that he was going to go head-to-head with the psychic hotlines. He asked for the support of his followers so that his daily program would telecast over the same secular television stations that broadcast the psychics' advertisements and infomercials. In reality, what he has done and is doing appears to be a "Christianized" version of the psychic hotlines. His demonstrations of the supernatural, such as healings, future telling, words of knowledge, trances, and other antics, are stock-in-trade in the occult world.

Hinn also, by virtue of his trance, gives to his faithful a skewed and unbiblical concept of inspiration. Divine inspiration is not robotic or mechanical. God did not use his prophets as mindless robots or mere drunken scribes. Those who spoke for Him were intellectually involved and knowledgeable in terms of what was being communicated. Paul wrote to the church at Corinth that "The spirits of prophets are subject to the control of the prophets" (1 Corinthians 14:32).

The Prophetic Beat Goes On

Undaunted by his dismal track record of failed prophecy and by the news media's debunking of his claim that a man was raised from the dead at one of his healing crusades, Hinn pressed on in 1999 with a divine revelation of worldwide resurrections.

"I'm telling you, I can feel the anointing talking here. People are going to be canceling funeral services and bringing their dead in their caskets, placing them — My God, I feel the anointing here — placing them before a television set, waiting for God's power to come through and touch them," Hinn told Paul and Jan Crouch and their Trinity Broadcasting Network viewing audience during the *Praise the Lord* show which originally aired live October 19, 1999.[12]

Of course, according to Hinn, the television sets will need to be tuned to TBN. "You're going to have people raised from the dead watching this network. ... People around the world who will lose loved ones will say to undertakers, 'Not yet, I want to take my dead loved one and place him in front of that TV set for 24 hours,'" Hinn announced to the network's followers.

Hinn also alleged that God was showing him "rows of caskets lining up in front of this TV set." "I see them bringing them closer to the TV set, and as people are coming closer, I see loved ones picking up the hands of the dead and letting them touch the screen and people are getting raised as their hands are touching that screen," Hinn said. "The word will spread that if some dead person be put in front of this TV screen, they will be raised from the dead — and they will be by the thousands," Hinn promised the Crouches and the viewers of their *Praise the Lord* show.

Still, there was much more of his divine revelation for Hinn to tell viewers of the world's largest network of religious stations. "TBN will no longer be just a television network, it will be an extension of heaven to earth. ... The Lord just said to me these words, ... 'TBN will not only be a Christian network, it will be an extension of heaven to the earth,'" he declared. Hinn went on to say, "So if you want to go to heaven, if you want to see heaven, if you want to taste heaven — turn on that channel because you will."

Once again Hinn's declarations put him more at home with the occult than a biblical setting. His concept that TBN is to become an open passage to a higher spiritual realm closely resembles an occult vortex known as a "Cone of Power," through which spiritual powers energize agents on earth.

Perhaps, Hinn should have stopped while he was ahead. As he prolonged his prophetic utterance, a verbal *faux pas* devastated any claim of a divine inspiration for his revelation. *"Now the Lord just told me — and I don't know whether this is true or not...,"* the careful listener will hear Hinn say during the TBN broadcast.

Thus, Hinn's revelation, which he claimed came through his anointing, is nothing more than imagination or fabrication — perhaps even demonic. It is not, in any manner, divine revelation. Moreover, Charismatics and TBN viewers alike are still burying their dead.

People need to wake up and apply the Scriptures to Hinn's false statements and to all false prophets. The Church need not be afraid of speaking out against false prophets who deliver false prophecies. Either God is wrong and has made a mistake, or the "prophet" is speaking presumptuously from his own mind. Going with God and His written Word is always the safe route. Theatrics and tabloid teasers do not belong in God's house.

Christians need to take seriously the words of H.M. Wolf as he points us to the Scripture:

> "In the NT false prophets were plentiful (1 John 4:1) and were compared with wolves in sheep's clothing

(Matt 7:15) and false teachers (2 Pet 2:1). ... Christ
warned of false prophets whose miracles would deceive
many in the end (Matt 24:24; Mark 13:22)."[13]

This time Hinn cannot blame his mistakes on an editor or
say it was a joke or that he is just a human, as he has in the
past. Throughout his prophetic statements cited above, Hinn
repeatedly claims a divine origin for his message by alleging:
"The Spirit of God tells me," or the "Lord says," or "I can
feel the anointing talking here." His words were all supposed
to be right from the throne room of God and he is pretending
to be God's conduit. He claimed them to be bona fide
prophetic utterances. They were supposed to be no less than
"the real thing." It is time for people to wake up!

The late PFO director, Bill Cetnar, repeatedly declared,
"Time is the enemy of a false prophet." Hinn's claim of
divine inspiration has succumbed to time, the mortal enemy
of a false prophet.

By now you would have thought Hinn would have learned
that all his documented falsehoods have a way of catching up.
Jeremiah and Moses said we are to judge self-professing
prophets on the basis of their accuracy. Paul instructed the
Church to "weigh carefully" what the prophets have said.
That is all that we have done.

Benny Hinn and the Bible

"From that moment on the Bible took on a whole new dimension. ... The Bible became alive. ... It was just by asking the Holy Spirit to open the Word to me. And He did. ... He was my comforter, my teacher, my guide."[1]

How one handles the Word of God reveals much about how the interpreter views the Bible, himself, and his audience. Therefore, we can expect to gain valuable insights into the phenomenon of Benny Hinn from such an investigation.

The foundations of modern biblical interpretation ("hermeneutics") were laid during the Renaissance and the Protestant Reformation. Prior to this time, much biblical interpretation was dominated by spiritualization and allegorization of the text in question. Authoritative figures, whose interpretations were often considered infallible, ruled over the hermeneutical landscape. The controlling principles of hermeneutics were: 1) personal authority, 2) mystical interpretations, 3) tradition, and 4) dogmatics (producing contrived biblical support for official church doctrines).

With the Renaissance and the Reformation, these controls were laid aside. The concept of the Priesthood of every believer, in which all have the right to approach Scripture directly without the mediation of official "authorities," was maintained. Mysticism, allegorization, and spiritualization gave way to the "grammatico-historical" method, in which the goal of the interpreter is to understand the text in light of its original background, and to allow the biblical authors to speak for themselves. The crucial question posed to each passage became, "What is the author trying to say?" rather than the old method, "How can we read this to support our doctrine?"

Tradition was discarded in favor of empirical evidence as a deciding factor in the interpretation of biblical texts.

The Reformers left to conservative Protestantism this great legacy, insisting on such basic principles as authorial intent (what the author intended to communicate to the original audience) and "the Analogy of Faith" (Scripture interprets Scripture). Further, they demanded that matters of faith and practice be determined by Scripture alone (*Sola Scriptura*) and by reference to the "Full Counsel of God" (taking *everything* the Scriptures say about a given subject, not simply one or two out-of-context passages).[2]

The battle for the Bible was won by the Reformers, but each subsequent generation has had to re-engage in this ongoing war. It appears that the present generation is not faring well in its battle over biblical interpretation.[3] More and more, the Protestant church of today is coming to resemble the church of the Middle Ages. In this age of high technology, information superhighways, and (supposed) rationalism, the Church is all too willing to yield its Priesthood of every believer status over to "professionals" who sway "laymen" not by the evidence, but by the force of their own personalities, by their own mystical experiences, and by their own subjective "insights." The limits of the interpreter's own (too often fertile) imagination frequently replace the "controls" of interpretation left to us by the Reformers.

Enter Benny Hinn. It goes unquestioned that he is the most popular figure in Christian media today.[4] He is humorous, charismatic, and *convincing*. Despite his admitted lack of formal Bible training and his doctrinal retractions of the past, he continues to speak with the utmost authority, boldly declaring that his teachings rest firmly on no less authority than the Word of God itself.

At the beginning of this study of Hinn and his hermeneutics (methods of interpretation), it appeared that there was no rhyme, reason, or consistent systematic approach to his Bible interpretations. It seemed his choice of Scriptures and how he handles them is simply a random, somewhat naive, "shotgun" approach which defies careful analysis and categorization. Upon greater scrutiny and further exposure to his written materials and taped and live broadcasts, however, a very consistent pattern became clearly discernible.

Hinn is working within the historical framework of conservative Protestantism. Therefore, he must base everything he says and does upon the Bible. Despite the fact that much of what he says sounds more Catholic than Protestant, he has, for whatever reason, decided to "play by the rules" of Protestantism. His constant appeal will be to the Scriptures that we all hold to be the *only* rule for matters of faith and practice. What separates him from Protestantism is not his constant appeals to the Bible as his authority; rather, it is the manner in which he *approaches* the Bible. What distances Hinn from historical orthodoxy is his *hermeneutical methodology*.

The passages dealt with below are representative of the vast majority of Hinn's interpretations. Admittedly, there are times when his preaching and teaching are biblically and theologically sound. These are in the minority, however, and do not reflect the true agenda that is at the heart of his ministry, namely the exaltation of the exegete.

In the world of biblical interpretation, the authority of the exegete (interpreter) has historically been established by his training, ecclesiastical investiture (delegated authority), and proven experience (time- and evidence-tested track record of reliability and consistency). Because these accepted avenues are unavailable to Hinn, he regularly appeals to three other criteria to establish his interpretive authority: 1) his claim to "insider's knowledge" of the biblical world, 2) his claim of divine origin of his interpretations, and 3) his claim of novelty (claim to exceptional spiritual intuition to reveal "new," "deeper," or "hidden" meanings of biblical texts which are not perceivable to the average Christian).

"Insider's Knowledge" of the Biblical World

Because Hinn was born and lived his first 14 years in Israel, he promotes himself as having greater insight into the biblical world. In his mind, this places his interpretive authority above laymen and scholars alike. Here, however, it is best to allow Hinn to speak for himself:

"Now. The Bible promises seven blessings to every giver and every one of them you ought to claim every time you give. Malachi 3:10 says, "'Bring ye all the tithe into the storehouse, that there may be meat in mine house, and prove me now herewith," saith the LORD of Hosts.' And here is the first blessing: 'If I will not open the windows of heaven.' Listen! Every time you give, God promises revival. 'Windows of heaven' deal with *revival*. And believe me when I tell you, *I am an Israelite, from Israel, and I can read this thing in Hebrew and tell ya. And I know the culture and the tradition and the mentality.* 'Windows' *always* deal with revival to the Jewish mind. *Always!* ...third... 'and I will *rebuke* the devourer for your sakes.' You know what the word 'rebuke' means? I, I looked it up. John [Avanzini], you, you would love this. It means 'I will *paralyze*.' 'I will *paralyze* the devourer' ...and the word 'paralyze' means 'putting him [the devourer] behind bars.' If you want the devil behind bars, start giving. God will paralyze him for you, for your sake. He'll quit eating your seed. ...fifth... it states, 'Neither shall your vine cast her fruit before the time in the field.' You know what that means? *'Vine'* deal withs [sic] family, your family. Jesus said, 'I am the vine, you are the branches,' right? That's family... Your vine, family will not forsake the children. What are the fruits of the vine? The children in the family. So what God's Word says is if we give, our children will never lack. ... Now this is something that the Holy Ghost said to me. He said, 'Every time you give, not only will *you* reap the harvest. Your *children*, when they grow up, will reap the harvest you are sowing for...' The seventh, I think, is the greatest blessing. He says, 'And ye shall be [a] *delightsome* land...' And the word 'delightsome,' I looked it up — *remember I told you I am from that part of the world.* The word 'delightsome' means *in Hebrew* 'highly desired.' God will highly desire you, which means He'll start using you... *It's in the Word. It's in the Word.* You know, every time I give, I tell the Lord, 'I want all seven Lord.'"[5]

In the evangelist's opening statement, Hinn established his belief in the Prosperity Gospel (give expecting to get some specific remuneration in return). This is a doctrine which he is on record as renouncing numerous times, but continues to promote in one expression or another.

"Windows of heaven" or "windows" do not "*always* deal with revival.*" In point of fact, there is not one place in the entire Bible which is even remotely suggestive of such a meaning. In most places, the reference is to literal windows (1 Kings 7:4, 5; Daniel 6:10, etc.). Three times the phrase "windows of heaven" is connected with *judgment* (Genesis 7:11; 8:2; Isaiah 24:18). In Ecclesiastes 12:3, "windows" is used metaphorically (symbolically) to refer to "eyes." The same phrase which occurs in Malachi 3:10 appears also in 2 Kings 7:2, 19. Here it is clear that the reference is to divine provision. This is clearly the intent of the statement in Malachi as well.

The statement, "I am an Israelite," is simply not correct. As much as Hinn might like to be, and as much as he might wish that his audience would think that he is, he is *not Jewish*. Although he was born in Israel, his ethnic identity is Arabic.

There are *no* authoritative Hebrew lexicons which attribute the meaning "to paralyze" to the word *ga'ar*.[6] In all instances in which this word occurs, "rebuke" is the proper rendering, with no other nuance connected to it.

One wonders, "If Hinn is an Israelite, and an expert in the Hebrew language, having spoken it from his youth,[7] why would he have to look this word up?" *Ga'ar* appears in the Bible 29 times,[8] and is used in spoken Hebrew today.[9]

The word *ocel* (devourer) appears in the Hebrew Bible 21 times in this form,[10] but never in a context which suggests that it might be understood as referring to the Devil. None of the authoritative Hebrew lexicons list such a meaning.[11]

Hinn's interpretation of vine/cast/fruit as referring to family/forsaking/children is simply arbitrary assignment of allegorical meanings to words which do *not* occur in an allegorical or symbolic context. The larger context clearly reveals that the vine referred to is a real vine. The prophet is here addressing the poor, agriculturally-oriented society of the post-exilic period, which was tithing in large measure directly from the produce of their fields. The reader will recall the phrases, "...that there may be *food* in my house" (v. 10) and *"fruits of* your *soil"* (v. 11), both of which speak of the literal harvest of the field. The word "fruit" in the phrase "neither shall your vine cast her *fruit* before the time in the field," although it appears in the KJV, is nevertheless *absent* in the Hebrew, in which Hinn claims the expertise of a native speaker. A literal translation would therefore read, "Your vine in the field will not *miscarry.*"[12]

Thus, Hinn has created an allegorical/spiritualized meaning for a word which does not even exist in the Hebrew text! This observation also serves to clarify the term "cast," which never has the sense of "forsake" ascribed to it by Hinn. Rather, here it is an agricultural term used to refer to grapes falling off before they are ripe.

Finally, with respect to children benefiting directly from the giving of their parents, this would appear to be in direct contradiction to the doctrine of personal responsibility taught by the Bible (e.g., Jeremiah 31:29; Ezekiel 18:2-20; Romans 2:6; 2 Corinthians 5:10; etc.). It seems to more closely resemble the Roman Catholic doctrine of "treasury of merits." It is clear that children benefit from the godly example when they see parents giving from a heart of gratitude, expecting nothing in return. It is *not* clear that they will benefit at all from the attitude encouraged by Hinn and other purveyors of the "Give-to-Get Gospel."

The following is another example of Hinn's "insider exegesis":

> "And one day He [Jesus] stood and said, 'I am the Way. I am the Truth. I am the Life.' You know why the Jews got angry with Him? ... *I am an Israelite. I know something that most Westerners don't know.* The reason they got angry with Him when He said, 'I am the Way, Truth, Life,' is because the tabernacle of Moses had three entrances. The gate was called 'The Way,' the holy place had a door called 'The Truth,' and the Holy of Holies had a veil called 'The Life.' When Jesus said, 'I'm the Way, Truth, and Life,' He was saying, 'I'm the

gate of the tabernacle, the door to the holy place, and
the veil to the Holy of Holies.' And they got angry at
Him. They said, 'How dare this man declare he's the
way to the Holy of Holies where the ark is!'"[13]

Hinn's failure to properly handle the Word of God is all
too obvious from his exegesis of John's narrative. First, the
"Jews" never got angry. They never heard Jesus say these
words (John 14:6). This teaching of Jesus was at the Last
Supper, attended only by Jesus and the disciples. From the
biblical account, it appears that the disciples accepted it
willingly, and loyally remained with Jesus until his arrest
(John 13:1 through 18:14). Since these "Jews" never heard
this teaching, they could not have asked the question put on
their lips, and thus added to the biblical account by Hinn.

Moreover, his comment, "I am an Israelite. I know
something that most Westerners don't know," is again very
telling. He seems to think his middle-eastern experience gives
him exegetical powers and perception beyond that of normal
men. This writer has lived and studied extensively in Israel,
and know of others who have had as much or more experience
as I, yet there is a difference. Neither I nor these others
regularly appeal to our experiences as an "insider" to create
the same "cult of personality" and sense of authoritative
definitiveness as does Hinn. Our interpretations must stand
or fall on the basis of the evidence we put forth to support
them. Nor are the mistakes made by other experts who have
first-hand experience with the land of the Bible so glaring and
so frequent when drawing from that experience as those of
Hinn.

It is instructive to note that the tabernacle was not in
existence during the earthly ministry of Jesus. The temple was
the edifice which was the visible representation of the
dwelling presence of God in Christ's day. Although this might
appear to be historical nit-picking, historical accuracy is the
least we should expect from one who touts himself as an
authority on the biblical world. In the time of Jesus, the ark
no longer resided in the Holy of Holies. According to the
contemporary historian Josephus, *nothing* was found in the

Holy of Holies at this time (*War* 5:219). It was not present when Pompey entered the Holy of Holies in 63 B.C. (*War* 1:152-153).

Therefore, the names of the three gates, or more appropriately, "entranceways" of the tabernacle is a moot issue, since the historical setting Hinn has recreated is impossible. Nevertheless, it is instructive to delve deeper into the origin of this "insider's knowledge" about the names of these "gates." The Bible itself offers no evidence by which to determine the names of the entranceways of either the tabernacle or the temple.

Likewise, there is no extra-biblical text (from the Apocrypha, Pseudepigrapha, Dead Sea Scrolls, Josephus, Philo, Rabbinic Literature, etc.) which ascribed *any* name to these places. Therefore, the origin of this material is the fertile imagination of the interpreter.

Further, when the Romans looted the temple at its destruction in A.D. 70, there is no mention of the Ark being among the treasures taken, although the lampstand(s) appear in this account (*War* 6:387-391). These also appear on the "Arch of Titus" in Rome, a monument constructed in commemoration of this event, yet the Ark of the Covenant is strangely absent. The rabbis of the time stated that the ark no longer resided in the temple after the time of King Josiah (Mishnah *Yoma* 5:2).

One final example will further illustrate Hinn's appeal to "insider's knowledge." Hinn offered *Praise the Lord* show viewers the following interpretation of the destruction of the Egyptian army at the Red Sea:

> "You talk about watching God divide an ocean, taking the wheels off the chariots of the Egyptians. And here this wall of ice, it was, by the way a wall of ice, if you read your Scriptures, that's right. The Hebrew word, and I can show it to you after the show, Paul [Crouch]. But the Hebrew word, uh-uh-uh-wh-when God divided the—that Red Sea, as the walls stood, it actually froze with God's breath. So when the—when the water came down it was ice coming that crushed the Egyptians. *It's in the Word. It's in the Hebrew.* You—it's not in the King

James, but *it's in the Hebrew* and I'll show it to Paul and he can show it to you after I'm all done, maybe next week. *You—you—you Hebrew scholars look me up, you'll find I'm right.*"[14]

We did. He was wrong again. Not only was he wrong about the meaning of words and the proper interpretation of this passage, but as is all too often the case when Hinn is involved, serious theological problems arise out of this manner of handling the Word of God.

A "strong east wind" is the agent God used to accomplish the miracle (Exodus 14:21). This is a well-known meteorological phenomenon of the Middle-East, both in antiquity and today. The normal air-flow, which moves from west to east, brings moisture and more moderate temperatures from the Mediterranean Sea. On the other hand, the "east wind" describes a fluctuation in the normal air-flow and moves from east to west. Called in Arabic *Hamseen*, it comes off the desert and is therefore unusually hot and arid.

This contrast was known by the writers of Scripture and is easily seen in passages such as Genesis 41:6; Exodus 14:21; Job 15:2; Isaiah 27:8; Ezekiel 17:10; 19:12; Hosea 13:15; and Jonah 4:8. The point here is that God would not send a hot wind to freeze anything. The passages given describe the drying, scorching, withering effect of the wind, not its cooling action. Anyone such as Hinn, who lived in Israel for 14 years, experienced at least 14 of these, and should know first-hand the devastating heat it brings in its wake.

Hinn further misses the term consistently used throughout the narrative: "waters" (14:22, 26, 28, 29; 15:1, 4, 5, 10, 19, 21; always plural in Hebrew). There is no indication that the actual state or make-up of the waters changed, since the term remains the same, and the number remains in the plural (i.e., it did not become a solid block of ice).

In addition, there are a number of terms which occur in the Old Testament describing the action of freezing or hardening, following the commonly used translations, and none of these appear in the passage in question. Examples of words available to the ancient author, but unused, include *davak* (2 Samuel 23:10), *yatsak* (Job 37:10), and *lachad* (Job 38:30). In addition to the action of freezing, the term "ice" (*kerach*) is also conspicuous in its absence. That the term was available and used in the Old Testament, even by Moses himself, is clear from its appearance in Genesis 31:40 (cf. Job 6:16; 37:10; 38:29; Psalm 147:17; and Jeremiah 36:30).

Also, in Exodus 15:4, 5, and 10 (cf. 14:26-28, 30; 15:19), the demise of the Egyptian army is described as "drowning." The Hebrew term *tava'* means "to sink" or "to sink down" (cf. Job 38:6; Psalms 9:15; 69:2, 14-15; Jeremiah 38:6, 22; Lamentations 2:9). Because this term is in the text in question and its meaning is abundantly clear, it is impossible to support the statement that "...it was ice coming [down] that crushed the Egyptians."

The "Full Counsel of God," and the "Analogy of Faith" or "Scripture Interprets Scripture," require that we fully investigate the testimony of the remainder of Scripture to determine what took place at the Sea. Moses, an eye-witness, describes the event in these terms, "I will sing unto the Lord...the horse and rider he has *thrown into* the *sea*" (Exodus 15:1; cf. v. 21). In verse 19 he states, "...the Lord brought back the *waters* of the sea upon them." Deuteronomy 11:4 states that God *"overwhelmed* them *with the waters* of the Red Sea." Joshua 24:7 notes that God *"brought the sea over them and covered them."* Nehemiah 9:11 adds that God *"cast* their pursuers *into the depths, as a stone into the mighty waters"* (i.e., they sank/ drowned). Psalm 78:13 reads, "[God] made *the waters* stand up *like a heap."* Psalm 78:53 adds that *"the sea overwhelmed* their enemies." Psalm 106:11 reminds us that *"the waters covered* their adversaries." Finally, Hebrews 11:29 informs us, "By faith the people crossed the Red Sea as if on dry land; but *the Egyptians*, when they attempted to do the same, *were drowned"* (cf. Wisdom of Solomon 10:19). The language employed by the majority of these passages is highly suggestive of death by drowning. At least two passages state it explicitly (Exodus 15:4, 5, 10; Hebrews 11:29).

The Holy Spirit will never reveal a meaning of a Scripture which contradicts a truth He has revealed in another

Scripture. When a seeming contradiction does occur, the problem must be said to originate in the human interpretation and not the divine interpreter of Scripture. The interpretation placed upon this Scripture by Hinn is not only impossible from the standpoint of philology, meteorology, and immediate context: it is also impossible because it contradicts the clear statements of other Scriptures.

Therefore, we can only infer from this that Hinn has effectively placed himself above Scripture in terms of the authority to interpret the acts and revelations of God. This almost has to be the case because of his reference to Hebrew to support his assertions, and his challenge to experts to prove him wrong. In this matter it will be difficult to allow him to pass off his heterodoxy as resulting from ignorance or lack of formal Bible training.

In his 1995 book, *Welcome, Holy Spirit*, he states that as a child he had already "mastered the Bible" and that he had "spent thousands of hours studying the Bible."[15] The argument he makes based on the Hebrew presupposes a certain amount of previous reading or research by which he came to his conclusions.

We must also point out one final problem that this exegetical blunder illustrates: Hinn does not know Hebrew to the extent that he purports. Almost every reference he makes to the Hebrew text contains errors a first-year student of Hebrew would not make. For example, on his personal broadcast of October 24, 1994, he stated that the Hebrew of Psalm 46:10 [v. 11 in the Hebrew Bible] reads, "Be still and know Jehovah Elohim." In actuality, the word "Jehovah" (or Adonai or Yahweh or any of its variant spellings) does not even appear in this passage. In the place where Hinn interjects the proper noun "Jehovah," one reads a common pronoun for the word "I," exactly as all the translations have it.

Time and again, he constantly states that he knows something to be the case because he is "from the land of the Bible," or because he is an "Israeli," an "Israelite," a "Hebrew," or a *"Sabra"* (a technical Hebrew term denoting a *native-born Israeli Jew*).[16] Only the first of these assertions is factual. He is not Jewish, despite these and other intentionally misleading statements. In his writings, he has admitted that he was born of a Greek father and an Armenian mother.[17] Even this statement, however, cannot be maintained in light of testimony, which shows that his father was a Jaffa-born Arab and his mother was a Ramallah-born Arab.[18]

These examples should be sufficient to discern the basic pattern. Nevertheless, readers will discover additional instances of this phenomenon below, in passages used to illustrate other aspects of Hinn's interpretive agenda.

Claim of Divine Origin

Hinn has established a consistent pattern of appealing to the divine origin of his interpretations as the source of his authority. In other words, Hinn regularly claims that he has been taught a deeper, clearer meaning of a Scripture by God/Jesus/the Holy Spirit. This is well-documented in the earlier part of his ministry. In 1991, however, it appeared that Hinn would renounce this aspect of his hermeneutical practices. He promised:

> "I'm not about to get up and say, 'God showed me,' because my days of doing that are over. I just believe you begin preaching what you feel and believe without having to say, 'God showed me.' Because then you're gonna look like an idiot, you know, if you get back two years later and say, 'God showed me—showed me something different.'"[19]

Despite the many and highly-publicized renunciations of this practice, Hinn continues his attempt to convince his listeners that he speaks with the greatest interpretive authority. Take, for example, his radicalization of the account of Jesus' healing of the blind man in John 9:1-34:

> "...one day [Jesus] saw a blind man. And He did this: He collected some mud and spit upon it and made clay and stuck it on the man's eyes. [Here Hinn makes two popping sounds with his mouth.] See if you can do that. I thought to myself, 'Why did Jesus do that? Why did He just not lay His hands and be healed? Why did

He have to make mud and spit on it and stick it on the man's eyes?' *And the Holy Spirit gave me a marvelous answer*. You remember when God made man and He squeezed mud into shape and He breathed on that? And he became a living soul. The reason Jesus put mud on a guy's eyes was not because the man was blind. It's because he had no eyes and He just gave him brand new ones. [Hinn repeats the popping sound.] He is the source of creation."[20]

Hinn's error here lies in his original point of departure. He questions, "Why did Jesus do that? Why did He just not lay His hands and be healed? Why did He have to make mud and spit on it and stick it on the man's eyes?" He approaches the Bible immediately looking for hidden, deeper meanings. The questions he asks of the text cannot be answered using the accepted methods of interpretation.

In fact, the information given and *not given* in the text shows the inappropriateness of the questions he asks. Answers to such questions were evidently not of interest, either to the characters in this story or to the writer who recorded it. Now, however, Hinn has created a niche, an opportunity for him to show off his subjective spiritual intuition. Stated another way, he is able to allow his fertile imagination to run free once again.

Another problem with the questions Hinn poses occurs on the theological level. Jesus did not *"have* to make mud and spit on it and stick it on the man's eyes." He did not *have* to do anything. He is divine; He has the authority to choose whatever method he wishes to accomplish His purposes.

A quick review of Jesus' healing techniques reveals incredible diversity. There is no pattern or paradigm discernible which Jesus might have intended to become normative. Nor are there any hidden meanings in the methods Jesus used. It is as though Jesus chose such a multiplicity of methods of healing for the express purpose of showing that there *is no "preferred" method and no deeper meaning hidden in the method*.

Hinn again claims that the Holy Spirit gave him this interpretation. Aside from the obvious ethical problem raised by the breaking of his promise (which he repeated time and time again) to not appeal to divine origin as the source of his interpretations, this "revelation" of the Holy Spirit again has serious theological consequences. Hinn claims that the Holy Spirit explained to him that Jesus placed the mud into the man's eye sockets because there were no eyes there. He "popped" the mud into the sockets and eyes appeared.

The Bible, however, states that Jesus "put clay *on [his] eyes*" (vv. 6, 11, 15), that the man was born *"blind,"* not *"without eyes"* (vv. 2, 13, 17, 18, 19, 20, 24, 25), and that Jesus *"opened,"* not *"created"* his eyes (vv. 10, 14, 17, 21, 26, 30, 32). The testimony here comes from *three* sets of witnesses: the man healed, the authorities, and the man's parents. They all use the same language to describe the same phenomena. The Holy Spirit inspired the biblical author to record the testimonies of these three. They are, therefore, infallible. Yet, we are told that the same Holy Spirit inspired the authoritative interpretation of Hinn, which is in direct contradiction to the repeated statements of Scripture.

More Reckless Bible Commentary

Another example of Hinn's irresponsible biblical exegesis and ignorance of Scripture is proven by his correlation of Moses with the two disciples who encountered the risen Christ on the road to Emmaus (Luke 24). Hinn again attributes his interpolation to the Holy Spirit, as he tells the Trinity Broadcasting Network audience:

> "And I compared Moses and his boldness to ask, 'What is your name?' to God, and took the story of the two on the road to Emmaus who never once said, 'Who are you?' When Jesus was walking with them, there [was] not one time [when] they said, 'Well, how do you know all this?' and 'Where are you from?' And frankly missed an incredible opportunity. *And the Holy Spirit made it so clear to us that these two were never mentioned again in the Bible. It's almost like they were dis — dishonored. We don't even know who they are. To this day we do not know their names.* And it's very clear that God Almighty, seeing that they've missed their incredible opportunity

to say, 'Who are you Lord?' *God wouldn't even honor them to give us their names.*"21

The scriptural record of the two disciples on the road to Emmaus and their encounter with the risen Christ in Luke 24:13-35 provides a portrait quite dissimilar from the one Hinn painted.

Here are just six facts from Scripture that Hinn disregards: 1) One of the disciples *is* named. His name is Cleopas (v. 18). 2) Their inability to discern that it was the Lord who walked with them was a result of divine intervention (vv. 16, 31). 3) The Lord went to great lengths to teach the pair from the Word (v. 27). 4) Their hearts burned as the Lord revealed the fulfilled Scriptures to them (v. 32). 5) The two disciples were not dishonored, but are again distinguished to witness the resurrected Lord when He appeared to His group of apostles (vv. 33-36). 6) Although not by name, these disciples are mentioned again in God's Word, as they would certainly be part of the collective number who witnessed the resurrected Christ described by Paul (1 Corinthians 15:5-8).

It is, without doubt, ironic that Hinn would contort this exact scriptural record. In verse 27, Luke tells us, "And beginning with Moses and all the Prophets, He *explained* to them what was said in all the Scriptures concerning Himself." The word "explained" in the text is the Greek word, *diermeneuo*, which is a strengthened form of the word for hermeneutics. Luke is telling us that Jesus carefully and thoroughly interpreted and explained the Word of God. How unlike the exegetical antics of Hinn.

On another broadcast, Hinn again addressed one of his favorite subjects: financial prosperity. Despite multiple renunciations of what is popularly called the "Faith Message," the "Confession Message," and the "Health and Wealth Gospel," Hinn gives his current understanding of Luke 6:38 and his two sources for that understanding:

> "It took *Oral Roberts*...to really wake me up on this thing. ... [He] came to my church...and says uh, 'Can I talk to you like my son?' ... He said, 'You take lousy

offerings.' ... I said, 'Doc, what do you mean?' He says, 'You know...all you did here this morning is emphasize the seed, but never the harvest.' And then he opened the Bible and showed me a portion of God's Word I'd seen a million times before. And here it was, Luke 6:38, 'Give and it shall be given unto you, good measure, pressed down, shaken together, running over shall men give into your bosom.' ... He said, 'Now how many times did Jesus say "Give"?' I said, 'One time.' He said, 'How many times did He say "Receive"?' ... Well, I began counting. Seven times, saints, seven times, and here they are. He said 'Give' one time and [counting on his fingers as he recites parts of the verse] 'it shall be given [raises one finger], unto you [raises a second finger], good measure [raises a third finger], pressed down, [raises a fourth finger], shaken together [raises a fifth finger], running over [raises a sixth finger], shall men give into your bosom [raises a seventh finger].' Seven times. ... He said, 'So what is the emphasis, on the seed or on the harvest? ... Begin to tell your people to expect the harvest ... you'll see a change in your church ... From now on begin to *tell* God what you want ... *tell* Him what you want.' And I said, 'Doc,' I said, 'Where is it in the Bible?' [Roberts showed it to him in Luke 6:38] ... *The Lord spoke so clearly to [me]...on that Sunday morning, and here's what God said. He* [God] *said*, 'Faith is not faith 'til you believe it.' ... It wasn't long, the entire congregation was doing the same thing, because like priest, like people. They follow what you do."22

The manner in which Roberts and Hinn arrive at the number seven and determine the emphasis in this passage being upon "receiving" has been labeled "atomistic exegesis." This method has never been employed in historical conservative Protestantism, but rather is a prominent feature of liberalism. When doctrine can be supported by reference to a phrase such as "unto you," the church is truly in a precarious position.

Oral Roberts, long-time proponent of the Prosperity Gospel, and "the Lord" are Hinn's authorities for this particular teaching. One is usually known by the company one keeps and the authorities one quotes. The reference to Roberts after Hinn's multiple renunciations of the Prosperity Gospel is therefore quite revealing in light of when this telecast aired. A second source for this teaching is "the Lord." Again, this is despite his numerous promises to avoid appeals to direct revelation in support of his interpretations of Scripture.

A part of this teaching is the heretical practice of *telling* God what you want. Not only is this also indicative of Hinn's continued belief in most aspects of Confession/Prosperity, but it is also in direct contradiction to the clear teachings of Scripture (Matthew 7:7, 11; 21:22; Luke 11:13; John 14:13-14; 15:7; 16:23-24; Ephesians 3:20; James 1:5-6; 4:3-4, 15; 1 John 3:22; 5:14-15).

Hinn's statement about the nature of faith reveals that he is still of the opinion that faith is an external, animated "power." His statement, which he attributes to God, "Faith is not faith 'til you believe it," resembles liberal existentialism (which has received the title *"rhema* knowledge" in charismatic circles) more than the biblical concept of faith as trust in a covenant-keeping God.

Moreover, Hinn's words, "like priest, like people," is an interesting figure of speech to be found on the lips of a Protestant minister. This would appear to be not only the result of the influence of his Catholic upbringing, but it also seems to be a clear indicator of the way he views himself today. He considers himself to stand in the role of the medieval priest, who has the sole authority to issue authoritative pronouncements with the full expectation that his flock will blindly follow. Although stated explicitly here, this attitude is implicit in all of his authoritative pronouncements.

On national television, Hinn shared an experience which should raise a red flag in the minds of all thinking Christians. In the course of describing a Catholic communion service in Amarillo in which he took part, he stated that he suddenly felt numb, then felt someone step in front of him. The sensation became so real that he then reached out and touched a robe, which had:

"...a silky feeling, a beautiful softness to the robe. ...
The next thing I was feeling was actually the form of a
body, the shape of a body. And my body...went totally
numb. ... *And God really gave me a revelation that night,*
that when we partake communion, it's not just
communion, Paul [Crouch]. We are partaking Christ
Jesus himself. He did not say, 'Take, eat, this *represents*
my body.' He said, 'This *is* my body, broken for you...'
When you partake communion, you're partaking
Christ, and that heals your body. When you partake
Jesus how can you stay weak? ... sick? ... And so
tonight, as we partake communion, we're not partaking
bread. We're partaking what *He* said we would be
partaking of: 'This is my *body*.'"[23]

Hinn here relates what can only be classified as a mystical
experience. He describes the sensations of feeling, touching,
and numbness. This experience will soon be seen to supersede
the teachings of Scripture and the historic interpretation of
most of Protestantism with respect to the meaning of the
elements of communion. It will also be seen as the foundation
upon which to base his doctrine of transubstantiation (the
Roman Catholic teaching that after the priest's blessing, the
bread and wine of communion literally become the body and
blood of Jesus).

After the ascension, there is no scriptural record of anyone
"feeling" the physical body of Jesus. This appears to be closer
to the mystical position of Roman Catholicism.

In this telecast, Hinn states that it was an authority no
less than God Himself who taught him that the true
interpretation of the elements is that the bread is literally
Jesus' physical body. Besides corresponding perfectly to the
Roman Catholic doctrine of transubstantiation, it also contradicts perfectly the clear teaching of Scripture.

In all five accounts of the Lord's Supper found in
Scripture, it is abundantly clear that Jesus breaks the bread
and commands all His apostles to partake therefrom. His own
physical body is still intact and present at the same time in
which he institutes these *symbolic* elements. Because Jesus is
physically present at the same time that the bread is

representing His body, there is sufficient evidence to infer the fundamental difference between His actual physical body and the symbol thereof.

These claims of the divine origin of Hinn's interpretations are simply the continuation of a pattern which goes back many years. In the past, Hinn has claimed or alluded to divine inspiration for such erroneous teachings as Jesus' rebirth in Hell,[24] that women originally gave birth out of their sides,[25] that the Godhead consists of nine persons,[26] that each member of the Godhead has a body,[27] and that Adam could fly and was capable of interplanetary travel.[28]

The only conclusion one can reach is that, with respect to his appeal to divine origin, neither his method nor his results have changed since his series of renunciations and promises of reform. It is also important to note that, in a number of the examples listed above, Hinn appeals to divine revelation to establish *doctrines* which are well outside the bounds of biblical Christianity.

Claim of Novelty

Novelty has always been an integral part of Hinn's ministry. This is evidenced by his words to his own flock, "Please, please, please, don't think OCC [Orlando Christian Center] is here to repeat something you've heard for the last fifty years. ... If we quit giving you new revelations, we're dead."[29]

Naturally, there is overlap between this category and his claim of divine origin for many of his interpretations. In this category, however, explicit claim to divine inspiration is not heard. Rather, the implication here is that Hinn possesses exceptional spiritual intuition which is available to none but the elite. What characterizes the following examples is that, outside Hinn's heightened subjective intuition, these "deeper" understandings of Scriptures would never have been discovered.

An example of this phenomenon may be observed in his comments about God teaching the Prosperity Gospel to Adam at the beginning of creation:

"God creates man and puts him in a Garden of Eden and introduces him to wealth. Because it [the Bible] declares, 'In that garden was gold, the most precious gold found on the planet.' ... Do you think that God put it there just to tell Adam, 'Here it is, just look at it, enjoy it?' No, no, no. God put it there to let him know that He's the God of abundance. Our God is not a poor God. He's the God of abundance, saints. ... We are not after money...but we *are*, hear this, we *are* after God. And the *Bible* says if you're after God, these things will be added unto you."[30]

The existence of gold in the Garden is not the emphasis of the biblical text. Despite its appearance in the narrative, it is not the biblical author's intention to suggest that God was using the presence of gold to teach Adam that He is a God of abundance. This interpretation is unique to Hinn; it will not be found among the Reformers or modern commentators.

The only mention of gold appears in Genesis 2:12, which is in the midst of a lengthy description of the physical characteristics of the Garden. If there is any emphasis to be discerned in the biblical narrative, the emphasis would appear to be upon the abundance of *water* (vv. 10, 11, 13, 14). Elsewhere in the Bible, this same emphasis is also evident (Genesis 13:10). From the order of the biblical narrative of creation, it would appear that God used the entire created order to show His abundant care for man, having created an environment which included all things necessary for human survival *before* the creation of man, that man might thrive and multiply.

That gold is simply descriptive in this passage, as opposed to Hinn's understanding that it represented financial prosperity, is evidenced in the observation that at this time there was no established economy in which gold might be perceived as having any more worth than any other commodity. His observation is motivated not by desire to read this passage in its historical context, but rather out of a desire to support his own heterodox doctrine of prosperity.

His observation that this gold was "the most precious gold found on the planet" is entirely without textual support. His sole intent is to heighten the importance of the part that "gold" plays in the narrative, and thus provide further support for his doctrine of prosperity.

His constant appeals to the Bible ("And the *Bible* says") are consistent throughout his interpretations. Because he has chosen to play by the rules of Protestantism, he must at least appear to base his teachings on the sacred texts. The reader should be alerted, however, by his use of this technique, and should be aware of Hinn's consistent track record of misreading and adding to the intent of the biblical authors.

Not content with rereading the intentions of Moses, at the end of the comment above, Hinn turns his attention to the words of Jesus in Matthew 6:33. He suggests that if we are seeking God, riches will follow. The intent of Jesus' statement in Matthew 6:33, however, when read in context, is that we should not worry (cf. vv. 25, 31, 34) about *physical necessities* (vv. 25-31). There is no promise in this text to suggest that godliness will automatically produce extravagant wealth. Here again we find evidence of the intentional misreading of a biblical text to support the doctrine of Prosperity which he claims to have renounced.

The following is an example of novel exegesis done to support what Hinn understands as an extra-biblical prophecy:

> "Really she [Kathryn Kuhlman] laid a foundation that God today is building on. ... You heard [her] prophecy. Now...we *will* see that happen, Paul [Crouch]. Before Jesus comes back, I am going to see that happen. ... I have begun to pray...that God will heal all. And why not? ...[In] Exodus 12...when they all partook of the Passover...a people who came out of slavery *should* be healed. In one glorious service before leaving Egypt, God healed them all...Psalm 105:37."[31]

The connection between the Passover event in Exodus 12 and Psalm 105:37 is novel exegesis at best. No reputable commentator has ever suggested such a connection, that would presuppose a great healing service at the first Passover observance in which every participant was healed. The original account in Exodus 12 mentions no such miracle.

Psalm 105:37, likewise, suggests no mass healing service.

If "Scripture interprets Scripture," we should read Psalm 105:37 with Isaiah 63:13-14, which refers to the same event. It is obvious from this second Scripture that, rather than referring to divine healing, both passages refer to God's enabling power granted to Israel, which heightened their human ability to travel over the rough desert terrain.

Hinn's teaching on the healing of all Christians is indeed true. The point at which it occurs, however, is the issue. According to Revelation 21:4, this will only take place in the eternal state. It makes no difference what Kathryn Kuhlman "prophesied," what Hinn's interpretation of that "prophecy" is, or what he wants, prays for, or thinks he will see. "All flesh is grass ... but the Word of *God* abides forever" (Isaiah 40:6-8).

In 1990, Hinn employed novel exegesis to further buttress his teaching on Prosperity:

> "We are going to believe that *in one year you'll be out of debt*. Now, that's in the Bible! Genesis 26 states that Isaac sowed in famine and reaped that same year. It said that he got a harvest that same year! If you want a harvest *this year*, it's gonna happen. *I was out of debt in one year*."[32]

After several professed personal reformations, little seems to have changed with Hinn. In 1994, he proclaimed:

> "And now here's something wonderful. The Bible says in Genesis 26 that in the same year Isaac sowed, he reaped. The same year. *Well, God Almighty wants to give you that miracle the same year you sow for it*. Let's believe Him tonight for it. And really, it's according to your faith."[33]

The reader should first notice the evidence in both citations of Hinn's pattern of referring to the Bible to establish the credibility of his pronouncements. In the way he grounds his beliefs in Scripture, however, he has exhibited questionable practices in other examples, and it is problematic in these instances as well.

Hinn cites Genesis 26:12 and the harvest of Isaac as paradigmatic for all believers in all ages. There are no authoritative commentators, however, who have ever come to such a conclusion. The context of the passage indicates that it is a straightforward historical report of a singular bountiful harvest. The novel interpretation placed on this passage by Hinn has no doubt been fueled by teachers of the Prosperity Gospel who have focused upon the term "hundredfold" which occurs in this verse.

Using this novel interpretation and application of Genesis 26:12, Hinn has established both doctrine and practice. It is important to note that his interpretations do not simply remain in the realm of academic curiosity. Rather, the very purpose of his novel interpretations is usually to support some doctrine which, in turn, informs us of how we are to live out our faith practically.

Hinn alludes to the fact that the very year he began to believe in an immediate hundredfold return, he himself was out of debt. He uses this personal experience to provide a further foundation upon which to teach that, if all others would adopt this same mindset, all would be out of debt in one year. This is an example of establishing matters of faith and practice on the basis of personal experience, which is not allowed under the principle of *Sola Scriptura*, the foundational Protestant belief that matters of faith and practice can be established by reference to the Bible alone.

In the 1990 citation, Hinn further reinforced his teaching of the Prosperity Gospel with other novel interpretations:

> "Jesus said this. Watch this. Now you all know the Bible. And you know Brother John [Avanzini], I. love when you teach on Prosperity, 'cause it gets me going! But there's one thing, there's one thing I always think about. Jesus said in Luke 6:38 what? 'Give.' Isn't that right? 'And it shall be given unto you, good measure, pressed down, shaken together, running over, shall men give into' What? [The audience answers, 'your bosom.'] Okay. *You give it with your hand, but when it comes back it'll take your bosom to carry it! Did you catch this? Brother,*

*you give with your hand, but when you get it back, your hand
isn't big enough!* [Other guests, hosts, and audience clap
to show their approval.]"[34]

Hinn again makes his traditional appeal to the Bible. He
suggests, however, that there is something that he has seen in
the Scripture which is not discernible to the average reader.

Hinn next expresses his love for the way which John
Avanzini teaches the Prosperity Gospel, but indicates that
even he has not intuited this novel interpretation from the
verse in question.

Then Hinn's presuppositions about giving require that he
add the words, "with your hand." This addition is necessary
to set up the comparison between the size of the hand and
the size of the bosom (lap). The reader should recognize,
however, that there is nothing in the text that limits the
activity of giving to money, which can be held in the hand
(and placed in offering plates!). The kind of giving encouraged
by Jesus in this passage is an attitude which incorporates all
areas of sacrificial giving. Likewise the comparison between
the size of the hand and the lap is fueled by Hinn's
presupposition about the hundredfold return. The reason the
Church Fathers, the Reformers, and modern commentators
who employ the grammatico-historical method never saw this
interpretation is because they were not driven by the
"give-to-get" mentality of proponents of the Prosperity
Gospel.

Returning to another favorite theme, Hinn wrote in 1993:

> "The prophet Jeremiah asked: 'Is there no balm in
> Gilead, / Is there no physician there? / Why then is
> there no recovery / For the health of the daughter of my
> people?' (Jeremiah 8:22). This Scripture contains a
> marvelous truth that holds a key to your healing.
> Jeremiah asks, 'Is there no balm in Gilead?' *The word
> balm in Hebrew speaks of healing. And the word Gilead
> speaks of worship. He is asking, 'Is there no healing in
> worship?' Of course there is.* And you need to act upon the
> knowledge that your worship brings healing. If you
> confess the Word and nothing seems to happen, begin
> to worship the Lord God of heaven."[35]

Hinn utilizes this text to support his belief that verbal praise of God brings physical healing. This is a teaching which is presently popular in charismatic circles, and especially among adherents of "Restoration Theology." Whether the concept is true or not is not at issue. The question we pose here is whether this verse can be used to support Hinn's assertion. His appeal is again to the Hebrew language which he purports to know so well. It must be stated, however, that in no authoritative lexical work is there any evidence to suggest that the name "Gilead" can ever be understood as symbolizing "worship."[36] This manner of spiritualization/ allegorization of a geographical point of reference was supposed to have been discarded in favor of a literal reading of the text at the Protestant Reformation. It is unfortunate that such exegetical practices are making a comeback after five hundred years.

Consider a similar example of novel exegesis:

> "In Old Testament times, if a person was sick he received a pain killer—myrrh. 'A bundle of myrrh is my beloved to me, / That lies all night between my breasts' (Song 1:13). When Christ was on the cross, He was offered myrrh. 'Then they gave Him wine mingled with myrrh to drink, but He did not take it' (Mark 15:23). It was customary to give such a drink to a person being crucified so that he would not feel the pain. Why did the Lord Jesus refuse it? Christ rejected the myrrh because He did not want to die without pain. ... *Christ is your 'pain killer,' ... He will lie beside you in your darkest hour to stop the hurt and bring you healing.*"[37]

The connection between the function of myrrh in Song of Solomon 1:13 and Mark 15:23 exists only in the mind of Hinn. Those who are familiar with the biblical world are well aware that myrrh has multiple uses. The function of myrrh in the passion narrative was indeed that of a pain killer. However, the myrrh referred to in Song of Solomon 1:13 clearly refers to its use as a perfume.[38]

The general context of Song of Solomon 1:12-14 provides conclusive proof that the purpose of "the bag of myrrh" was not to give relief from the pain of breast cancer or some other malady, but rather was intended to exude a pleasing aroma. The word "myrrh" here is synonymous with "nard," "fragrance," and "cluster of henna blossoms," none of which contain pain-relieving qualities.

By this time, the reader has seen enough examples of this approach used so often by Hinn. The methods by which he accomplishes his intentions are now obvious. It is no longer enough for laymen to read debates between supposed experts who hold opposing views. At some point the reader must exercise his belief in the Priesthood of the believer, and engage in the argument himself.

The interpretive practices of Hinn are helping to lead the church back into mysticism, "papal" authority figures, and confusion. The infallibility of the Word is assailed as ambiguity is introduced by the contradictions inherent in most of his interpretations. His approach places the authority of the interpreter over the divinely inspired authority of the biblical authors. His emphasis on "rhema," or experiential knowledge, leads us back into liberalism and existentialism. Allegorization, spiritualization, and constant appeal to "insider" and "revelation" knowledge undermine authorial intent. Such methods are regularly employed by pseudo-Christian cults, and destine those who embrace them to spiritual slavery. Jesus taught, "You shall know the truth, and the truth shall make you free" (John 8:32). Unfortunately, the opposite is also true.

Hermeneutics That Harm

In the previous chapter, numerous examples of Benny Hinn's interpretations were discussed, which pointed to a logical, systematic attempt to establish himself as an authoritative biblical commentator. The primary purpose of this chapter is to investigate the effect Hinn's hermeneutics (methods of interpretation) have on doctrine and practice.

To a select few who have questioned the unorthodox teachings of Benny Hinn, the faith healer has claimed lack of formal Bible training as a primary reason for his unbiblical declarations:

> "You know, in a way, I really envy those who have had Bible training. ... I was really hoping I could go to Bible school or something. But it never really happened that way."[1]

> "But I knew so little about biblical teaching at that time."[2]

Yet to the thousands of patrons of Hinn's books and telecasts, a quite different scenario is painted. In his 1995 publication, *Welcome, Holy Spirit*, he claims that:

> "After over a decade of Bible instruction [combined with] a lifetime of living in the Holy Land ... you could say I had mastered the Bible. ... I have spent thousands of hours studying the Bible and reflecting on practically every word."[3]

In the previous chapter, an entire section was devoted to examples of Hinn's appeal to exceptional "insider's knowledge" of the biblical world.

Hinn has even enlisted testimony from some of his "partners in ministry" to further boost his credentials as an authoritative interpreter of Scripture. In a testimonial advertisement for Hinn's ministry, actress Donna Douglas said:

> "The *insight* that Benny has into the Scriptures is absolutely amazing to me."[4]

The hermeneutical or interpretive framework of Hinn is not simply a matter of academic curiosity. Historically, those who have departed from the commonly accepted and time-tested methods of legitimate Bible interpretation have erred sooner or later in matters of faith and practice. Hinn is no exception.

Hinn's past unorthodox theology is well documented. As sensational as his aberrations were, and as much criticism as they attracted, the reader should be aware that despite his rhetoric to the contrary, many of his positions have remained unchanged. A prime reason for this is that his basic hermeneutical methodology (interpretive approach) has remained the same. Because it has not changed, his core beliefs about the nature of the Bible, its message, and the character of God remain unaltered.

Additions and Changes to the Biblical Text

Hinn is a man of great conviction. He believes so strongly in the correctness of his theological presuppositions that he has gone so far as to actually *change* or *add to* biblical revelation to support them. For example, in the past, he has said with respect to Job's declaration, "The Lord giveth and the Lord taketh away" (Job 1:21):

> "I have news for you. That is not Bible. That is not Bible. The Lord giveth and *never* taketh away!"[5]

Hinn's edict caused him embarrassment. In 1993, he apologized for his criticism of Job's pronouncement and said:

> "Now let me tell you something else I said once that I so regret I said. Poor Job, I hope he's still my friend in

heaven. ... I made a statement one day, I said uh, something about Job, 'The Lord giveth and the Lord taketh away," that he was in unbelief."[6]

To support his belief in the lordship/dominion of man over the earth, Hinn added this statement to the text of Genesis, "[God told Abram He] could not touch this earth 'til a man gave it back to Him."[7]

In 1991, Hinn wrote that on the basis of Ephesians 5:23, all Christians should pray, "You are the savior of my [physical] body." In support of this statement, he reread the biblical text, "He Himself being the savior of *my body*." Hinn's rendering is in opposition to the inspired words of Paul, "*the* body," which in context, refers to the Body of Christ, the Church. Based on his change/addition to the text, Hinn concludes, "If Jesus Christ is the savior of the body, then your body ought to be made whole."[8] This is a perfect example of the equation: additions/changes to the text result in faulty exegesis (interpretation), which in turn results in erroneous faith and practice.

In the past, Hinn's additions to biblical revelation have not been limited to a word or two. In a fund raising homily for the Trinity Broadcasting Network, Hinn introduced an entirely new concept to the Church, which the Holy Spirit supposedly confirmed by direct revelation, and further supported by reference to the Scriptures:

> "I want to break *the Devil of Poverty* tonight. *You say, 'Well, Benny Hinn, I don't believe there's a demon of poverty.'* Oh, yes there is. Do you realize that...in my bedroom I had a vision. Now...if you have troubles with this, it's your problem. But I woke up one night and saw a man in my bedroom and you say, 'Wow!' Look, I've seen more visions than you realize and those things, when you deal with the supernatural, supernatural visions are just common things, all right? I saw in my bedroom a man standing mocking me. He was thin and his clothes were torn off. And the Spirit of God said, 'That's the Devil of Poverty.' And I sat up in bed—I wasn't asleep; I wasn't dreaming—that thing was *there*. And I said, 'I rebuke you in Jesus' name.' And

the Holy Ghost stopped me and said, 'You're rebuking
it wrong. ... You don't rebuke with saying, "I rebuke."
You rebuke with, "Thus saith the Lord!" Use the Word
against that devil.' ... And you know what I did? I said,
'The Bible says,' just like Jesus said, 'It is written.' And
when I did that, that thing vanished. And from that
day 'til this, I'm telling you, I'm telling the truth, I
don't have debts." [The clear implication is that this
should be done by all Christians, and they will become
free of debt, too.][9]

Just after his extrabiblical revelation about the existence of
this special spirit-being, its purpose, his explanation from the
Scriptures on how to deal with that spirit, and what result it
will have in the life of the believer, Hinn continues on the
themes of prosperity and healing:

> *"Make a pledge, make a gift. Because that's the only way
> you're going to get your miracle.* Miracles don't happen
> when you lay around and say, 'Let me feel something.'
> Miracles happen when you *do* something, and then you
> [sic] gonna get it. Then you [sic] gonna feel it. *The man
> at the Gate Beautiful never got healed...while he was sitting.
> No. He was healed as he stood.* The Bible says Peter *picked
> him up* and while he stood the power of God hit him. *As
> you give, the miracle will begin.* All right, so get to the
> phones and get busy."[10]

The above passage to which Hinn refers appears in Acts
3:1-11. In verses 6 and 7, the origin of both the faith and the
action is Peter, not the man about to be healed. An unbiased
reading of verses 7 and 8 contradict Hinn's assertion that God
responded to the man standing up, and that he was healed *"as
he stood."* This rereading constitutes yet another addition to
the inspired biblical record. Verse 8 specifically states, "and
leaping up he stood..." Therefore, in verse 7, it would appear
that Luke is trying to say that the miracle took place before
the man stood, at the approximate time that Peter began to
lift him up.

Thus, rather than an objective reading of the text in
question, Hinn's interpretation appears to be driven by his

theological presupposition that people must first exhibit faith and then put that faith into physical action before they can become candidates for healing. This would appear to be in closer conformity to the Roman Catholic emphasis on works, rather than to biblical revelation.

Richard Mayhue has noted these presuppositions on the part of Hinn.[11] After careful analysis of the entire Bible, however, Mayhue demonstrates conclusively that effort, and even faith, on the part of the afflicted is not a prerequisite for healing, according to the biblical pattern.[12] From examples such as the Creation, the Flood, the raising of Lazarus and Jairus' daughter, and other biblical miracles, it is clear that God does not require human action or faith in order to display His power.

Elsewhere in the same homily, Hinn observes:

> "The same way you activate your faith for a physical miracle, you activate your faith for a financial miracle. When you want a miracle physically, you have to move your arms, your legs, whatever. Jesus saw one day a man with a withered hand. He said, 'Stretch it!' OK. *How do we get a financial miracle? By giving! That activates our faith!* That gets our faith loose! ... Every time I put my tithe in...or an offering, I say, 'Thank you for my harvest.' Audibly, I say it. Audibly. 'Thank you for my harvest.'"[13]

In Hinn's interpretation of the healing of the man with the withered hand, Jesus commands, "Stretch it!" His understanding of this command is clearly the same as that delineated in his previous comment: you must begin to move the ailing part before God will heal it. In other words, the same presuppositional error he exhibited above is evident in this example as well. In place of the clear intent of the command (to expose the ailing limb for all to see), Hinn has added a theological significance to the act which exists in his belief system, but which is not readily evident in the text itself.

Having committed one error of interpretation, Hinn compounds the problem by applying the principle of "action to energize faith" to the action of *giving*. Because the concept is unbiblical with respect to the physical realm, it only follows that the same concept is unbiblical when applied to the financial realm.

Hinn has again illustrated his belief that faith is an external creative force which has to be "activated" and "loosened." In addition, his emphasis upon the importance of the spoken word in this process is at the very heart of the Confession/Faith Message, and not that of the Bible.

The Bible has strong words to say about the negative results which follow when God's revelation is supplemented by man. Most interpreters living on this side of the Reformation are deterred by the warnings found in Scriptures such as Deuteronomy 4:2; 12:32; Proverbs 30:6; Revelation 22:18; etc. It is quite telling that Hinn is not.

Continued Expressions of Heterodox Theology

The Nature of Christ. For a season, Hinn became less bold than to add to the Bible outright. By employing his own brand of pre-Reformation hermeneutics, however, he still manages to support all of his favorite doctrines. For example, Hinn continues to teach that Jesus actually became sin, and took on the nature of Satan himself:

> "Now the Lord said to Nicodemus, 'As Moses lifted up the serpent, so shall the Son of Man be lifted up.' You know, that verse...years ago used to bother me. ... I thought, 'Why the Lord [sic] comparing Himself to a snake?'... Well—I—someone put in my hand a book by Martin Luther, the great reformer. And I'm riding on a bus...reading this book called *Justification by Faith* by Martin Luther. ... In this book he says, 'There is a verse in the Bible that used to bother me.' ... I was so amazed, I spoke out and said, 'You, too?' [Laughter.] ... God used his book to give me an *incredible* truth. Martin Luther says in his book, he says, 'The Holy Spirit showed me what Jesus meant in this.' And he goes into describing the fact that *serpents are symbols of sin in the Bible,* that the lowest animal on earth is the snake, and *the lowest thing on earth is sin, and that Jesus became the*

lowest thing on earth when he took our sin, and gave the Scriptures how, 'He who went to the lowest became the highest and fills all in all,' and so on. Powerful! And somehow I began to understand, dear God! *Jesus was made sin for me!*"[14]

Analogies used by authors of Scripture are usually of such a nature that, when every aspect of the analogy is taken to its logical conclusion, the analogy breaks down. By use of the word "As," Jesus has set up an analogy. His intent is to draw Nicodemus' attention to the fact that He will be "lifted up" for the purpose of healing in a manner similar to an event which happened under the ministry of Moses. When the analogy is taken to the extreme, Jesus must then be analogous to the serpent, and since serpents are symbolic of sin, Jesus must become sin or sinful. A similar example of the danger of pressing analogies too far appears in the parable of the unjust judge (Luke 18:1-8). If the analogy is pressed to the extreme, the unjust judge must be interpreted as an allusion to God, which is contradictory to His character as revealed elsewhere in Scripture (e.g., Deuteronomy 32:4, etc.).

Hinn also notes that his source for this teaching is the book, *Justification by Faith,* by the great reformer Martin Luther. He states that Martin Luther wrote that he was troubled by the same passage which concerned him. Further, he asserts that Luther was led to the correct interpretation by divine revelation from the Holy Spirit.

To set the record straight, it must be observed that Martin Luther never wrote a book entitled *Justification by Faith.* Nor did the great reformer ever express confusion about the meaning of this text. Nor did Luther claim divine revelation for his interpretation of John 3:14. In no place in his works does Luther ever suggest that Jesus took on a sin nature or the nature of Satan. What Luther *does* say is that, as He hung on the cross, He was "regarded" as evil, despised, and "an archvillain" *by ungodly, worldly men* in fulfillment of Isaiah 53:12, etc. He states uncategorically that Christians:

> "Must even then learn to ignore this figure and outward appearance of Christ. ... I will still regard this

> vile worm as the Savior...not as a worm, serpent...devil.
> ... The *world* regards Him as an accursed, damned man.
> ... In reality, of course, He is not a serpent; He is the
> lamb of God. ... Christ is not a serpent, a vile worm...a
> dragon, or a demoniac, as His slanderers claim. ... *Let
> them perish!*"[15]

Quite the opposite of supporting Hinn's interpretation, Luther places a curse upon those who hold such views!

If the origin of this interpretation is not Martin Luther, where could Hinn have obtained such an unbiblical view of the nature of Christ? This doctrine originated with the mystic E.W. Kenyon, and was probably passed on to Hinn in the teachings of faith teachers such as Kenneth Hagin, Frederick Price, and Kenneth Copeland.[16] That Hinn continues to draw from his roots in the Faith movement, after his claim of personal reformation, should be an indication to all interested that his past repudiations have been in word only.

As in the case with Hinn's interpretation of the "prophecy" of Kathryn Kuhlman,[17] Hinn exhibits the same problem interpreting the communication of Martin Luther, as well. In other words, whether the communication under consideration is from 1400 B.C., A.D. 30, A.D. 1500, or A.D. 1970, the theological agenda of Hinn is of paramount importance, not the intentions of the original communicator. Individuals who exhibit a pattern of misconstruing messages such as this should be approached with great caution.

All Christians Should Walk in Divine Health. It is well-known that, in the past, Hinn taught that no Christian should ever be sick and should walk in divine health. One of the ways he grounds this in Scripture is by drawing an analogy between the Church and Israel at the time of the Exodus. In essence, because all Israel was healed in the Exodus, all members of the Church should also be healed. He taught this in his 1993 book, *Lord, I Need a Miracle.*[18]

He reiterated this teaching, however, in December 1994:

> "When Israel came out of Egypt, God performed an
> incredible miracle. And that is when *He healed all of
> Israel.* I mean the Bible says, 'Not one feeble among

them were traveled [sic] when they came out.' But what happened? ... the amazing thing is, in Exodus 12 we find they ate the lamb and the blood was sprinkled on the doorposts. And the cross was presented to Israel. Even though they did not know it, it was because of eating the lamb, it was the first Passover, is what brought that great miracle. ... The Israelites were all healed when they ate the Passover. *When people are saved they ought to be healed at the same time.* ... The Bible says, 'When He brought them out.' ... The reason so many are not healed, they're not *out* yet. In Psalm 105:37 it says, 'When God brought Israel out of Egypt.' ... Then it says, 'there was not one feeble among all the tribes.' [Paul Crouch interjects, 'And Egypt is a type of sin.'] Egypt is a type of the world. The reason they are not healed is that they aren't brought out yet. ... God healed all under the law. Why not all under grace? It is God's will to heal. ... When, when, when Jesus said to the man, 'I will. Be thou clean,' that was clearly a promise. He said, 'I will.' Well, if He'll heal one, He'll heal two. If He heals two, He'll heal three. If He heals three, He'll heal four. *Otherwise He's a respecter of persons.* ... *when we take that bread [of the Lord's Supper], we should get our healing at that [moment].* ... When they [Israel] ate the Passover, they were all healed. That's when the miracle took place in Egypt."[19]

What should be observed here is that this passage evidences Hinn's continued belief in the Faith Message, and that he goes so far as to suggest that those who are not healed when partaking of communion are still living in sin or are not saved. In some respects, this would appear to be an even more radical position than he espoused before he "renounced" the Faith message.

With respect to his statement, "God healed all under the law. Why not all under grace?" Hinn has begun with one false premise and preceded to build another on top of it. It is a matter of the biblical record that not all saints were healed or walked in continual divine health, in either the Old Testament or the New Testament. The same situation may safely be said to exist today.

When Jesus said, "I will," or better, "I want to," it was in response to the sick man's statement, "Lord, if You want to, You can make *me* clean." In Jesus' response to the man, He said, "I want to. Be *thou* (singular) clean" (Matthew 8:3). In context, Jesus' statement was to this one man. It was not a blanket "promise" which extends to all people, in all places, in all ages. If Benny Hinn were to apply this same methodology to all the words of Jesus, he would have to sell all that he has and give it to the poor (Matthew 19:16-21).

When God expresses His sovereignty, it is never at the expense of other aspects of His character (e.g., His justice). To suggest such, and thus remove the sovereignty of God, is to create a theological impossibility.

Equally important, the Lord's Supper is not a magical ritual. The will of God cannot be manipulated or dictated by our consumption of the elements of bread and wine. This assumption by Hinn is again dependent upon his faulty interpretation of Exodus 12 and Psalm 105:37, and therefore must be judged illegitimate.

Hinn further advocated the same teaching to Trinity Broadcasting Network viewers in reference to the fulfillment of a statement (which Hinn calls a "prophecy") by the late Kathryn Kuhlman, to the effect that there will be end-time services in which everyone will be healed. Hinn states that this prophecy will be fulfilled in his services:

> "Now, we are going to see that happen. We *will* see that happen, Paul [Crouch]. Before Jesus comes back, I am going to see that happen. ... I have begun to pray...that God will heal all. And why not? ... *Exodus 12...when they all partook of the Passover ... a people who came out of slavery should be healed in one glorious service before leaving Egypt.* God healed them all. ... Psalm 105:37."[20]

Transubstantiation. Hinn has also aligned himself with a medieval superstition by promoting the Roman Catholic doctrine of transubstantiation. This doctrine teaches that the elements of communion are changed into the literal body and blood of Christ.

He informed a Trinity Broadcasting Network audience:

> "*God really gave me a revelation*...that when we partake communion, it's not just communion, Paul [Crouch]. We are partaking Christ Jesus himself. He did not say, 'Take, eat, this *represents* my body.' He said, 'This *is* my body, broken for you...' When you partake communion, you're partaking Christ, and that heals your body. When you partake Jesus, how can you stay weak? ... sick? ... And so tonight, as we partake communion, we're not partaking bread. We're partaking what *He* said we would be partaking of: 'This is my *body*.'"[21]

Confession, Prosperity and Commanding God. Part and parcel with Hinn's teaching on the divine health of all Christians is his continued emphasis on the importance of positive confession as a means to obtain and keep one's healing.

In 1990, with reference to Proverbs 13:22, Hinn encouraged his studio and viewing audience to confess:

> "Say after me, all of you, everybody say it, 'The wealth of the wicked is mine.' [The audience repeats.] One more time. [The audience repeats.] One more time. [The audience repeats.]"[22]

Likewise, with regard to Numbers 14:28, Hinn offered this interpretation:

> "'If you'll say it, I'll do it,' that's what God says. ... So when you confess it, you are activating the supernatural force of God. Do you know that *confession activates heaven? Confession releases the spirit world*. I'm telling you. Do you know, Paul [Crouch], something? A witch told me ... 'As a witch I used to kill birds with words. ... There are three words they [witches] continually speak on your life and every Christian: poverty, death and sickness.' ... And then suddenly a Scripture popped into my mind. ... 'No weapon formed against thee shall prosper,' — Isaiah 54 — 'and every tongue that shall arise against thee in judgment thou shalt *condemn*.' ... I said to the Lord, 'Lord, how do I condemn?' He [God] said, 'With words.'... *And do you know what the Holy Spirit said to me?* He said, 'If witches can speak death,

you can speak life. If they can speak poverty, you can speak prosperity.' *And the Spirit of the Lord said to me, He said, 'Words activate heaven.'* Jesus said, 'The words that I speak, they are spirit; they are life.' When you speak, you speak spirit, you speak life. ... We confess tonight that we *are* blessed. We *are* prosperous."[23]

The context of Numbers 14:28 is negative. God is actually judging the people for their ungodly murmuring. Hinn announces, "When you confess it you are activating the supernatural forces of God ... confession activates heaven ... releases the spirit world." Faith as an external force, and human ability to manipulate the supernatural by words, are beliefs common in pagan magic, but are entirely foreign to biblical faith.

The historical position of the orthodox Christian church has no place in its doctrine of revelation for theology to be informed by the faith or practice of those involved in the occult. Revelations, experiences, and practices of witches are of no consequence to the faith and life of a New Testament believer. To think that the Holy Spirit would agree with revelation derived from the occult, and then use this revelation as a basis for further extrabiblical revelation, which in turn informs faith and practice, is blasphemous beyond words. This is another teaching which Hinn has never disavowed.

As much as Hinn would like to believe that we are of like nature with Christ, we are not Jesus. Our words are not "spirit and life." We are not "little gods" and do not speak with the same life-giving, creative authority with which He spoke. No amount of wishful thinking or exegetical gymnastics will place man above the status in which God placed him within the created order. He reserves this privilege for Himself alone. To usurp this privilege makes us not one in nature with God, but rather one in nature with the generation of the tower of Babel (Genesis 11:1-9) and Lucifer (Isaiah 14:12-15).

In several of Hinn's post-reformation proclamations, he again affirmed his continued belief in the doctrine of Confession:

"It is God's will to heal...but...we as believers must claim the promises. ... You take the Word and say, 'You said in Your Word,' and something happens. ... Healing is ours. It's a part of our inheritance. There is a place for violent faith. ... If we get that kind of faith, we're gonna see miracles. Sometimes it's not enough to say, 'Lord, heal me.' ... Sometimes it takes, it takes aggressive faith. The Bible says, 'The prayer of faith will save the sick.' Not just prayer, the prayer of faith. That prayer must be full of faith and power to bring salvation from that sickness. And sickness, Paul [Crouch], is limited death. Think about it. When a body is sick, that sick part is dying. That's limited death. God wants to give us life. 'I have come that they might have life and have it more abundantly.'"[24]

"...violent faith. I think the time has come that we take what is ours aggressively. You see, God will not give you anything until you go after it hard. ... People are tired of hearing, 'Maybe.' They want to hear the positive. God will do it no matter what the devil does, no matter what the world says, no matter what the skeptic says. *God will do it!"*[25]

"I believe it is not only God's will for you to be healed, but *it is His will that you live in health until He calls you home (see Job 5:26). ... I am not one who prays, 'If it be your will, Lord, grant healing to this person.' It is His will! You will never hear me pray such faith-destroying words as 'If it be Your will, Lord, heal them.'* God intends for you to rise and be healed. Today. Tomorrow. Always!"[26]

These fresh proclamations are no different in substance than those made in his 1991 book, *"Rise & Be Healed!"*:

"Ladies and gentlemen, saint of God, healing *is* the will of God for you. *Never, ever, ever go to the Lord and say, 'If it be thy will...' Don't allow such faith-destroying words to be spoken from your mouth. When you pray 'if it be your will, Lord,' faith will be destroyed. Doubt will billow up and flood your being. Be on guard against words like this which will rob you of your faith and drag you down in despair.* It is His will. Jesus said, 'I will.'"[27]

In 1993, Hinn approvingly recounted an incident in the life of heretic William Branham in which Branham began to *demand* his healing on the basis of Isaiah 45:11:

> "Then he [Branham] said, 'Lord, if the Word is health to all *my* flesh, I will stand on Your Word that says "concerning the work of My hands, you command Me"' (Isa. 45:11). *The Lord did not say to 'ask,' He said 'command Me.'* And that is what Branham did. God promised it and the evangelist commanded Him to do it."[28]

Another of Hinn's discourses included the statement:

> "You can tell God what you want. You just express your faith in what you want. ... You can tell God what you want."[29]

Hinn lays down "simple" laws which, if obeyed, "you will live in health. *And when sickness comes, you'll command it to leave your body.*" On the basis of Exodus 15:26, one of Hinn's conditions or laws is *Heed*:

> "You must 'hearken' to the voice of the Lord. In Hebrew, the word means both to 'hear and declare.' You must hear it, *speak it, and confess it.* The importance of this first step cannot be overlooked."[30]

On the basis of Jeremiah 17:5, Hinn continues to believe and teach that healings, once obtained, may be lost as a result of lack of faith:

> "*The Lord not only wants you to receive your healing, He wants it to continue. Here are seven specific ways you can keep your healing.* 1. *Trust in God.* 'Cursed is the man who trusts in man / And makes flesh his strength, / Whose heart departs from the LORD' (Jer. 17:5)."[31]

The thread of commonality which binds all these pronouncements together is Hinn's undaunted commitment to the doctrine of Positive Confession. It makes no difference to what length he has to go to make the Scriptures say what he needs them to say. It matters not that he has to cite a known heretic to establish authority for his pronouncements.[32] No leap of logic is too great for this mentality. Positive confession accentuates an unbiblical emphasis on works, and results in unbiblical doctrines such as the possibility of "losing a healing."[33] Even the concept of the "Full Counsel of God" is run over roughshod (Matthew 26:39; James 4:3, 4, 15; 1 John 5:14; etc.) in every attempt to establish the theological agenda of the interpreter.

After numerous renunciations of the Prosperity Gospel, little seems to have changed with Hinn. In April 1994, he proclaimed:

> "And now here's something wonderful. The Bible says in Genesis 26 that in the same year Isaac sowed, he reaped. The same year. *Well, God Almighty wants to give you that miracle the same year you sow for it.* Let's believe Him tonight for it. And really, it's according to your faith."[34]

A New Twist on an Old Issue. For a season, Hinn appeared to tone down his flamboyant style and his doctrinal rhetoric, possibly because of his status as an ordained minister of the Assemblies of God. Perhaps this allegiance would finally put him on the road to reform. Then, in February 1995, he announced:

> "My friend, if you've had, hear this, if you've had a face-to-face encounter — *my, I feel the anointing under this!* — if you've had a face-to-face encounter with Christ Jesus, you *cannot* turn away from Him! You *can't* turn your back and live the old life again! *It's impossible!* Peter said, 'They have gone from us, for they were never a part of us. The dog has gone back to its vomit.' If you go back to the old life, I don't think you've ever met the Redeemer."[35]

Many readers will not have a problem with Hinn's espousal of the doctrine of "Eternal Security." Numerous denominations hold this as a cardinal tenet of their belief system. These same religious bodies would, however, have a problem with the fact that Hinn has attributed 1 John 2:19 to

Peter (especially since he claimed to be under the "anointing"). They, too, may have concerns about Hinn's citation of 2 Peter 2:22, since this has historically been used against the doctrine of Eternal Security (cf. the larger context of 2 Peter 2:20-22). More appropriate to support a belief in Eternal Security would have been a passage such as John 10:28-29 or 11:26.

What is even more significant is that Hinn signed a doctrinal statement in order to qualify for ordination with the Assemblies of God, which singles out the doctrine of Eternal Security as a doctrine which *cannot* be believed by its ordained ministers. Indeed, all Pentecostals and most Charismatics (along with Methodists, Freewill Baptists, etc.) have rejected belief in Eternal Security *on the very basis of Scriptures like 2 Peter 2:22!*

Conclusions

From a brief survey of the variety of the dates of the citations in this investigation, it should be abundantly clear to those who wish to know the truth, that Hinn has not changed *any* of his teachings, despite his many promises. If the premise of this study is correct, that the interpretive framework of any individual lies at the heart of his ministry, Hinn's inability to change his theological positions makes perfect sense. His theology *cannot* change until his interpretive practices come into line with those of historical orthodoxy.

Hinn has the cart in front of the horse. His agenda drives his hermeneutics. His need to produce novel interpretations, to establish his own credibility/authority, and to support his heterodox theological agenda are the motivating forces which keep his hermeneutics in a deplorable state. He is, therefore, trapped. His theology cannot change until he changes his interpretive approach, and he cannot change his interpretive approach because his theology is dependent upon it.

Hinn's popularity is a visible reminder of the poor spiritual health in which the Church finds itself today. That one man can create a "cult of personality," an elite priesthood which can pronounce authoritative interpretations binding upon thousands of believers, is almost inconceivable. Such popularity is a sad indication of the willingness of the majority to follow any authoritative voice which feeds the carnal craving of so many in the body of Christ for the "new."

His past explanations of heterodoxy as resulting from lack of formal training, would appear to be a step in the right direction. His actions, however, such as his successful circumvention of the educational requirements for ordination in the Assemblies of God, indicate that his priorities lie elsewhere. Nevertheless, his observation is still legitimate, and should encourage clergy and laymen alike to develop a strong foundation in both theology and hermeneutics.

Finally, we must reject both the methods and the results of ministers whose track records indicate a cavalier regard for the Word of God (see 2 Corinthians 2:17; 4:2; 2 Timothy 2:15; 2 Peter 1:20; etc.). In order for the Church to enjoy a sustained, truly biblical revival, we must first return to the concepts of *Sola Scriptura*, "Scripture interprets Scripture," "the Priesthood of the Believer," and evidentially based interpretation. If we do, the blessings of God are sure to follow. As we exalt His Word above personalities, agendas, human emotion, personal experience, and opinion, God will also exalt us. If we do not heed the call to another Protestant Reformation, we are doomed to return to the spiritual darkness of the Middle Ages.

Is Benny Hinn's "Fire" Anointing Really Just the Emperor's New Clothes?

Faith healer Benny Hinn is a man with an "anointing" for all seasons. Like Baskin-Robbins has flavors of ice cream, Hinn has anointings. There is one for almost everyone's taste. Following the run-away success of his book, *Good Morning, Holy Spirit*, his second volume for Thomas Nelson Publishers, titled simply *The Anointing*, introduced readers to an unembellished anointing — perhaps the "vanilla" of his other anointings.

Hinn has also pitched a "Double Portion Anointing," which included the macabre tale of visiting graves of the late faith healers Kathryn Kuhlman and Aimee Semple McPherson, where he is said to have felt "terrific" and "incredible" anointings.[1] People, he claims, have been physically healed by visits to Kuhlman's grave because of the anointing that lingers there. "Totally healed by God's power," he alleges. He said he planned to take some of his ministerial staff to these graves so that they can feel these "incredible" and "amazing" anointings for themselves.

Then, at his 1992 miracle crusade in Little Rock, Arkansas, Hinn demonstrated a "fresh" anointing, which left bodies strewn across the stage and on the floor — more casualties than a Rambo movie. In Little Rock, the anointing was so strong and powerful it supposedly radiated from his suit coat. Scores of victims hit the floor, slain in the Spirit, as he took off his suit coat and swung it like a baseball bat at the onslaught of people, including ministers, charging onto the stage. The feats of baseball legends Mark McGwire and Sammy Sosa pale in comparison.

Now comes what appears to be the *pièce de résistance* of anointings — the "fire" anointing. Those attending his 1998 Anaheim Miracle Crusade got to experience the phenomenon firsthand. Other Hinn enthusiasts were treated to the spectacle during an airing of his *This Is Your Day* television broadcast.

Hinn told viewers, "That incredible anointing that hit at one point in that service is something that I'll never forget as long as I live." He then divulged, "Listen saints, what we're about to show you we rarely ever show on any program. The fire of God hit and the Lord kept saying to me, 'Say, *Fire!* Speak the word, *Fire!*' And as I did you're about to see the results. You may never be the same again after this."[2] Thus, under God's direction, Hinn becomes one of the very few who is permitted to yell "Fire!" in a crowded building.

Hinn told the crusade audience that, "We're about to receive a revelation of Him, for I believe the Body of Christ is ready now for a fresh manifestation of Christ."[3] These comments assault the Word of God and its sufficiency as revelation of the person and work of the Lord Jesus Christ. In addition, these statements also gain a greater allegiance to Hinn by his followers as he sets himself up as the conduit of this "fresh manifestation." But Hinn's campaign was not finished:

> "There's coming a time in our lives as believers when we're going to have a fresh revelation of who He is. And we're going to come into a new walk with Him. Remember, He declared we would be baptized with fire. Fire. ... Ladies and gentlemen, I want you to know, the day will come when the fire of God's presence will visibly appear in public meetings. You may have never heard that before — it's biblical. ... We've known the baptism of the Holy Ghost, but we have not yet known the fire. And I'm here to tell you in Southern

California, God is about to visit you and the whole Church with fresh fire."[4]

The Church, according to Hinn, is lacking and deficient because of the absence of this "fire" anointing. He explains: "The reason the Church has not known fullness of liberty, the reason the Church has had partial liberty, is because we have not known the fullness of fire. The anointing as fire is coming to your life."[5] Hinn tells us that this new "fire" anointing will burn away bondage and sin.

This declaration immediately raises two very elementary questions. First, what has happened to the blood of Jesus Christ that we now need "fire" to burn away sin? (1 Peter 1:18-19). And secondly, more specifically for Hinn and his enthusiasts, is his 1993 volume, *The Blood*, now null and void? In this work Hinn claims, "The Holy Spirit showed me how powerful God's blood covenant is."[6] Hinn said in the book that *the blood* "would lead you to a greater freedom in Christ than you have ever experienced,"[7] give "God's protection for your household,"[8] and offers "Freedom from feelings of guilt over past sin."[9] Evidently, the Holy Spirit is now *showing* him something different.

The bottom line is that, for Hinn and his followers, it is never enough. There always has to be something fresh, something never heard before, something more powerful, something the next guy does not have. And as such, tragically, there is a distorting and discounting of the true power of the Holy Spirit through a steady and progressive means of biblical sanctification in a believer's life. It is very sad to realize how the likes of Hinn steadily infect and erode the Church, and distort the blessed anointing which is promised and which we already possess (1 John 2:20). Hinn and his devotees are simply not, as New Testament professor Thomas R. Edgar astutely cautions, "satisfied by the promise of the Spirit."[10]

What transpired at Hinn's meeting at Anaheim's Arrowhead Pond Arena is beyond belief and description. It demonstrates a man out of control, and further displays just how deceived his followers are as they drink in his "fire" anointing and go along with the "show." Hinn exhibits mannerisms and voice inflections that would cause mortal fear and spiritual trepidation to most individuals. *"Get my children up here! ... Get my wife up here!"* he thunders in a deep and almost demonic voice.[11] Like in Little Rock, bodies are strewn across the stage and in the choir section under the influence of his new anointing.

As Hinn runs back and forth across the stage, people are slain under the fire anointing as he yells, screams, physically seizes, and near head-butts his victims. Once on the platform, his wife, Suzanne, and daughters and son are also subjected to the same intense and forceful handling of a man gone wild. *"Fire, I said! Fire, I said! Fire, I said!"* he roars to his wife as she succumbs to the floor for a second time.[12] One by one, and most by name, Hinn calls people to the stage for targets of his powerful anointing. His family, his staff, his ministerial colleagues and their families, and his prominent friends all help to create a scene beyond belief and hard to describe.

The entire pathetic spectacle is classified by Hinn as the "power of God," and he further flaunts to his viewing audience and his crusade associates David Palmquist and singer Steve Brock:

> "I don't understand why sometimes the anointing comes that mighty and strong. All I know is it's been absolutely incredible. It's been incredible. I have never known the anointing, gentlemen, like I saw it that meeting, especially during that period in that service on Friday night when literally every part of my body was electrocuted with God's [power]."[13]

His associates agree. "The pure power of God," Brock exults. It "just breaks the chains that bounds [sic]. It sets us free," the singer further asserts. "I've never seen you like that before," his associate pastor Palmquist maintains.[14]

True to form, Hinn glamorized his "fire anointing" crusade. A year after the Anaheim crusade, Hinn described further the event to the readers of his 1999 autobiography:

> "That night I felt led to ask my children to come to the platform — I was going to introduce them to the

audience. However, God had something else in mind. The moment they approached me in the center of the stage, the anointing became so strong that when I turned toward them, all four of my children fell to the floor. There were Jessica, Natasha, Joshua, and Eleasha, slain in the Spirit by the power of God. It was a beautiful sight, and I began to weep before the Lord."[15]

Here, Hinn demonstrates just how far from reality he can take his readers. As noted above, the broadcast of the crusade depicted a man out of control with stage mannerisms and voice inflections which would strike mortal fear into most individuals. It was not a simple matter of wanting to bring his children on stage for an introduction. *"Get my children up here! ... Get my wife up here!"* he wildly commanded in a deep voice. As his family was ushered onto the stage, bodies were already strewn across the platform.

In his autobiography, he further evaluates the event by claiming, "God did an amazing work that night. When they returned to Orlando their Christian witness took on a boldness we had never seen — and the effects of that meeting are still evident."[16] The last part of Hinn's comment may well be one of the more honest statements he has ever made. The harsh and abusive conduct by Hinn toward his family — which is a clear reality on the crusade's video highlights — could very well have left "effects of the meeting [which] are still evident."

Perhaps Hinn's admission on a *Praise the Lord* show is a more legitimate and candid description of his "fire" anointing:

"I am not the same man under the anointing as I am now. I mean—believe me when I tell you I do not even identify with the Benny Hinn you see on television. Because it's a different man, it's not me. *My children are afraid of me under the anointing.* What they do not know is I'm afraid of the anointing too."[17]

The whole "fire" anointing episode (and really all of Hinn's claimed anointings) is nothing more than a contemporary retelling of the 1837 parable, "The Emperor's New

Clothes," by Hans Christian Andersen. The tragedy in all this is that it is no longer just a fairy tale.

If you recall, Andersen tells the story of an emperor who was well known for his desire for new clothes. So much so that, "he spent all his money in order to obtain them; his only ambition was to be always well dressed. ... He had a coat for every hour of the day." His appetite for new garments gave great opportunity for the unscrupulous. One day, two swindlers came to the emperor's city and bragged of their ability to weave for him the "finest cloth to be imagined." The emperor gave them a large sum of money and set them to the task. The suit that was to be made would not only be exceptionally beautiful, but would be unseen by those unfit for their offices or the unpardonably stupid.

All the emperor's money and the fine materials made their way, not into the new clothes, but into the knapsacks of the two perpetrators. "How well they look! How well they fit! ... What a beautiful pattern! What fine colours! That is a magnificent suit of clothes!" the swindlers boasted to the emperor. There were, in fact, no new magnificent garments at all, and the emperor paraded naked under the pretense of being adorned with his new clothes. In town, everyone was frightened to admit that they saw nothing, for fear of being thought unfit or stupid. They were unable to see anything, yet who were they to say? As the emperor marched unclothed, attendants behind him with outstretched hands pretended to carry the train of his new clothes. Everyone just went along with the show.

Finally, a little child revealed the "naked truth." "But he has nothing on at all," the child cried. The young boy's declaration finally permeated the crowd until all agreed, "He has nothing on at all!" Yet the emperor thought to himself, "Now I must bear up to the end," as he and his servants marched on with even greater dignity.

Unlike the Andersen parable, the misfortune with Hinn's anointing is that his faithful flock refuses to admit the naked truth: There simply is *no* anointing. They continue persistent and passionate in their desire not to be thought stupid or unfit — or even worse, unspiritual!

The Charismatic decree, heard over and over again, no doubt reverberates in their thinking. They have been victimized into thinking that questioning his anointing is tantamount to touching God's anointed, doing God's prophets harm, or blaspheming the Holy Spirit. The employment of such verses of Scripture (1 Chronicles 12:22, Psalm 105:15, Matthew 12:31), used out of context, is equal to nothing less than spiritual terrorism.

Hinn is able to engage the power of the mind in his approach to the miraculous and his anointings. His onstage persona creates a highly charged level of suggestibility, and with this he is able to initiate desired responses and activity from his faithful. Hinn sets himself up with a "Heads I win, tails you lose" environment. If one goes along with his anointing, telling of its wonders and falling to the ground (being "slain in the Spirit"), you confirm his claim that the power of God is being imparted through him ("Heads I win"). But if you do not succumb to his anointing and fail to go under, you are the one who is thought to be spiritually deficient, with perhaps sin or Satan as the cause of your dormancy to his anointing ("Tails you lose").

There are many small details recorded on the video which demonstrate the human element and theatrics in all of this. They are, for the most part, missed by the unobservant eye. One classic moment is when one of Hinn's female victims, half-sitting, half-laying on the stage after being "slain" under the alleged power imparted by Hinn, misreads a cue. Hinn comes near her and dispenses the "fire" anointing and she immediately flops back down. However, Hinn was not imparting the "powerful" anointing at her, but towards his associate minister David Palmquist. *Fire on David, Fire!"* Hinn screams at Palmquist, as he complies and also goes under the power.

Hinn's wife, Suzanne, leaves tell-tale signs as well for the careful observer. There are two instances where she takes time to adjust her clothing after she has been slain and knocked to the stage floor. This is hardly activity one would expect from someone truly impacted under the numbing power of Hinn's Holy Ghost fire anointing. Another instance is by a woman, who before "falling" under the power, makes a quick glance behind herself to insure that a "catcher" is in position and ready to catch her and lay her gently to the floor as she swoons. This quick glance action should have well been taken by another of Hinn's female players as the "catcher" missed his cue and allowed her to crash to the stage floor unrestrained. She is a clear example of how one has a better chance of being hurt, rather than healed, at a Hinn Miracle Crusade.

Yves Brault, author of *Behind the Scenes — The True Face of the Fake ~~Faith~~ Healers*, and himself a victim for several years of Hinn's seductive and deceptive power, also recognized the faith healer's orchestration. Brault observed:

> "To understand the recent performance of Benny Hinn at the Arrowhead Pond Arena, we must signal the promise he had made on September 9, 1998, on his daily program: 'You mark my word. The next three crusades: Birmingham, Anaheim, and Orlando, we are gonna see unusual creative miracles. Notable miracles. God in those crusades will do what hasn't happened in all the 24 years of ministry I've been in.'"[18]

He also urges:

> "Since there was no notable creative miracles, Benny had to 'create' an entertaining show of his own. What better way than the 'slaying in the spirit' method. Some observations: First he called the preachers on stage who naturally cooperated, then several staff members who know the drill well. His music director, Jim Cernero, standing at his pulpit leading the choir has his name loudly called as Benny throws the 'fire anointing' at him, indicating it's his turn to go down. A subtle trick to warn one who is not facing the show. Cernero's knees bend but he doesn't fall, as there is no 'catcher' in the vicinity."[19]

Brault also made similar observations concerning the performance of Hinn's family members:

> "Then came the turn of Benny's own children. 'Get my children up here,' he said. They seem so perturbed, as wishing they were somewhere else. His wife Suzanne is also called on stage like a slave. Benny, raging like he's about to hit her, knocks her down screaming, 'Fire, I said, fire I said, fire I said.' Suzanne acquiesces and falls, but not without stretching her jacket down as she hits the ground. Conscious of her outfit, and fully aware of the scheme, she and other staff members participated in a performance that once again misled multitudes."[20]

Perhaps Hinn's "fire" anointing, and the claim of its supernatural superiority, will soon fade into the background. Yet tragically, through his many and varied exploits, his followers have lost as much spiritually as the United States, in the 1990s, lost morally by way of the exploits of the leadership of this country.

What's next for Hinn? Only time will tell. But, no doubt, tomorrow will bring a new and improved, more powerful, more important anointing to his followers, who fill auditoriums across the country and the world, for his miracle crusades. Yet, it is more than time for the devotees of Hinn to stop and listen to the voice of reason: "He has no anointing; the emperor has no clothes."

Appendix A ———————————

The Orlando Christian Center: "Where you're only a visitor once"

EDITOR'S NOTE: Orlando Christian Center (OCC, later known as World Outreach Center and World Outreach Church) in Orlando, Florida, was home base for faith healer Benny Hinn for nearly two decades. According to Thomas Nelson Publishers' promotional materials and other reports, Hinn founded the church in March 1983, with 250 people and at one time claimed more than 10,000 in attendance each week. On August 12, 1992, Personal Freedom Outreach (PFO) Director Kurt Goedelman and former PFO Director Paul Blizard went to Orlando to see the church and hear Hinn preach. What follows is a "first-person" account of their visit written by Blizard.

We found a beautiful complex full of apparently happy worshipers. But visitors beware — one may be subject to search by Hinn's police force: "OCC Security." As we entered the building to attend a Wednesday evening service, we saw uniformed and plainclothes security personnel equipped with walkie-talkies and earpieces. They gave us the once-over as we entered.

"It is somewhat unnerving to enter a 'church' and see uniformed guards," I said to my colleague, Kurt Goedelman.

When entering the bookstore in the foyer, we noticed stacks of Hinn's books on the floor, along with Benny Hinn Ministry T-shirts and bumper stickers. In spite of Hinn's statement in an October 28, 1991, *Christianity Today* interview, where he said, "I no longer believe the faith message. I don't think it adds up," the bookstore carried a wide assortment of word-faith titles by authors such as Charles Capps, Kenneth Hagin, and Kenneth Copeland.[1] Also on the shelves was Rebecca Brown's bizarre, *He Came to Set the Captives Free.*

About 45 minutes before the service, we sat down in the fifth row from the front. We conversed with people in the nearby pews. One person spoke enthusiastically of Hinn's claim that his father had been mayor of Jaffa, Israel, "for 10 years," and of his Greek heritage.

We also asked this person about Hinn's claim to have seen the face of Jesus appear on the wall of the church. He pointed to a blank wall where the apparition had been seen. "It was there for thirty days. The mouth and eyes even moved," he said. When asked if he had witnessed the event, he replied: "That was before I was a member, but it is on videotape." We asked if the tape was available for viewing or purchase. He replied, "Pastor Benny does not want it released."

A couple turned around and enthusiastically asked: "Is this your first visit to OCC?" "Yes," answered Goedelman. The man continued, "Pastor Benny always says, 'At OCC, you're only a visitor once.'" The excited couple then turned around again, anticipating Hinn's entrance.

The service began, and near the end of a series of songs, while "heads were bowed and eyes closed," Hinn made his entrance. Diamonds and gold glittered as he waved his arms, continuing to lead the singing. Giant TV screens gave everyone in attendance a close-up.

Following several church formalities and announcements, Hinn began preaching his "sermon."

It was a familiar theme: "Touch not mine anointed." Hinn hopscotched through the Bible, trying to prove his point. It was obvious he was angry at his critics and wanted his congregation to share in that anger.

Hinn began the message with the preface that video cameras might have to be turned off because he had some things to say that he did not want taped. This is when we began to take notes. Hinn began to decry the "persecution" he was receiving.

He told a story of an incident with a customs agent at a Chicago airport. Hinn said:

> "Those people are mean up in Chicago, just because I am a preacher they gave me a hard time. I told that customs man 'I want to see your supervisor!' When I got into the supervisor's office he said to me, 'You're just like [Jim] Bakker.' That made me so angry — If I could have killed him, I would have!"

As shocking as these words are coming from a supposed preacher of the Gospel, "death" and the judgment of death was a central theme of his message: death to all "persecutors" and all those who question Hinn and his teaching. Hinn continued:

> "Now I'm going to tell you that God prophetically is showing us in the Psalms, that the body of Jesus Christ in America will sooner or later become militant, and say: 'We've had it! You touch us one more time and DROP DEAD, BROTHER.'"

Hinn continued to spew out his purported divine judgments:

> "If you pray, 'get 'em,' nothing can prevent that from happening, but God has allowed enough grace that you can say, 'Lord forgive them,' and God will not allow anything to happen to them; it's really up to you. God has given you the choice whether He should judge them or not; it's in your hands."

Not only did Hinn say that he and his church will have license to pronounce death on persecutors, but maintained that they did not have to forgive those who persecuted them. Hinn, in his teaching, twisted the words of Jesus on the cross where Jesus said, "Father, forgive them; for they know not what they do." Hinn said, "Now you say, 'Well, I forgive them,' you can and you must, but there's a place you don't say, 'Father, forgive them.'"

Hinn then contended that if the person "knows" what he is doing, he is to be turned over to God for retribution. Hinn said:

> "Christian, wake up. God is not mush — mush stuff; there is wrath with God; there is justice with God. We all think of the Lord as being some weakling! I've had people tell me, 'Well, Benny Hinn, forgive them.' I said, 'You don't know the scriptures! You forgive them only when they know not what they do.'"

Hinn further maintained:

> "There are folks out there that are persecuting you, not knowing what they are doing; you must forgive them, and you must say, 'Father, forgive them.' There's folks running around, attacking you, know exactly what they're doing. I have two of 'em who've done that to me. The Lord reward them. I pray that in my own prayer time; I said, *'Lord, don't forgive them, let 'em have it!'* [Congregation applauds] Hey, Hey, Hey that's in the Word."

I was so shocked by this teaching that I gasped, catching the attention of the couple in front us. They turned around, and I whispered to them, "That teaching is wrong; Jesus said to forgive those who persecute you." The couple snapped their heads back around.

The service concluded with Hinn's altar call:

> "Remember this, Numbers chapter 12, Korah and his company stood against Moses and were judged. Remember Numbers 16; even his own sister Miriam was struck with leprosy for attacking her brother, God's servant. You will not escape, even though you're a saint; there is punishment for those who'll touch God's servants. It's very serious. So tonight I'm gonna ask every person who will say, 'I've attacked ministers,' I want you right now to make your way down to this front."

We then went to the front, not in response to Hinn's call, but to get a photograph of Hinn. A worker told us to stand by a particular door and Hinn would pass there.

As we stood waiting, we noticed people with hearing aids, some on crutches and two young people in wheelchairs. For all his cross-country traveling on healing campaigns, many in his own congregation apparently go without healing.

When Hinn passed, I asked, "How about a picture?" When he saw the camera, he insisted that we step up on stage to get a better shot. One of Hinn's attendants snapped the photo of him with his arms around us, two of the kind of people he was denouncing only five minutes before. So much for spiritual discernment.

We went to the crowded foyer to buy a recording of the service and found ourselves surrounded by Hinn's security force.

"What's the problem?" they asked us.

One of the patrol identified himself as "head of security" and again asked, "What's the problem?"

"We're just trying to buy some tapes," Goedelman replied.

"I understand you have a tape recorder," he said as he reached and tried to confiscate Goedelman's camera, which had a zippered case. "What's that, what's that? Is that a tape recorder?"

"No," Goedelman said, "it's a camera."

The guard wasn't satisfied until he saw the camera removed from its case. Then he pointed at Goedelman's Bible and asked, "What's that? Is that a tape recorder? What is that?" Goedelman opened the zippered cover to reveal his Bible.

"What is going on here?" I asked.

"We had a complaint from some longtime members that there was a problem with you two," the guard said. "And that's what we're trying to find out. Just what is the problem?"

We surmised that the couple who sat in front of us during the service had been upset by my spontaneous critique of Hinn's teaching on forgiveness, and had reported us to security.

"What problem *would* there be?" I asked.

"I don't know, that's what we're trying to find out," the security guard answered.

"This is really strange. We traveled all the way down here to hear Benny Hinn preach, we hear a message, and we are detained by security guards. I would like to know, what *is* going on here? What kind of a church is this?" I asked.

The guard then said, "You can leave now! Leave the property!" A uniformed guard followed us to our car and took note of our license plate as we left the parking lot.

In the wake of our reception at OCC, we can only agree with the couple who said, "Pastor Benny always says 'At OCC, you're only a visitor once.'"

Appendix B —————————————————

The Hurt of Healing

Faith healing is big business. Oral Roberts in the 40s and 50s, Kathryn Kuhlman in the 60s and 70s, and, of course, Benny Hinn in the 90s, are but a few of the key players in a half-century of jam-packed meetings and crusades. Today, the healing business is not only marketed through books and tapes, but with modern technology, unashamedly merchandised on television. But is it really all that it appears to be?

Those who view telecasts such as Hinn's *This Is Your Day* see spectacular displays of apparent miracle after miracle, without being aware that the programs have been carefully edited. What they see is Hinn running back and forth upon the stage, counting empty wheelchairs, roaring, "This is your night for a miracle. Look at someone next to you and say it!" What they do not see is the number of victims leaving the crusade in the same wheelchair in which they arrived, or with the same physical affliction.

In March 1995, when Hinn brought his traveling "healing" road show to the Assemblies of God "Signs and Wonders Conference" in Springfield, Missouri, M. Kurt Goedelman and W.E. Nunnally, two of this book's coauthors, waited at the church auditorium's two exits at the conclusion of the service, watching to see how many empty wheelchairs left the building. Although dozens of occupied wheelchairs made their way from the crusade, not a single empty one passed through either of the two exits.

Not only is what the television audience sees edited, what the live audience sees is carefully staged. Those who are terribly deformed, children with Down's syndrome, amputees and the like, are kept from the stage and out of sight of TV cameras.

Journalist Carol McGraw of the *Orange County (California) Register*, discovered this painful reality when she reported on Jordan Sheehan. Jordan, at the time of her report, was a 2-year-old who suffered severe brain damage as a result of a fire. He was in a coma for two months. He cannot swallow, talk, or move. Jordan's parents and grandparents thought that if they could get the child to Hinn's healing crusade and have him prayed over, the miraculous would surely come upon the child. But, according to McGraw's report, Jordan never experienced the miraculous touch from Hinn, and he and his family were cautiously kept from the stage.[1]

This restricted perspective is not unique to the contemporary faith healing scene. According to Wade H. Boggs:

> "Mrs. Aimee Semple McPherson's practices also left much to be desired. Before the sick were entitled to stand in her healing line, she required them to apply for a card from her mother, Mrs. Kennedy, who permitted only those who appear to be good healing risks to present themselves on stage for anointing and prayer."[2]

And then there are other maneuvers that make the healer appear more competent than he is. Hinn and his ilk are skilled in working their followers into a pinnacle of mental, physical, and spiritual frenzy. Yet these periods of pandemonium in emotion-packed auditoriums are never the time or place to pronounce terminal diseases cured. In many cases, the complicated diagnosis of these illnesses required days, weeks, and even months by trained and skilled medical personnel with the latest in equipment. To claim a healing without the benefit of the same procedures and care is nothing less than foolish and misleading. Boggs says of this gimmick:

> "It is extremely easy for the layman to be misled regarding the exact nature of a disease. No layman is qualified either to diagnose his own sickness, or to determine whether he is completely healed. Public

testimonials of healing at moments of great excitement
and emotional stress are worthless. ... Most often, the
improvement lasted only as long as the spell of
excitement lasted."[3]

Although written nearly a half century ago, Boggs' words
are just as, if not more so, applicable today. The heightened
emotional level created among the crowds of people attending
such crusades places the faith healer in a win/win situation. In
what can be regarded as sheer acts of desperation, the sick
take that "leap of faith," hoping the miraculous will
materialize, thereby allowing the faith healer to parade them
as a trophy back and forth across the stage. The 20,000-plus
faithful in the arena, in addition to the potential millions
viewing by telecast or videotape, believe a healing really has
occurred.

However, when the victim returns home and the reality of
the affliction remains, no one is the wiser. And even if the
truth leaks out, it is easy to shift blame back to the afflicted
one's unconfessed sin or lack of faith or, if all else fails, Satan
himself.

Less than a year before her own death, Kathryn Kuhlman
brought one of her healing services to St. Louis. One driver
from a fleet of chartered buses that brought people to the
meeting from a near 200-mile radius of the city, was reported
to have said:

> "'She doesn't always succeed,' said a driver from
> Chester. 'My bus was pretty quiet on the way home last
> year [after her service]. But for some of those people a
> little inspiration does wonders, if only for a little while.
> I had a guy last year who was dying of cancer. He got
> up on the stage and said he was healed. He died a week
> later.'"[4]

To the thousands packed in the auditorium, this man with
terminal cancer was just one of many who supposedly walked
from the service healed of his infirmity. In reality, he was not,
despite Kuhlman's declaration: "God ... has more than
enough healing power for everyone in this great auditorium."[5]

This same scenario can be applied to untold thousands, perhaps millions.

Apologist Robert M. Bowman, in a brief, yet powerful, article, presents a biblical exegesis of James 5 that rebuts the more prominent expressions of the healing proponents. His examination of twelve faulty concepts commonly presented within the faith healing camp shows there is no support from this epistle for modern faith-healing crusades. The most salient points are:

> "(1) There are no **itinerant healing ministries**, since in James elders are called to come to the sick (v. 14); the sick are not called to come to the tents of the healer. (2) There are no **gifted healers in the congregation**, since again it is 'the elders' without distinction that are to be called; evidently people with gifts of healing (I Cor. 12:9) were not common. (3) There are no **healing services**, since again the elders are called to the sick. Scheduling the Holy Spirit to come to one's church at 7:00 p.m. on Thursday nights to perform healings is alien to the Bible."[6]

Christians can and should look to God for healing. And yes, sometimes our petition for physical deliverance may be granted through the miraculous. God is not restricted by the limitations and inabilities of the medical profession. However, other times it may not be His will to intervene supernaturally. For God has also provided gradual healings through doctors and medicine. And then there is the tenable reality that perhaps it is not God's will to heal at all. Ephesians 4 contains no office of "healer." Healers are, in reality, a 20th century mania for mysticism and media. Healers thrive in that artificial environment.

Faith healers purport to *pray for* the afflicted, but their conduct demonstrates that they *prey upon* the afflicted. As the smoke clears and the dust settles on the healing crusades, the disappointment left behind has, in so many cases, resulted in tragic consequences. False hope is no hope at all. Expectations that are based upon promises from the seducing minds of faith healers, and not upon the sure Word of God, will eventually lead one into the depths of despair and depression.

It is cruel to impart the physically impaired with yet another affliction. Those who leave these crusades without healing now face not only physical infirmity, but doubts about their spiritual well-being. This can be debilitating to their faith if they come to believe that God does not love them as much as the others who left the crusade apparently healed.

The theology of the "health gospel" is itself unhealthy and will inevitably lead to a sick Church. Richard Mayhue, vice president and dean of The Master's Seminary, considers the Church's lack of discernment and naiveté:

> "Tragically, our world offers very convincing counterfeits of the real thing. Even more tragic, in our eagerness to see God work, we as Christians sometimes flock to anyone who claims a miraculous healing. In doing so, we trivialize genuine divine healing — we accept man's deceitful illusions in place of God's divine intervention."[7]

Christians should not disparage claims of supernatural healing when the people of God sincerely pray. Churches should regularly seek God on behalf of the bruised and hurting. These things should not be abandoned because of the deluge of counterfeits and charlatans targeting the gullible. We must avoid the hurt of this artificial healing and avoid the "superstars" who perpetuate that hurt.

Endnotes

Chapter 1

1. Hinn is a man so careful about his image that for many years he did not want his Arabic birth name, Toufik, to be known. "But my first name I—which I will not tell you. No, you're not gonna find out. Too bad. But my nickname as a child was, Tou Tou," he told his Orlando congregation ("Personal Testimony Benny Hinn," July 19, 1987). After his birth name was disclosed in earlier editions of this book and in the newsletter publications of Personal Freedom Outreach, Hinn acknowledged the name he was called as a child (even into his high school years) in chapter 2 of his 1999 autobiography, *He Touched Me*.

2. The term "mystical Christian movement" could designate those in the contemporary Church who hold to the Word-Faith, Manifested Sons of God, Kingdom Now, Dominionist, and/or Latter Rain type of Charismaticism.

3. Benny Hinn, *Good Morning, Holy Spirit*. Nashville: Thomas Nelson Publishers, 1990, pg. 22.

4. Ibid., pg. 29.

5. Ibid., pp. 39, 43.

6. Ibid., pg. 56.

7. Benny Hinn, *War in the Heavenlies*. Winter Park, Fla.: Benny Hinn Ministries, Inc., 1984, pp. 16-17.

8. Benny Hinn, "Personal Testimony Benny Hinn," Orlando Christian Center, Orlando, Fla., July 19, 1987. Tape #A071987, tape on file.

9. Ibid.

10. Emanuel Swedenborg, *Heaven and Its Wonders and Hell*. New York: Swedenborg Foundation, 1960, Division 280, pp. 155-156.

11. *Good Morning, Holy Spirit*, op. cit., pg. 56, emphasis added.

12. Jay E. Adams, *Christian Living in the World*. Woodruff, S.C.: Timeless Texts, 1998, pp. 43-44.

13. Ibid., pg. 44.

14. *Good Morning, Holy Spirit*, op. cit., pg. 17.

15. "Personal Testimony Benny Hinn," op. cit.

16. Benny Hinn, *He Touched Me*. Nashville: Thomas Nelson Publishers, 1999, pg. 11.

17. Ibid.

18. *Good Morning, Holy Spirit*, op. cit., pg. 18.

19. *He Touched Me*, op. cit., pg. 13.

20. *Good Morning, Holy Spirit*, op. cit., pg. 28.

21. *Vestigia*, 1972 Yearbook of Georges Vanier Secondary School, North York, Toronto, Ontario, Canada.

22. *Recommendations and Information for Secondary School Organization leading to*

Certificates and Diplomas, Circular H.S.1 1972/73, Ontario Department of Education.

23. Peter Whelan and Aubrey Wice, "Faith healing: the power of belief," *Toronto Globe and Mail*, Dec. 25, 1976.

24. "Seneca College of Applied Arts and Technology, Calendar 1971-1973," Admissions Policies, pg. 31.

25. Randy Frame, "Same Old Benny Hinn, Critics Say," *Christianity Today*, Oct. 5, 1992, pg. 54.

26. *He Touched Me*, op. cit., pg. 48.

27. "Personal Testimony Benny Hinn," Orlando Christian Center, op. cit.

28. Ibid.

29. Ibid.

30. Benny Hinn, *The Anointing*. Nashville: Thomas Nelson Publishers, 1992, pg. 30.

31. Audio tape made of a Sept. 3, 1991, three-way telephone interview involving Randy Frame, J. Rodman Williams, and Benny Hinn in preparation for Frame's article which appeared in the Oct. 28, 1991 issue of *Christianity Today*, "Best-selling Author Admits Mistakes, Vows Changes," pp. 44-45. Transcript of tape on file.

32. *The Anointing*, op. cit., pg. 22.

33. *He Touched Me*, op. cit., pg. 80.

34. Robert M. Bowman, Jr., *Orthodoxy and Heresy*. Grand Rapids: Baker Book House, 1992, pp. 40-41, italics in original.

35. Ibid., pg. 42.

36. *The Anointing*, op. cit., pg. 52.

37. Ibid., pg. 55.

38. Ibid., pg. 86.

39. Ibid., pg. 52.

40. Jamie Buckingham, *Daughter of Destiny*. Plainfield, N.J.: Logos International, 1976, pp. 153, 149.

41. Ibid., pp. 2-3.

42. Ibid., pp. 76-77, 78.

43. *He Touched Me*, op. cit., pg. 120.

44. Benny Hinn sermon, *Double Portion Anointing*, Part #3, Orlando Christian Center, Orlando, Fla., April 7, 1991. From the series, *Holy Ghost Invasion*. TV#309, tape on file.

45. Benny Hinn, *This Is Your Day*, Trinity Broadcasting Network, June 11, 1997, tape on file.

46. Gerhardt Kittel, *Theological Dictionary of the New Testament*. Grand Rapids: Wm. B. Eerdmans Publishing Co., 1972, Vol. IV, pg. 770.

47. Ibid., pg. 781.

48. Ibid., pg. 793.

Chapter 2

1. Benny Hinn, Orlando Christian Center, sermon on 2 Corinthians 5:17, "New Creation in Christ," exact date unknown, ca. late 1988, tape on file.

2. Ibid.

3. Benny Hinn, Orlando Christian Center broadcast, Trinity Broadcasting Network, Dec. 9, 1990.

4. See further, Stephen F. Cannon, "Old Wine in Old Wineskins," *The Quarterly Journal*, October-December 1990, pp. 1, 6-12, and "Kansas City Fellowship Revisited," *The Quarterly Journal*, January-March 1991, pp. 4, 7-9.

5. See further, Stephen F. Cannon, "The Presumptuous Teachings of the Word-Faith Movement," *Personal Freedom Outreach Newsletter*, October-December 1986, pp. 4-6.

6. Benny Hinn sermon, ca. late 1988, op. cit.

7. Benny Hinn, *Our Position In Christ*, six tape audiocassette series, "Our Position In Christ," Part 1, Tape #A031190-1.

8. Benny Hinn, "A New Spirit," Orlando Christian Center broadcast, Trinity Broadcasting Network, Oct. 13, 1990, video tape on file.

9. Ibid.

10. William Alnor, "Leading Charismatic Denies the Historical Doctrine of the Trinity on National Television." News release dated Oct. 15, 1990.

11. Ibid.

12. Cited in ibid.

13. Benny Hinn, "Benny Hinn Testimony," Grace World Outreach, Saint Louis, Mo., March 4, 1983, audio tape on file.

14. Benny Hinn, *Good Morning, Holy Spirit*. Nashville: Thomas Nelson Publishers, 1990, pg. 66.

15. Ibid., pg. 85.

16. Benny Hinn, "Great Miracle Service," Church on the Rock, Rockwall, Texas, June 21, 1990, video tape on file.

17. Ibid.

18. Benny Hinn sermon, ca. late 1988, op. cit.

19. Orlando Christian Center broadcast, Dec. 9, 1990, op. cit.

20. Benny Hinn sermon, ca. late 1988, op. cit.

21. Orlando Christian Center broadcast, Dec. 9, 1990, op. cit.

22. Benny Hinn sermon, ca. late 1988, op. cit.

23. "Our Position In Christ," Part 1, op. cit.

24. Ibid.

25. There are several modern English versions that either translate the second occurrence of *hamartia* as sin offering or supply that rendering in the margin as an alternate translation. See especially: *The New International Version; The New Testament: A Translation in the Language of the People* (Charles B. Williams); and *The Revised Version, New Testament of 1881*.

26. See 1 Corinthians 1:30; Hebrews 7:26; 9:14; 1 Peter 1:18,19; etc.

27. Brian Onken, "The Atonement of Christ and the 'Faith' Message," *Forward*, Christian Research Institute Magazine, Vol. 7, No. 1, pg. 12.

28. Cited in ibid., pg. 13.

29. James Oliver Buswell, Jr., *A Systematic Theology of the Christian Religion*. Grand Rapids: Zondervan Publishing House, 1977, Vol. 2, pg. 68.

30. Benny Hinn, sermon given at the "Spiritual Warfare Seminar," Jubilee Christian Center, San Jose, Calif., May 2, 1990.

31. Benny Hinn, "Praise-A-Thon," Trinity Broadcasting Network, Nov. 6, 1990, video tape on file. The original live broadcast of Hinn's sermon was during Trinity Broadcasting Network's "Praise-A-Thon," April 1990. This date is established by Hinn's comment that Paul Crouch spends the least amount of air time soliciting funds, according to a current Newsweek magazine. The issue of the magazine with the fund raising statistics was April 9, 1990 (pg. 8). The entire segment includes not only the teaching that Christians are "little gods" and "little christs" espoused by Hinn but also the prosperity gospel teaching. In addition, he labels those who question his teachings as "morons." An abbreviated version of the segment was also repeatedly aired during TBN's "Praise-A-Thon," November 1994.

32. Benny Hinn, "God Super Being," Orlando Christian Center broadcast, Trinity Broadcasting Network, Oct. 20, 1990, video tape on file.

33. Benny Hinn, Orlando Christian Center broadcast, Trinity Broadcasting Network, Dec. 1, 1990.

34. "Praise-A-Thon," Nov. 6, 1990, op. cit.

35. "Spiritual Warfare Seminar" sermon, op. cit.

36. "Our Position In Christ," Part 1, op. cit.

37. Benny Hinn sermon, Dec. 1, 1990, op. cit.

38. "Spiritual Warfare Seminar" sermon, op. cit.

39. "Thomas Nelson Clarifies Hinn's Holy Spirit Book," *Christian Retailing*, March 15, 1991, pg. 8.

40. Ibid.

41. Ibid.

42. On March 13, 1992, with no warning, William D. Watkins was terminated from his position as managing editor of the book division of Thomas Nelson Publishers. Because of Hinn's unorthodoxy, Watkins had requested permission to be excused from handling any more of the faith healer's projects. Thomas Nelson officials contended that no employee has ever been "fired" for refusing to work on a Benny Hinn book. See further, *Cornerstone* magazine, Vol. 22, Issue 101, pp. 29-33.

43. Letters, along with photocopies of corrections of Hinn's book, were sent to Christian Research Institute, Religion writer William Alnor, *Christianity Today*, and others. Copies of letters on file.

44. Adelle M. Banks, "Pastor Sells His Books, But Not All Buy His Ideas," *The Orlando Sentinel*, March 2, 1991, pg. D-8.

45. News & Views, "Hinn's Book Clarified," *Charisma*, April 1991, pg. 28.

Chapter 3

1. Benny Hinn, *Good Morning, Holy Spirit*. Nashville: Thomas Nelson Publishers, 1990, pp. 27-32.

2. Benny Hinn, "Benny Hinn Testimony," Grace World Outreach, Saint Louis, Mo., March 4, 1983, cassette tape on file.

3. *Good Morning, Holy Spirit*, op. cit., pg. 29.

4. Benny Hinn, "Personal Testimony Benny Hinn," Orlando Christian Center, July 19, 1987, #A071987, cassette tape on file, emphasis added.

5. Ibid.

6. *Good Morning, Holy Spirit*, op. cit., pp. 29-30.

7. Ibid., pg. 31.

8. Benny Hinn, *He Touched Me*. Nashville: Thomas Nelson Publishers, 1999, pg. 49, italics in original.

9. Ibid., pp. 50-51.

10. Benny Hinn, *War in the Heavenlies*. Winter Park, Fla.: Benny Hinn Ministries, 1984, pp. 116-117, bold and upper case type in original.

11. Ibid., pg. 115, (emphasis added).

12. *Good Morning, Holy Spirit*, op. cit., pp. 42-43.

13. Ibid., pg. 175.

14. Ibid., pp. 173-175 (also see pp. 46-47).

15. Ibid., pp. 174-175.

16. Benny Hinn, *Praise the Lord* show, Trinity Broadcasting Network, May 12, 1999, video tape on file.

17. Steve Chambers, "Preacher inspires many followers, and skeptics," *The Star Ledger* (Newark, N.J.), July 21, 1999, pg. 12.

18. *Webster's New World Dictionary of the English Language*. Cleveland: Simon and Schuster, 1984, "truth," pg. 1528.

19. W.E. Vine, *Expository Dictionary of New Testament Words*. Westwood, N.J.: Fleming Revell, 1966, pg. 158.

20. Ibid.

21. Kenneth S. Wuest, *Word Studies in the Greek New Testament*. Grand Rapids: Wm. B. Eerdmans Publishing Company, 1952, Vol. 2, "The Pastoral Epistles in the Greek New Testament," pg. 158.

22. Craig Hawkins, *Witchcraft*. Grand Rapids: Baker Book House, 1996, pg. 15.

Chapter 4

1. Benny Hinn, "Personal Testimony Benny Hinn," Orlando Christian Center, July 19, 1987, Tape #A071987, tape on file.

2. Benny Hinn, *The Anointing*. Nashville: Thomas Nelson Publishers, 1992, pg. 29.

3. Jacket of cassette tape, "Personal Testimony Benny Hinn," Orlando Christian Center, op. cit., emphasis added.

4. "Personal Testimony Benny Hinn," op. cit.

5. Ibid.

6. Benny Hinn, *Good Morning, Holy Spirit*. Nashville: Thomas Nelson Publishers, 1990, pg. 21.

7. "Personal Testimony Benny Hinn," op. cit., emphasis added.

8. *Good Morning, Holy Spirit*, op. cit., pg. 27.

9. *The Anointing*, op. cit., pg. 34; *Good Morning, Holy Spirit*, op. cit., pg. 5.

10. *Good Morning, Holy Spirit*, op. cit., pp. 44-46.

11. Copy of letter on file.

12. Phone conversation with David Lockwood, July 26, 1992.

13. Phone conversation with Jim McCalister, Aug. 20, 1992.

14. Phone conversation with Merv Watson, Aug. 19, 1992.

15. Phone conversation with Merv Watson, Nov. 10, 1992.

16. Phone conversation with Mike MacLean, Oct. 10, 1992.

17. Ibid.

18. Phone conversation with Paul Pynkoski, Aug. 20, 1992.

19. Norman Snider, "Benny Hinn, Miracle Man," *Toronto Globe and Mail Fanfare*, Feb. 15, 1978, pg. 11.

20. *Good Morning, Holy Spirit*, op. cit., pp. 44-46.

21. Benny Hinn, *Praise the Lord* show, Trinity Broadcasting Network, Oct. 23, 1992, video tape on file.

22. Ibid.

23. Stephen Strang, "Practicing What We Preach," *Charisma*, June 1993, pg. 10.

24. Interview by Stephen Strang, "Benny Hinn Speaks Out," *Charisma*, August 1993, pg. 26.

25. Ibid., emphasis added.

26. Benny Hinn, *He Touched Me*. Nashville: Thomas Nelson Publishers, 1999, pg. 19.

27. Ibid., pp. 36-37.

28. Ibid.

29. Ibid., pg. 87.

30. Benny Hinn, *Praise the Lord* show, Trinity Broadcasting Network, Jan. 28, 1993, video tape on file.

31. Factual Report Aviation Accident/Incident, National Transportation Safety Board, Form 6120.4, "Narrative Statement of Pertinent Facts, Conditions, and Circumstances" states on page 9: "At 0035 [12:35 a.m.], the flight controller observed the flight approaching the airport at 200 feet MSL (45 feet AGL). This was the last time that the aircraft's target was observed on the radar scope." See also, Danny Powell, "Six Survive Avon Plane Crash," *The News-Sun*, Avon Park, Fla., June 1, 1983, pg. A-3.

32. "Six Survive Avon Plane Crash," op. cit., pg. A-1. Also "6 injured in twin-engine plane crash," *The Orlando Sentinel*, Orlando, Fla., May 27, 1983, pg. B-2.

33. Pilot/Operator Aircraft Accident Report, National Transportation Safety Board, Form 6120.1, pg. 5.

34. Ibid.

35. "Six Survive Avon Plane Crash," op. cit.; "6 injured in twin-engine plane crash," op. cit.

36. "6 injured in twin-engine plane crash," op. cit.

37. "Six Survive Avon Plane Crash," op. cit.

38. Ibid.

39. Florida Hospital, phone conversation with Records Department, Feb. 8, 1993.

40. Sheriff Department, Highlands County, Sebring, Florida, Offense-Incident Report, Case No. 83-05-0830, pg. 6.

41. "Personal Testimony Benny Hinn," op. cit.

42. Ibid.

43. Benny Hinn, *This Is Your Day*, Trinity Broadcasting Network, Oct. 22, 1997.

44. David Lees, "Blow me down Jesus," *Saturday Night* magazine, December 1994/January 1995, pg. 52.

Chapter 5

1. Benny Hinn, *Good Morning, Holy Spirit*. Nashville: Thomas Nelson Publishers, 1990, pg. 18.

2. Benny Hinn, *The Anointing*. Nashville: Thomas Nelson Publishers, 1991, pg. 21.

3. Hinn twice makes this claim on his 1987 testimony tape (Benny Hinn, "Personal Testimony Benny Hinn," Orlando Christian Center, July 19, 1987, #A071987) and then again on another testimonial recording from Orlando Christian Center with no date, but with tape number 315 and a copyright of 1990 on the cassette sleeve.

4. Dan Kurzman, *Genesis 1948*. New York: DaCapo Press, 1992, pg. 182.

5. Ibid., pg. 188.

6. Kathryn Kuhlman, *I Believe In Miracles*. New York: Pyramid Books, 1969, Foreword, pg. 11. Kuhlman's father was mayor of Concordia, Mo., when she was a child. According to Concordia's City Hall, Joe Kuhlman served as the city's mayor from 1922 until 1924 and then again from 1926 until 1932.

7. See further: Sanya Hamadi, *The Character and Temperament of the Arabs*. New York: Twayne Publishers, 1960.

8. *Good Morning, Holy Spirit*, op. cit., pg. 19.

9. "Jaffa Signs Surrender Terms," *Palestine Post*, May 14, 1948, pg. 1.

10. See further, Efraim Orni and Elisha Efrat, *Geography of Israel*. Jerusalem: Israel Universities Press, 1976, pg. 336; Karl Baedekers, *Baedekers Israel*. Englewood Cliffs, N.J.: Prentice Hall, no date, "Tel Aviv-Jaffa," pp. 227-231; A. Lewensohn, *Massada Guide to Israel*. Israel: Massada Ltd. Publishers, 1985, "Tel Aviv-Jaffa," pp. 480ff; and *The Encyclopaedia Judaica*. New York: The Macmillan Company, Vol. 15, "Tel Aviv," pp. 916ff.

11. David K. Shipler, *Arab and Jew: Wounded Spirits in a Promised Land*. New York: Viking Penguin, 1987, pg. 428.

12. Ibid., pg. 429.

13. Some other of the helpful reference works surveyed include *Politics in Palestine 1939-1948* by Issa Khalif; *My Life* by Golda Meir; *The Siege* by Conner Cruise O'Brien; and *Biographical Dictionary of the Middle East*.

14. See further, James McDonald, *My Mission To Israel 1948-1951*. New York: Simon and Schuster, 1951.

15. See further, Conner Cruise O'Brien, *The Siege: The Saga of Israel and Zionism*. New York: Simon and Schuster, 1987, pp. 424-434, and Dan Kurzman, *Genesis 1948: The First Arab-Israeli War*. New York: New American Library, 1992, pp. 6, 31-37.

16. Neil Tilbury, *Israel: A Travel Survival Kit*. Oakland, Calif.: Lonely Planet

Publications, 1993, pg. 228.

17. A.P. Anthony, *The 1936 Year Book and Almanac of the Holy Land.* Chicago: Holy Land Almanac, Inc., 1936, pg. 123.

18. Shabtai Teveth, *Ben Gurion and the Palestinian Arabs.* New York: Oxford University Press, 1985, pp. 174-175.

19. Tom Segev, *1949: The First Israelis.* New York: The Free Press, 1986, pg. 75.

20. Issa Khalif, *Politics in Palestine: Arab Factionism and Social Disintegration 1939-1948.* Albany, N.Y.: State University of New York Press, 1991, pp. 67, 99.

21. *Good Morning, Holy Spirit,* op. cit., pp. 19-20.

22. See further, Joan Peters, *From Time Immemorial.* New York: Harper Collins Publishers, Inc., 1985.

23. *Good Morning, Holy Spirit,* op. cit., pg. 20.

24. Ibid., pp. 18, 37.

25. Benny Hinn, *Praise the Lord* show, Trinity Broadcasting Network, Oct. 23, 1992, video tape on file.

26. Benny Hinn, *Good Morning, Holy Spirit,* draft manuscript submitted to Thomas Nelson Publishers, ca. Sept. 1989, pg. 23.

27. *Good Morning, Holy Spirit,* op. cit., pg. 20.

28. Additional documents which claim to validate Costandi Hinn's political status in Tel Aviv-Jaffa were promised to the authors by Christopher Hinn during an Oct. 7, 1992 phone conversation. These additional documents have never been received.

29. Interview by Stephen Strang, "Benny Hinn Speaks Out," *Charisma & Christian Life,* August 1993, pg. 26.

30. Letter from Stephen Strang to M. Kurt Goedelman, Oct. 12, 1993.

31. Benny Hinn, *He Touched Me.* Nashville: Thomas Nelson Publishers, 1999, pg. 4.

32. Ibid., pg. 8.

33. Ibid., pg. 9.

34. Ibid.

35. Ibid., pg. 14.

36. Ibid., pg. 18.

37. Ibid., pg. 45.

38. Ibid., pg. 4; see also pg. 15.

39. Ibid., pg. 40.

40. Ibid., pg. 18.

41. Ibid., pg. 42.

42. Ibid.

43. See further, Fouad Ajami, *The Dream Palace of the Arabs.* New York: Vintage Books, 1998, pp. 74-75.

44. *He Touched Me,* op. cit., pg. 13.

45. *Good Morning, Holy Spirit,* op. cit., pg. 20.

46. *He Touched Me,* op. cit., pg. 13.

47. Ibid., pg. 14.

Chapter 6

1. Benny Hinn, "Double Portion Anointing," Orlando Christian Center sermon, April 7, 1991, VT#309, video tape on file.
2. Benny Hinn, *Praise the Lord* show, Trinity Broadcasting Network, Nov. 9, 1990, video tape on file.
3. Ibid.
4. There is scriptural precedence for publicly naming those who publicly teach contrary to Scripture. The Apostle Paul gave us the names of those who were causing both himself and the church great problems through false doctrine: "This charge I commit unto thee, son Timothy, according to the prophecies which went before on thee, that thou by them mightest war a good warfare; Holding faith, and a good conscience; which some having put away concerning faith have made shipwreck: Of whom is Hymenaeus and Alexander; whom I have delivered unto Satan, that they may learn not to blaspheme" (1 Timothy 1:18-20); "But shun profane and vain babblings: for they will increase unto more ungodliness. And their word will eat as doth a canker: of whom is Hymenaeus and Philetus; Who concerning the truth have erred, saying that the resurrection is past already; and overthrow the faith of some" (2 Timothy 2:16-18); and "Alexander the coppersmith did me much evil: the Lord reward him according to his works: Of whom be thou ware also; for he hath greatly withstood our words" (2 Timothy 4:14-15).
5. Benny Hinn, *Miracle Invasion*, daily television broadcast for Oct. 25, 1990.
6. Benny Hinn, Melodyland Christian Center, "World Charismatic Conference," Aug. 7, 1992, audio tape of cited statements on file.
7. Paul Crouch, *Praise the Lord* show, Trinity Broadcasting Network, Oct. 23, 1992, video tape on file.
8. Benny Hinn, *Praise the Lord* show, Trinity Broadcasting Network, Oct. 23, 1992, video tape on file.
9. Orlando Christian Center, Aug. 12, 1992. Wednesday evening service attended by Personal Freedom Outreach directors Paul R. Blizard and M. Kurt Goedelman.
10. Oct. 7, 1992 phone conversation between PFO directors G. Richard Fisher and M. Kurt Goedelman, and Benny Hinn Ministry representatives Christopher Hinn and Attorney Stephen W. Beik. The call was in response to charges made by PFO challenging the historical accuracy of Benny Hinn's claims in his publications and cassette tapes.
11. Benny Hinn, Orlando Christian Center sermon, "The Apple of God's Eye," Aug. 12, 1992, #T081292, audio tape on file.
12. Benny Hinn, *Praise the Lord* show, Trinity Broadcasting Network, Sept. 10, 1999, video tape on file.
13. Ibid.
14. Ibid.
15. Ibid.
16. Benny Hinn, *Our Position In Christ*, six tape audio cassette series, "Our Position In Christ," Part 1, Tape #A031190-1.

17. Ibid.

18. Marc Galanter, *Cults: Faith, Healing, and Coercion.* New York: Oxford University Press, 1989, pp. 6-7.

19. Stanley M. Burgess, Gary B. McGee, and Patrick H. Alexander, editors, *The Dictionary of Pentecostal and Charismatic Movements.* Grand Rapids: Zondervan Publishing House, 1988, pg. 789.

20. Flo Conway and Jim Siegelman, *Snapping.* Philadelphia: J.B. Lippincott Company, 1978, pp. 51-52, expletives deleted, italics in original.

21. Benny Hinn, *The Anointing.* Nashville: Thomas Nelson Publishers, 1992, pg. 177.

22. Mike Thomas, *Florida Magazine*, "The Power and The Glory," Nov. 24, 1991, pp. 8, 11.

23. John Camp, "The Miracles and the Money," *CNN/Time Impact*, March 16, 1997, video tape on file.

24. John Iwasaki, "Benny Hinn offers 'miracles'," *Seattle Post-Intelligencer*, Aug. 22, 1997, pg. C1.

25. Jeffrey Weiss, "Evangelist Hinn shares plans for healing center," *The Dallas Morning News*, Oct. 30, 1999, pg. 31A.

Chapter 7

1. Randy Frame, "Best-selling Author Admits Mistakes, Vows Changes," *Christianity Today*, Oct. 28, 1991, pp. 44, 46, and "Same Old Benny Hinn, Critics Say," Oct. 5, 1992, pp. 52-54; "Hinn Answers Critics, Evangelist vows to make reforms after CBS investigation," *Charisma*, May 1993, pg. 69; Paul Galloway, "Turnabout, Benny Hinn repents," *Chicago Tribune*, June 27, 1993, Tempo section, pp. 1, 7; and James D. Davis, "The Reformation of Benny Hinn," (Orlando) *Sun-Sentinel*, Aug. 22, 1993, pp. 1E, 4E are some examples.

2. The video, *The Many Faces of Benny Hinn*, is produced by *The Door Magazine* and the Trinity Foundation in Dallas. The Trinity Foundation is an organization with a national hotline to assist victims of televangelist abuse. It also assists the media with investigations of fraud and abuse by televangelists like Benny Hinn, Robert Tilton, and others. The video is available from Personal Freedom Outreach (PFO) in Saint Louis.

3. The first edition of this book was published in 1994. Prior to its initial publication, early research material and conclusions were published in *The Quarterly Journal*, the newsletter publication of PFO. Further research about Hinn was also published in the *Journal*, prior to being included in subsequent editions of this book.

4. Benny Hinn, "Special Message to Believers," Orlando Christian Center sermon, May 30, 1993, video tape on file.

5. Ibid.

6. Ibid.

7. Ole Anthony, "A tale of two televangelists," *The Dallas Morning News*, March 8, 1993.

8. "Turnabout, Benny Hinn repents," op. cit.

9. Interview by Stephen Strang, "Benny Hinn Speaks Out," *Charisma*, August 1993, pp. 22-29.

10. Benny Hinn, sermon on Ezekiel (no title available), Orlando Christian Center, ca. June 1987, audio tape on file.

11. "Benny Hinn Speaks Out," op. cit., pg. 24.

12. Benny Hinn, "God's Super Being," Orlando Christian Center broadcast, Trinity Broadcasting Network, Oct. 20, 1990, video tape on file.

13. "Benny Hinn Speaks Out," op. cit., pg. 25.

14. Benny Hinn, "A New Spirit," Orlando Christian Center broadcast, Trinity Broadcasting Network, Oct. 13, 1990, video tape on file.

15. Benny Hinn, Orlando Christian Center sermon, June 21, 1987, audio tape on file.

16. Benny Hinn, "Our Position in Christ," six tape audio cassette series, *Our Position in Christ*, Part 1, Tape #A031190-1.

17. Benny Hinn, "Praise-A-Thon," Trinity Broadcasting Network, Nov. 9, 1990, video tape on file.

18. Ibid.

19. "Best-selling Author Admits Mistakes, Vows Changes," op. cit., pg. 44.

20. Ibid.

21. Audio tape made of a Sept. 3, 1991, three-way telephone interview involving Randy Frame, J. Rodman Williams, and Benny Hinn in preparation for Frame's article which appeared in the Oct. 28, 1991 issue of *Christianity Today*, "Best-selling Author Admits Mistakes, Vows Changes," pp. 44-45. Transcript of tape on file.

22. "Same Old Benny Hinn, Critics Say," op. cit., pg. 53.

23. "Benny Hinn Speaks Out," op. cit., pg. 28.

24. Benny Hinn, "Praise-A-Thon," Trinity Broadcasting Network, Nov. 2, 1999, video tape on file.

25. *Inside Edition*, March 2, 1993, report produced by Steve Wilson and Charles Delaklis, video tape on file.

26. Benny Hinn, *Praise the Lord* show, Trinity Broadcasting Network, March 4, 1993, video tape on file.

27. "Turnabout, Benny Hinn repents," op. cit., pp. 1, 7.

28. The Kansas City Miracle Crusade, July 16, 1993, was personally attended by author M. Kurt Goedelman.

29. Advertisement in *Celebrate Jesus* magazine, Benny Hinn Media Ministries, Vol. 3, No. 2, pg. 9.

30. "Benny Hinn Speaks Out," op. cit.

31. Ibid., pg. 25.

32. Ibid.

33. "Special Message to Believers," op. cit.

34. "Benny Hinn Speaks Out," op. cit., pg. 24, italic in original.

35. Benny Hinn, "Who is This Jesus?" recorded at San Antonio Miracle Crusade, March 1994, video tape on file.

36. Ralph Earle, editor, *Adam Clarke's Commentary on the Bible*. Grand Rapids: Baker Book House, 1967, pg. 126.

Chapter 8

1. "Benny Hinn Seeks Credentials with the Assemblies of God," *The Centralite*, Springfield, Mo.: Central Bible College, Vol. 48, No. 1, Sept. 9, 1994.
2. "Hinn is in," *The Centralite*, Vol. 48, No. 2, Sept. 29, 1994.
3. Ibid.
4. Benny Hinn, *1995 Signs and Wonders Conference*, Tape #95C52/761122, Michael Cardone Media Center. Video tape and transcript on file.
5. Benny Hinn, *The Anointing*. Nashville: Thomas Nelson Publishers, 1992, pg. 98.
6. *Signs and Wonders Conference*, op. cit., emphasis added.
7. Benny Hinn, *Good Morning, Holy Spirit*, draft manuscript submitted to Thomas Nelson Publishers, ca. Sept. 1989, pg. 109.
8. Benny Hinn, *Good Morning, Holy Spirit*. Nashville: Thomas Nelson Publishers, 1990, 1st Edition, pg. 86.
9. Benny Hinn, *Good Morning, Holy Spirit*. Nashville: Thomas Nelson Publishers, 1990, 8th Edition, pg. 86.
10. *Good Morning, Holy Spirit*, draft manuscript, op. cit., pg. 101.
11. *Good Morning, Holy Spirit*, 1st Edition, op. cit., pg. 81.
12. *Signs and Wonders Conference*, op. cit., emphasis added.
13. Benny Hinn, "A New Spirit," Orlando Christian Center broadcast, Trinity Broadcasting Network, Oct. 13, 1990, video tape on file.
14. Benny Hinn, *Praise the Lord* show, Trinity Broadcasting Network, Oct. 23, 1992, video tape on file.
15. Interview by Stephen Strang, "Benny Hinn Speaks Out," *Charisma* magazine, August 1993, pg. 25, emphasis added.
16. *Signs and Wonders Conference*, op. cit.
17. "People & Events, News Briefs...," *Charisma* magazine, May 1995, pg. 74.
18. *Signs and Wonders Conference*, op. cit.
19. Ibid.
20. Larry Thomas, *The Inkhorn*. Excelsior Springs, Mo.: Amazing Grace Ministries, Vol. 8, No. 1, January 1997, pg. 46.
21. For a critical analysis of the "Pensacola Revival," see further, G. Richard Fisher and M. Kurt Goedelman, "The Murky River of Brownsville — The Strange Doctrine and Practice of the Pensacola Revival," *The Quarterly Journal*, Vol. 17, No. 2, pp. 1, 12-22.

Chapter 9

1. P.J. Kavanagh, *A G.K. Chesterton Anthology*. San Francisco: Ignatius Press, 1986, pg. 282.
2. Jane Watrel, "Whistle Blower" segment, WFTV-Channel 9, Orlando, Fla., June 27, 1996, video tape on file.
3. Ibid.
4. Ibid.

5. Ibid.

6. Ibid.

7. Ibid.

8. Jane Watrel, "Whistle Blower" segment, WFTV-Channel 9, Orlando, Fla., December 18, 1996, video tape on file.

9. Jane Watrel, "Whistle Blower" segment interview with Benny Hinn, WFTV-Channel 9, Orlando, Fla., December 1996 (exact date of broadcast unknown), Orlando, Fla., video tape on file.

10. Henry Pierson Curtis, "Hinn's foes to settle suit with sheriff in Orange," *The Orlando Sentinel*, Nov. 20, 1998.

11. Ibid.

12. Ricky L. Johnston, "Nine Judas'." A one-page document dated Nov. 3, 1998 and filed with the "Mediation Settlement Agreement" from the United States District Court, Middle District of Florida, Orlando Division," copy on file.

13. Henry Pierson Curtis and Mark Pinsky, "Nightmare of heroin hits Hinn ministry," *The Orlando Sentinel*, Dec. 2, 1998.

14. Ibid.

15. Ibid.

16. Ibid.

17. Benny Hinn, *He Touched Me*. Nashville: Thomas Nelson Publishers, 1999, pg. 169.

18. Ibid.

19. "Nightmare of heroin hits Hinn ministry," op. cit.

20. Benny Hinn Miracle Crusade highlights, Trinity Broadcasting Network, date unknown, tape on file, emphasis added.

21. Henry Pierson Curtis, "Benny Hinn tries to keep ex-aide quiet," *The Orlando Sentinel*, Dec. 9, 1998.

22. Ibid.

23. Ibid.

24. Henry Pierson Curtis, "Hinn church at odds with lawyers," *The Orlando Sentinel*, Dec. 11, 1998.

25. Ibid.

26. Comedy Central, *The Daily Show*, "God Stuff" segment for June 21, 1999, video tape on file.

27. Benny Hinn, *Praise the Lord* show, Trinity Broadcasting Network, May 12, 1999, video tape on file.

28. Patrick Johnstone, *Operation World*. Seattle: Youth With a Mission, 1993, pp. 438-441. See also *The NIV Study Bible*, Map 12: Christianity in the World Today, which indicates the Christian population of Papua New Guinea in 1982 as "Over 90%."

29. *Praise the Lord* show, May 12, 1999, op. cit.

30. "Hinn's crusade gets Catholic rebuff," *Post-Courier* (Papua New Guinea), April 29, 1999.

31. See further, G. Richard Fisher, "Words of Knowledge: Mystical or Statistical? — The Truth Behind the Sham," *The Quarterly Journal*, January-March 1994, pp. 4, 12-13.

32. Peter Symonds, "Australian connection in PNG corruption scandal," Workers News Online, International News, December 17, 1997 - January 28, 1998. Available online at: **http://www.sep.flex.com.au/wn/wn171297/png.html**.

33. *Praise the Lord* show, May 12, 1999, op. cit.

34. "Bishop: Government must go," *Post-Courier*, Jan. 4, 1999.

35. Benny Hinn Ministries web site, "Papua New Guinea Crusade exceeds all expectations," **http://www.bennyhinn.org/pngnews.asp**.

36. Personal correspondence from a Pacific news reporter to authors, 14 July 1999. Quoted by permission.

37. Ibid.

38. "Call for PNG not to grant US televangelist broadcast license," *Pacific Islands Report*, radio news item, June 4, 1999.

39. Ibid.

40. Steve McGonigle, "What happened to Hinn's promised healing center?", *The Dallas Morning News*, June 23, 2002.

41. Ibid.

42. Ibid.

43. Ibid.

44. Ibid.

Chapter 10

1. Mike Thomas, "The Power and The Glory," *Florida Magazine*, Nov. 24, 1991, pp. 10, 12.

2. *National & International Religion Report*, Sept. 21, 1987.

3. "The Power and The Glory," op. cit., pg. 13.

4. People & Events, "Hinn Faces Suit After Woman Dies," *Charisma & Christian Life*, January 1988, pp. 54-55.

5. Benny Hinn, December 1992, "Houston Miracle Crusade" segment shown on *Inside Edition*, March 2, 1993, report produced by Steve Wilson and Charles Delaklis, video tape on file.

6. *Inside Edition*, op. cit.

7. Benny Hinn, *Praise the Lord* show, Trinity Broadcasting Network, March 3, 1994, video tape on file.

8. Ibid.

9. Benny Hinn, Signs & Wonders Conference, General Session, March 9, 1995. Video tape #95SWC52, video tape on file.

10. Benny Hinn, *Welcome, Holy Spirit*. Nashville: Thomas Nelson Publishers, 1995, pg. 50, italics in original.

11. *Inside Edition*, July 28, 1994, video tape on file.

12. Ibid.

13. Charles B. Clayman, *The American Medical Association Home Medical Encyclopedia*. New York: Random House Publishers, 1989, pg. 871.

14. David N. Holvey, editor, *The Merck Manual of Diagnosis and Therapy*. Rahway, N.J.: Merck and Co., 1972, see pp. 1215-1218.

15. Doctors Kate Lorig and James F. Fries, *The Arthritis Helpbook*. Reading,

Mass.: Addison-Wesley Publishing Co., 1990, pg. 226.

16. Dana Sobel and Arthur Klein, *Arthritis: What Works*. New York: St. Martin's Press, 1992, pg. 181.

17. Hank Hanegraaff, *Christianity in Crisis*. Eugene, Ore.: Harvest House Publishers, 1993, pg. 341.

18. Ibid.

19. *Udfordringen*, 15 September 1994, Side 2. Translated from Danish by Suresh Jeyasingham for PFO.

20. *Welcome, Holy Spirit*, op. cit., pg. 230.

21. Ibid., pg. 231.

22. Ibid.

23. Ibid.

24. Ibid.

25. Ibid., 233-234.

26. Ibid., pg. 234.

27. Ibid.

28. Ibid., pg. 235.

29. Fax copy of May 19, 1995 letter on file.

30. Richard Mayhue, *The Healing Promise*. Eugene, Ore.: Harvest House Publishers, 1994, pp. 59-60.

31. John Camp, "The Miracles and the Money," *CNN/Time Impact*, March 16, 1997, video tape on file.

32. Ibid.

33. Ibid.

34. "Four Die Waiting for 'Miracle' Cures," Reuters News Service, May 4, 2000.

35. Ibid.

36. "Sick baby dies at Benny Hinn crusade," *Daily Nation News*, May 2, 2000.

37. "Four Die Waiting for 'Miracle' Cures," op. cit.

38. "Did Jesus Christ come to Nairobi?" *Kenya Times*, June 22, 1988.

39. Ibid.

40. Personal correspondence from *Daily Nation News* reporter Tom Nyongesa, May 15, 2000.

41. Mark O'Keefe, "Debate continues whether faith healers perform miracles — or just perform," *The Grand Rapids Press*, Sept. 21, 1996, pg. B1.

42. Quentin Schultze, *Televangelism and American Culture*. Grand Rapids: Baker Book House, 1991, pp. 69-95.

Chapter 11

1. "Heart Condition Forces Holyfield Into Retirement," *St. Louis Post-Dispatch*, April 27, 1994, pg. 1D.

2. Evander Holyfield, *Praise the Lord* show, Trinity Broadcasting Network, June 16, 1994, video tape on file.

3. Ralph Cipriano, "Former champ has faith God has healed his heart," *Philadelphia Inquirer*, June 12, 1994, pg. B1.

4. *Praise the Lord* show, June 16, 1994, op. cit.

5. Matt Winkeljohn, "Holyfield pleased, but comeback talk premature," *Atlanta Journal-Constitution*, June 17, 1994, pg. D16.

6. Wayne A. Robinson, *Oral: The Warm, Intimate Unauthorized Portrait of a Man of God*. Los Angeles: Action House Publishers, 1976, pg. 4, italics in original.

7. Ibid., pg. 9.

8. Matt Winkeljohn, "Holyfield decision: 'I'm going to fight,'" *Journal-Atlanta Constitution*, June 21, 1994, pg. D1.

9. Benny Hinn, *Praise the Lord* show, Trinity Broadcasting Network, Dec. 6, 1994, video tape on file.

10. Jeff Schultz, "Holyfield's doctor says 'stiff heart' was judgment call," *Atlanta Journal-Constitution*, Dec. 3, 1994, pg. C2.

11. Jeff Schultz, "Misdiagnosis linked to post-fight drugs," *Atlanta Journal-Constitution*, Dec. 28, 1994, pg. G1.

12. Jeff Schultz, "Thankful Holyfield holding no grudges," *Atlanta Journal-Constitution*, Nov. 25, 1994, pg. D3.

13. Jeff Schultz, "Nevada OK certain for Holyfield return," *Atlanta Journal-Constitution*, Dec. 27, 1994, pg. D3.

14. Terrence Moore, "Healthy or not, Holyfield should hang up gloves for good," *Atlanta Journal-Constitution*, Jan 8, 1995, pg. F3.

15. "Thankful Holyfield holding no grudges," op. cit.

16. Ralph Ellis, "Holyfield paternity suit settled," *Atlanta Journal-Constitution*, Oct. 22, 1998.

17. William Plummer and Krista Reese, "'I thank the Lord for using me as his vessel,'" *People*, Dec. 2, 1996, pg. 54.

18. Jeff Schultz, "Holyfield's toughest foe is infidelity," *Atlanta Journal-Constitution*, Sept. 22, 1998.

19. Ralph Ellis, "Holyfields agree to settle; pastor off the hook with judge," *Atlanta Journal-Constitution*, March 11, 2000.

20. Ibid.

21. News Service Briefs: "Judge says no jail time for Creflo Dollar," *Charisma*, May 2000, pg. 50.

22. Benny Hinn, *Praise the Lord* show, Trinity Broadcasting Network, Aug. 9, 1994, video tape on file.

23. Ibid.

24. Ibid.

25. Benny Hinn, *He Touched Me*. Nashville: Thomas Nelson Publishers, 1999, statement found on the rear dust cover.

26. Ben Vereen, *The Suzanne Somers Show*, July 29, 1994, video tape on file.

27. Ibid.

28. Ibid.

29. See further, John P. Juedes, "Mail Order Christianity — Is a Word from Unity a Word from God?" *Personal Freedom Outreach Newsletter*, January-March 1987, pp. 4-6.

30. J. Gordon Melton, editor, *The Encyclopedia of American Religions*. Tarrytown, N.Y.: Triumph Books, 1991, Vol. 2, pg. 259.

31. Ibid.

32. *Praise the Lord* show, Aug. 9, 1994, op. cit.

33. See further, G. Richard Fisher, "The Life and Time of Golden Girl and Globetrotter Ruth Ward Heflin," *The Quarterly Journal*, January-March 2001, pp. 5-11.

34. Benny Hinn, *This Is Your Day*, March 29, 2000, video tape on file.

35. Henry Gordon, "Faith healer's empty miracles," *The Toronto Star*, Oct. 3, 1992, pg. J14.

Chapter 12

1. Audio tape made of a Sept. 3, 1991, three-way telephone interview involving Randy Frame, J. Rodman Williams, and Benny Hinn in preparation for Frame's article which appeared in the Oct. 28, 1991 issue of *Christianity Today*, "Best-selling Author Admits Mistakes, Vows Changes," pp. 44-45. Transcript of tape on file.

2. Benny Hinn, "Because of Christ's Blood," *Charisma*, November 1993, pg. 34.

3. Benny Hinn, *The Blood*. Orlando: Creation House, 1993, pp. 22-23.

4. Ibid., pg. 69.

5. Ibid., pg. 73.

6. Ibid., pg. 57.

7. Ibid., pg. 73.

8. Ibid., pg. 65.

9. Ibid., pg. 67.

10. Ibid., pg. 68.

11. Ibid., pg. 71.

12. Ibid., pp. 71-72.

13. "Because of Christ's Blood," op. cit., pg. 39.

14. *The Blood*, op. cit., pp. 23-24.

15. Philip Schaff, *History of the Christian Church*. Grand Rapids: Wm. B. Eerdmans Publishing Co., 1907, Vol. 5, pg. 847.

16. Louis Bourdaloue in Grenville Kleiser, *The World's Great Sermons*. New York: Funk and Wagnalls, 1908, Vol. 2, pp. 198-199.

17. Benjamin B. Warfield, *Counterfeit Miracles*. Edinburgh, England: The Banner of Truth Trust, 1918, pp. 96-97.

18. Alan Richardson and John S. Bowden, *The Westminster Dictionary of Christian Theology*. Philadelphia: Westminister Press, 1983, pg. 460.

19. Arnold A. Dallimore, *George Whitefield*. Westchester, Ill.: Cornerstone Books, 1980, Vol. 2, pp. 327.

20. Ibid., pg. 326, ellipsis in original.

21. Ibid.

22. Essek W. Kenyon, *New Creation Realities*. Lynnwood, Wash.: Kenyon's Gospel Publishing Society, 1945, pg. 44.

23. Ibid., pg. 129.

24. Ibid., pg. 131.

25. M.R. DeHaan, *The Chemistry of the Blood*. Grand Rapids: Zondervan Publishing Co., 1943, pg. 28.

26. H.A. Maxwell Whyte, *The Power of the Blood*. Springdale, Pa.: Whitaker

House, 1973, pg. 18.

27. Ibid., pg. 64.

28. Ibid., pp. 39-40.

29. Ibid., pg. 53.

30. Ibid., pg. 54.

31. Ibid., pg. 87.

32. Ibid.

33. "Because of Christ's Blood," op. cit., pg. 39, and *The Blood*, op. cit., pp. 21-22.

34. *The Blood*, op. cit., pp. 82-83.

35. Millard Erickson, *Introducing Christian Doctrine*. Grand Rapids: Baker Book House, 1992, pg. 250.

36. Joseph Thayer, *A Greek-English Lexicon of the New Testament*. New York: American Book Company, 1886, pg. 15.

37. Merrill C. Tenney, editor, *The Zondervan Pictorial Encyclopedia of the Bible*. Grand Rapids: Zondervan Publishing House, 1975, Vol. 1, pp. 626-627.

38. J.C. Macaulay, *Expository Commentary on Hebrews*. Chicago: Moody Press, 1978, pg. 129.

39. Everett F. Harrison, editor, *Baker's Dictionary of Theology*, Grand Rapids: Baker Book House, 1960, pg. 100.

40. *The Westminster Dictionary of Christian Theology*, op. cit., pg. 76.

41. J.D. Douglas, editor, *The New Bible Dictionary*. Grand Rapids: Wm. B. Eerdmans Publishing Co., 1962, pg. 160.

42. Trent C. Butler, editor, *Holman Bible Dictionary*. Nashville: Holman Bible Publishers, 1991, pg. 201.

43. See further, Bob Banner, editor, *Critique, A Journal of Conspiracies and Metaphysics*. Santa Rosa, Calif.: The Critique Foundation, Issue 7-E, Spring/Summer 1982, pg. 71.

44. Arthur Custance, *The Seed of the Woman*. Brockville, Ontario: Doorway Publications, 1980, pp. 444-452.

45. Oral Roberts and Benny Hinn, *Miracles Yesterday, Today & Forever!* Gener8Xion Entertainment, Inc., 1994, two-video tape set. Trinity Broadcasting Network also distributed a one-hour "Special TBN Edition" of the presentation as a donation gift to its supporters.

46. See also 1 Peter 2:5; Hebrews 4:14-16; 13:15-16; Revelation 1:6; 5:10 and 20:6.

47. Albert Barnes, *Barnes' Notes on the New Testament*. Grand Rapids: Kregel Publications, 1966, pg. 1406, italics in original.

48. Gerhardt Kittel, *Theological Dictionary of the New Testament*. Grand Rapids: Wm. B. Eerdmans Publishing Co., 1972, Vol. 3, pg. 250.

49. B.K. Kuiper, *The Church in History*. Grand Rapids: Wm. B. Eerdmans Publishing Co., 1964, pg. 167.

50. Daniel G. Reid, Robert D. Linder, Bruce L. Shelley, and Harry S. Stout, editors, *The Dictionary of Christianity in America*. Downers Grove, Ill.: InterVarsity Press, 1990, pg. 939.

51. Ibid.

52. Tim Dowley, editor, *Eerdmans' Handbook to the History of Christianity*.

Grand Rapids: Wm. B. Eerdmans Publishing Co., 1977, pg. 373.

53. W.E. Vine, *The Expanded Vine's Expository Dictionary of New Testament Words*. Minneapolis: Bethany House Publishers, 1984, pg. 13.

54. Henry Gariepy, *100 Portraits of Christ*. Wheaton, Ill.: Victor Books, 1993, pg. 183.

55. Jack Hayford, Foreword, *The Blood*, op. cit., pg. 12.

56. Evander Holyfield, *Praise the Lord* show, Trinity Broadcasting Network, June 16, 1994, video tape on file.

57. See further, G. Richard Fisher, "Words of Knowledge — Mystical Or Statistical, The Truth Behind the Sham," *The Quarterly Journal*, January-March 1994, pp. 4, 12-13.

58. See David E. Harrell, Jr., *Oral Roberts — An American Life*. San Francisco: Harper and Row Publishers, 1985.

59. *Miracles Yesterday, Today & Forever!* op. cit.

60. *Oral Roberts*, op. cit., pg. 51.

61. See further, Stephen F. Cannon, "A Prophet Sent From God? Examining the Life and Claims of William M. Branham," *The Quarterly Journal*, October-December 1988, pp. 1, 8-9.

62. *Oral Roberts*, op. cit., pg. 150.

63. Ibid., pg. 230.

64. Ibid., pg. 291.

65. Ibid., pg. 424.

66. Ibid., pg. 353.

67. Ibid., pg. 427.

68. Ibid.

69. See further, M. Kurt Goedelman and G. Richard Fisher, "The Latter Rain Movement — Showering Heresy on the Church for Nearly Fifty Years," *The Quarterly Journal*, April-June 1995, pp. 4, 10-12, and J. Gordon Melton, *The Encyclopedia of American Religions*. Tarrytown, N.Y.: Triumph Books, 1991, Vol. 1, pp. 46-47.

70. Dr. W.E. Nunnally, letter to Thomas Trask, July 1994, pg. 2, copy on file.

71. Lewis Sperry Chafer, *Systematic Theology*. Dallas: Dallas Seminary Press, 1948, Vol. 7, pg. 257.

72. Loraine Boettner, *Studies in Theology*. Phillipsburg, N.J.: The Presbyterian & Reformed Publishing Company, 1947, pg. 246.

73. See, for example, Benny Hinn, *Praise the Lord* show, Trinity Broadcasting Network, May 12, 1999 and July 25, 2000. Video tapes on file. The July 25, 2000 program has been rebroadcast numerous times on TBN.

74. Finis Dake, *Dake Annotated Study Bible*. Lawrenceville, Ga.: Dake Bible Sales, 1963, pp. 1, 54.

75. *Praise the Lord* show, May 12, 1999, op. cit.

76. See further, Weston W. Fields, *Unformed and Unfilled — The Gap Theory*. Phillipsburg, N.J.: Presbyterian and Reformed Publishers, 1978, pp. 5-47.

77. John Davis, *Paradise to Prison — Studies in Genesis*. Grand Rapids: Baker Book House, 1982, pg. 44.

78. *Unformed and Unfilled*, op. cit., pg. 45.

79. Bernard Ramm, *The Christian View of Science and the Scriptures*. London: Paternoster Press, 1965, pp. 134-135.

80. *Unformed and Unfilled*, op. cit., pp. 221-222.

81. Ibid., pg. 222.

82. Henry Morris, *Studies in the Bible and Science*. Philadelphia: Presbyterian and Reformed Publishing, 1966, pp. 31-33.

83. See W.E. Vine, *Vine's Complete Expository Dictionary of Old and New Testament Words*. Nashville: Thomas Nelson Publishers, 1985, pp. 51-52.

84. *Paradise to Prison — Studies in Genesis*, op. cit., pg. 44.

85. *Unformed and Unfilled*, op. cit., pg. 112.

86. C.F. Keil and F. Delitzsch, *Commentary on the Old Testament*. Grand Rapids: William B. Eerdmans Publishing Company, 1985, Vol. 1, pp. 48-49.

87. *Paradise to Prison — Studies in Genesis*, op. cit., pg. 45.

88. Ibid., pg. 46.

89. Benny Hinn, *War in the Heavenlies*. Winter Park, Fla.: Benny Hinn Ministries, 1984, pg. ii.

90. Ibid., pp. 16-17.

91. Kurt Koch, *Occult ABC*. Grand Rapids: Kregel Publications, 1993, pg. 222.

92. Craig Hawkins, *Witchcraft*. Grand Rapids: Baker Book House, 1996, pg. 75, emphasis added.

93. See, for example, *The Ryrie Study Bible*, New Testament, 1978, Revelation 1:10, pg. 1895.

94. John Walvoord, *The Revelation of Jesus Christ*. Chicago: Moody Press, 1966, pg. 42.

95. Gerhard Kittel, *Theological Dictionary of New Testament Words*. Grand Rapids: Eerdman Publishing Co., 1968, Vol. 6, pg. 449.

96. William Henrikson, *More Than Conquerors*. Grand Rapids: Baker Book House, 1983, pp. 55-56.

97. Alexander Maclaren, *Expositions of Holy Scripture*. Grand Rapids: Baker Book House, 1984, pg. 145.

98. See further, Leonard George, *Alternative Realities*. New York: Facts On File, 1995, pp. 204-208.

Chapter 13

1. Benny Hinn, *This Is Your Day*, Trinity Broadcasting Network, June 11, 1997, video tape on file.

2. Ibid.

3. Ibid.

4. Benny Hinn, Honolulu Crusade, February 28, 1997. Transcript of Hinn's comments made by Mike Oppenheimer, Let Us Reason Ministries. Audio tape and transcript on file.

5. Ibid., emphasis added.

6. Ibid.

7. Ibid.

8. Ibid.

9. Phone call from M. Kurt Goedelman to Benny Hinn Media Ministries, July 25, 1997, confirmed that Hinn's organization is not making available, nor will be making available, tapes from the 1997 Honolulu Crusade.

10. See Hank Hanegraaff, *Counterfeit Revival*. Dallas: Word Publishing, 1997, pp. 168-169.

11. Benny Hinn sermon, *Double Portion Anointing*, Part #3, Orlando Christian Center, Orlando, Fla., April 7, 1991. From the series, *Holy Ghost Invasion*. TV#309, tape on file.

12. Israel Pocket Library, *Religious Life and Communities*. Jerusalem: Keter Books, 1974, pg. 154.

13. Leonard George, Ph.D., *Alternative Realities*. New York: Facts on File, 1995, pg. 55.

14. Adam Clarke, *The Holy Bible with a Commentary and Critical Notes*. New York: Abingdon Press, no date, The Old Testament, Vol. 2, pg. 525, commentary note on 2 Kings 13:21, italics in original.

15. See further, *The Zondervan Pictorial Encyclopedia of the Bible*, Vol. 4, pg. 401, and *Biblical Demonology* by Merrill Unger, pp. 143-164.

16. Henry A. Ironside, *Expository Notes on the Prophet Isaiah*. New York: Loizeaux Brothers, 1952, pp. 55-56.

17. See, for example, Leviticus 19:31; 20:6, 27; Deuteronomy 18:10-11.

18. J.R. Dummelow, *A Commentary on the Holy Bible*. New York: Macmillan Company, 1958, pg. 97.

19. Merrill Unger, *Biblical Demonology*. Wheaton, Ill.: Scripture Press, 1952, pg. 148.

20. Ibid., pg. 152.

21. W.E. Vine, *Vine's Complete Expository Dictionary Of Old And New Testament Words*. Nashville: Thomas Nelson Publishers, 1985, pp. 241-242.

22. Ibid., pg. 242.

23. J.D. Douglas, editor, *New 20th-Century Encyclopedia of Religious Knowledge*. Grand Rapids: Baker Book House, 1991, pg. 782.

24. Alan Morrison, *The Serpent and the Cross*. Birmingham, England: K&M Books, 1994, pg. 142.

25. Frank S. Mead, *Handbook of Denominations in the United States*. New York: Abingdon Press, 1965, pg. 206.

26. J. Stafford Wright, *Man in the Process of Time*. Grand Rapids: Wm. B. Eerdmans Publishing Company, 1956, pp. 107, 109-110, italics in original.

27. *Counterfeit Revival*, op. cit., pp. 127-128.

28. Benny Hinn, *Larry King Live*, CNN, April 23, 1998, video tape on file.

29. Ibid.

30. Ibid.

31. Felician A. Foy, editor, *1983 Catholic Almanac*. Huntington, Ind.: Our Sunday Visitor, Inc., 1983, pg. 288.

32. Ibid.

33. Ibid.

34. Ibid., pg. 289.

Chapter 14

1. Stephen F. Cannon, "A Prophet Sent from God? Examining the Life and Claims of William M. Branham," *The Quarterly Journal*, October-December 1988, pg. 9.

2. Steven Lawson, "What Hollywood Forgot to Show," *Charisma and Christian Life*, April 1990, pg. 66.

3. Ibid.

4. Ibid.

5. Benny Hinn, prophetic sermon (no title available), Dec. 31, 1989, Orlando Christian Center, audio tape on file.

6. Benny Hinn, *Praise the Lord* show, Trinity Broadcasting Network, June 11, 1996, tape on file.

7. Stephen Strang, "Boycott Disney?" *Charisma* magazine, August 1996, pg. 88.

8. A few months later, Hinn excited viewers of TBN's "Praise-A-Thon" when he proclaimed: "The Lord is really coming back, I'm telling you. I'm gonna prove to you from the Word tonight that we have less than two years. And I'm not saying I'm 100% sure, but that thing is getting so close it's scaring the life out of me and shaking my bones. Yes sir, there are scriptures to prove it" (Benny Hinn, "Praise-A-Thon," Nov. 9, 1990, video tape on file).

9. See Chapter 4, pp. 46, 48.

10. David Hagopian and Douglas Wilson, *Beyond Promises*. Moscow, Idaho: Canon Press, 1996, pg. 245.

11. Kurt Koch, *Occult ABC*. Grand Rapids: Kregel Publications, 1986, pg. 219.

12. Apparently the program has become a favorite of TBN or its viewing audience as it has replayed several times on TBN, including Jan. 7, 2000.

13. Merrill C. Tenney, editor, *The Zondervan Pictorial Encyclopedia of the Bible*. Grand Rapids: Zondervan Publishing House, 1975, Vol. 2, pg. 496.

Chapter 15

1. Benny Hinn, *Good Morning, Holy Spirit*. Nashville: Thomas Nelson Publishers, 1990, pp. 14-15, italics added.

2. For further reading on the history and nature of proper hermeneutics, see James Barr, *The Semantics of Biblical Language*. London: Oxford University Press, 1961; Gordon Fee and Douglas Stuart, *How to Read the Bible for All It's Worth: A Guide to Understanding the Bible*. Grand Rapids: Zondervan Publishing Co., 1993; D.A. Carson, *Exegetical Fallacies*. Grand Rapids: Baker Book House, 1984; Walter C. Kaiser, Jr., and Moisis Silva, *An Introduction to Biblical Hermeneutics: The Search for Meaning*. Grand Rapids: Zondervan Publishing Co., 1994; Grant Osborne, *The Hermeneutical Spiral: A Comprehensive Introduction to Biblical Interpretation*. Downers Grove, Ill.: InterVarsity Press, 1991; Moisis Silva, *Has the Church Misread the Bible?: The History of Interpretation in the Light of Current Issues*. Grand Rapids: Academie Books,

1987; Henry A. Virkler, *Hermeneutics: Principles and Processes of Biblical Interpretation*. Grand Rapids: Baker Book House, 1981.

3. David F. Wells, *No Place for Truth: Whatever Happened to Evangelical Theology?* Grand Rapids: Wm. B. Eerdmans Publishing Co., 1993, pp. 95-136.

4. Richard Mayhue, *The Healing Promise*. Eugene, Ore.: Harvest House Publishers, 1994, pp. 32-33. See his excellent overall critique of Hinn's ministry on pp. 32-35, and illusionist André Kole's analysis on pp. 42-61.

5. Benny Hinn, "Praise-A-Thon," Trinity Broadcasting Network, Nov. 6, 1990. See Endnote 31 of Chapter 2 for additional information concerning the original broadcast date of this fund raising sermon by Hinn.

6. Francis Brown, S.R. Driver, and Charles A. Briggs, *The New Brown - Driver - Briggs - Gesenius Hebrew and English Lexicon*. Lafayette, Ind.: Associated Publishers and Authors, 1980, pg. 172, henceforth referred to as BDB; William L. Holladay, *A Concise Hebrew and Aramaic Lexicon of the Old Testament*. Grand Rapids: Wm. B. Eerdmans Publishing Co., 1971, pg. 63, henceforth referred to as Holladay; Ludwig Koehler and Walter Baumgartner, *Lexicon In Veteris Testamenti Libros*. Leiden: E.J. Brill, 1958, pg. 191, henceforth referred to as K-B.

7. Benny Hinn, *The Blood*. Orlando: Creation House, 1993, pg. 19.

8. Abraham Even-Shoshan, *A New Concordance of the Bible*. Jerusalem: Kiryat Sepher Publishing House, 1982, pp. 241-242, henceforth referred to as E-S. My [Dr. Nunnally's] second-year Hebrew students are required to know all words in the Hebrew Bible which occur 25 times or more.

9. Reuben Alcalay, *The Complete Hebrew-English Dictionary*. Jerusalem: Massada Publishing Company, 1981, pg. 376, henceforth referred to as Alcalay.

10. E-S, op. cit., pg. 57.

11. BDB, op. cit., pp. 37-38; Holladay, op. cit., pg. 15; K-B, op. cit., pp. 43-44.

12. Cf. K-B, op. cit., pg. 969; BDB, op. cit., pp. 1013-1014; Holladay, op. cit., pg. 369.

13. Benny Hinn, Orlando Christian Center broadcast, Trinity Broadcasting Network, March 28, 1994, emphasis added, video tape on file. Taken from a sermon, "Who is this Jesus?" from the March 3-4, 1994, San Antonio Miracle Crusade.

14. Benny Hinn, *Praise the Lord* show, Trinity Broadcasting Network, July 14, 1994, emphasis added, video tape on file.

15. Benny Hinn, *Welcome, Holy Spirit*. Nashville: Thomas Nelson Publishers, 1995, pp. 57, 199.

16. Cf. *Webster's Ninth New Collegiate Dictionary*, pg. 1034; Alcalay, op. cit., pg. 2150.

17. *Good Morning, Holy Spirit*, op. cit., pp. 16-17. The reedited version reads the same as the original. In *The Blood*, op. cit., pg. 18, he also admits that his family was not Jewish.

18. Benny Hinn, *He Touched Me*. Nashville: Thomas Nelson Publisher, 1999, pp. 5-6.

19. Audio tape made of a Sept. 3, 1991, three-way telephone interview involving Randy Frame, J. Rodman Williams, and Benny Hinn in preparation for Frame's article which appeared in the Oct. 28, 1991 issue of *Christianity Today*, "Best-selling Author Admits Mistakes, Vows Changes," pp. 44-45. Transcript of tape on file.

20. Benny Hinn, OCC broadcast, March 28, 1994, op. cit., emphasis added.

21. Benny Hinn, *Praise the Lord* show, Trinity Broadcasting Network, May 12, 1999, emphasis added, video tape on file.

22. The original recording of this segment was during TBN's "Praise-A-Thon," April 3-9, 1994. This date has been established upon the following: 1) Hinn mentions at the beginning of his discourse the healing of a small boy in Argentina; and 2) at the conclusion of his discourse he says he was in Costa Rica a few weeks prior. Hinn's *Celebrate Jesus* magazine (Vol. 4, No. 1, 1994) gives a foreign mission report which details a February 1994 "first time" trip to Costa Rica and a mid-March 1994 crusade in Argentina. Also, the June 1994 *Praise the Lord* newsletter featured a photograph of Hinn praying over the financial pledges, an event which happened at the conclusion of the video segment. This segment also aired on August 2, 1994, during TBN's Macedonian Fund Raiser, and was rebroadcast during TBN's "Praise-A-Thon," November 1994.

23. Benny Hinn, *Praise the Lord* show, Trinity Broadcasting Network, Dec. 27, 1994, emphasis added.

24. Benny Hinn, *Our Position in Christ*, six tape audiocassette series, "Our Position in Christ," Part 1, Tape #A031190-1.

25. *Our Position in Christ* series, "An Heir of God," Part 5, Tape #A031190-5.

26. Benny Hinn, "A New Spirit," Orlando Christian Center broadcast, Oct. 13, 1990, video tape on file.

27. Ibid.

28. Benny Hinn, *Praise the Lord* show, Trinity Broadcasting Network, Dec. 26, 1991.

29. Benny Hinn, Orlando Christian Center broadcast, Trinity Broadcasting Network, Dec. 12, 1990.

30. TBN's "Praise-A-Thon," April 1994, op. cit.

31. *Praise the Lord* show, Dec. 27, 1994, op. cit. That Hinn believes there will come a time when no Christian will be sick is also evidenced in his 1992 report of this same "prophecy" by Kuhlman in his book, *The Anointing* (Nashville: Thomas Nelson Publishers, 1992), pp. 146-147. Here, however, he quotes Kuhlman as saying, "There will not be one sick saint in the body of Christ." In the excerpt of the tape of that meeting which was shown by TBN on Dec. 27, 1994, it is clear that this is Hinn's interpretation of what Mrs. Kuhlman said, and not her own words or intentions. Her hope/ assertion was that there would come a time in her ministry that all individuals who came to some specific meeting would be healed. It is evident that Hinn has trouble not only in ascertaining the meaning of ancient texts such as the Bible, but also the meaning of contemporary

communications as well.

32. TBN's "Praise-A-Thon," Nov. 6, 1990, op. cit., emphasis added.

33. TBN's "Praise-A-Thon," April 1994, op. cit., emphasis added.

34. TBN's "Praise-A-Thon," Nov. 6, 1990, op. cit., emphasis added.

35. Benny Hinn, *Lord, I Need a Miracle*. Nashville: Thomas Nelson Publishers, 1993, pg. 75, emphasis added.

36. BDB, op. cit., pp. 167-168; Holladay, op. cit., pg. 61; K-B, op. cit., pp. 185-186.

37. *Lord, I Need a Miracle*, op. cit., pg. 76, emphasis added.

38. Any Bible handbook or dictionary will reveal such usage. For example see Merrill F. Unger, *Unger's Bible Dictionary*. Chicago: Moody Press, 1976, pg. 1140.

Chapter 16

1. Audio tape made of a Sept. 3, 1991, three-way telephone interview involving Randy Frame, J. Rodman Williams, and Benny Hinn in preparation for Frame's article which appeared in the Oct. 28, 1991 issue of *Christianity Today*, "Best-selling Author Admits Mistakes, Vows Changes," pp. 44-45. Transcript of tape on file.

2. Benny Hinn, Signs & Wonders Conference, General Session, March 9, 1995. Video tape #95SWC52, video tape on file.

3. Benny Hinn, *Welcome, Holy Spirit*. Nashville: Thomas Nelson Publishers, 1995, pp. 57, 199.

4. Video vignette from the 1994 "Covenant Partners In Ministry Conference on the Holy Spirit," featured on the Orlando Christian Center broadcast, Trinity Broadcasting Network, Feb. 20, 1995.

5. Benny Hinn, Orlando Christian Center broadcast, Trinity Broadcasting Network, Nov. 3, 1990.

6. Benny Hinn, Orlando Christian Center broadcast, Trinity Broadcasting Network, June 13, 1993.

7. Benny Hinn, Melodyland Christian Center, "World Charismatic Conference," Aug. 7, 1992. Cassette tape of cited statements on file.

8. Benny Hinn, *"Rise & Be Healed!"* Orlando: Celebration Publishers, Inc., 1991, pg. 64.

9. Benny Hinn, "Praise-A-Thon," Nov. 6, 1990, Trinity Broadcasting Network, emphasis added. In a Nov. 9, 1990, version of this story, the Holy Spirit gave him different directions, and his address to this demon contained only the "blessings of God." See Chapter 7 (pp. 85-86) for a transcript of the alternate episode.

10. TBN's "Praise-A-Thon," Nov. 6, 1990, op. cit., emphasis added.

11. Richard Mayhue, *The Healing Promise*. Eugene, Ore.: Harvest House Publishers, 1994, pg. 33.

12. Ibid., pp. 91, 102, 134, etc.

13. TBN's "Praise-A-Thon," Nov. 6, 1990, op. cit., emphasis added.

14. Benny Hinn, *Praise the Lord* show, Trinity Broadcasting Network, Dec. 6, 1994, emphasis added. This unbiblical doctrine has been repeated time

and again by Hinn. See for example Benny Hinn, Orlando Christian Center broadcast, Trinity Broadcasting Network, Dec. 9, 1990. See also Chapter 2 (esp. pp. 20-24).

15. *Luther's Works*, edited by Jaroslav Pelikan and Helmut T. Lehmann. 55 volumes. St. Louis: Concordia Publishing House, 1955-1986, 22:341-344.

16. See E.W. Kenyon, *New Creation Realities: A Revelation of Redemption*. Seattle: Kenyon's Gospel Publishing Society, 1964, pg. 44; Kenneth E. Hagin, *The Name of Jesus*. Tulsa: Kenneth Hagin Ministries, 1981, pg. 31; Frederick Price, "Identification, Number 3." Inglewood, Calif.: Ever Increasing Faith Ministries, 1980, tape FP545; Kenneth Copeland, "What Happened from the Cross to the Throne." Fort Worth: Kenneth Copeland Ministries, 1991, audiotape #02-0017.

17. See Chapter 15, endnote 31.

18. Benny Hinn, *Lord, I Need a Miracle*. Nashville: Thomas Nelson Publishers, 1993, pp. 63, 64, and 67.

19. *Praise the Lord* show, Dec. 6, 1994, op. cit., emphasis added. See also, Benny Hinn, *Praise the Lord* show, Trinity Broadcasting Network, Jan. 24, 1995, where he expressed the same unbiblical concept. See further comments regarding Hinn's use of Exodus 12 and Psalm 105:37 (cf. Isaiah 63:13-14) in Chapter 15, pp. 229-230.

20. Benny Hinn, *Praise the Lord* show, Trinity Broadcasting Network, Dec. 27, 1994, emphasis added.

21. Ibid., emphasis added. See Chapter 15, pp. 225-227 for additional comments.

22. TBN's "Praise-A-Thon," Nov. 6, 1990, op. cit.

23. Ibid., emphasis added.

24. *Praise the Lord* show, Dec. 6, 1994, op. cit., emphasis added.

25. Benny Hinn, Orlando Christian Center broadcast, Trinity Broadcasting Network, Sept. 26, 1994, emphasis added.

26. *Lord, I Need a Miracle*, op. cit., pg. 63, emphasis added. See also, *Praise the Lord* show, Jan. 24, 1995, where Hinn expresses the same unbiblical concept.

27. *"Rise & Be Healed!"*, op. cit., pg. 37, emphasis added.

28. *Lord, I Need a Miracle*, op. cit., pp. 74-75, emphasis added.

29. Benny Hinn, "Praise-A-Thon," April 1994, Trinity Broadcasting Network.

30. *Lord, I Need a Miracle*, op. cit., pp. 72-73, emphasis added.

31. Ibid., pg. 100, emphasis added.

32. *Dictionary of Pentecostal and Charismatic Movements*, op. cit., pp. 95-97; C. Douglas Weaver, *The Healer-Prophet, William Marrion Branham: A Study of the Prophetic in American Pentecostalism*. Macon, Ga.: Mercer University Press, 1987; and Stephen F. Cannon, "A Prophet Sent from God? Examining the Life and Claims of William M. Branham," *The Quarterly Journal*, October-December 1988, pp. 1, 8-9.

33. See further, *The Healing Promise*, op. cit. Mayhue proves conclusively that there is no healing in the biblical record which was subsequently reversed for any reason (pp. 34-35).

34. TBN's "Praise-A-Thon," April 1994, op. cit., emphasis added.
35. OCC broadcast, Feb. 20, 1995, op. cit.

Chapter 17

1. For further details about Hinn's claim of graveside anointings, see Chapter 13, pp. 180-182.
2. Benny Hinn, *This Is Your Day*, Trinity Broadcasting Network, Nov. 12, 1998, video tape on file.
3. Ibid.
4. Ibid.
5. Ibid.
6. Benny Hinn, *The Blood*. Orlando: Creation House, 1993, inside front dust cover.
7. Ibid.
8. Ibid., back dust cover.
9. Ibid.
10. Thomas R. Edgar, *Satisfied by the Promise of the Spirit*. Grand Rapids: Kregal Resources, 1996. This volume is a sane and biblical treatise of the subject, and a breath of fresh air into a Church gone mad by the antics of Hinn and others.
11. *This Is Your Day*, Nov. 12, 1998, op. cit.
12. Ibid.
13. Ibid.
14. Ibid.
15. Benny Hinn, *He Touched Me*. Nashville: Thomas Nelson Publishers, 1999, pg. 196.
16. Ibid.
17. Benny Hinn, *Praise the Lord* show, Trinity Broadcasting Network, Sept. 10, 1999, video tape on file, emphasis added.
18. Comments to Kurt Goedelman from Yves Brault regarding the *This Is Your Day* broadcast, January 1999, letter on file.
19. Ibid.
20. Ibid.

Appendix A

1. Subsequent visits in June 1995 and August 1997 by M. Kurt Goedelman revealed that the church's bookstore continues to sell assorted titles by Capps, Hagin, and Copeland, in addition to works by David (Paul) Yonggi Cho, E.W. Kenyon, Finis Dake, and others.

Appendix B

1. See further, *Orange County Register*, Anaheim, Calif., Dec. 5, 1995, Accent, "Faith in His Hands," pp. 1, 6.

2. Wade H. Boggs, *Faith Healing and the Christian Faith*. Grand Rapids: Baker Book House, 1955, pg. 21.

3. Ibid., pp. 22, 30.

4. Gary Ronberg, "Praying, Hoping, Waiting...", *St. Louis Post-Dispatch*, St. Louis, Mo., May 4, 1975, pg. G11.

5. Ibid.

6. Robert Bowman, Jr., *The ApoLog*, May 1996, pg. 1, emphasis in original.

7. Richard Mayhue, *The Healing Promise*. Eugene, Ore.: Harvest House Publishers, 1994, pg. 39.

Index ———————————————

Toufik Benedictus Hinn Arrives December 3, 1952 – *The hospital in Jaffa, Israel, where Benny was born and where his mother, Clemence, is said to have had a dream of Jesus in response to her petition for a son to be born. The facility was converted into a mental hospital and then later abandoned.*

The Mayor's Mansion – *The building in Jaffa, Israel, which housed the Greek Orthodox Club. It was in the basement of this structure where the Hinn family lived. Benny alleges it to be a "wonderful home" made possible by his father's position of "mayor" of the city. Benny also claims it was here, at age 11, that Jesus appeared to him in a vision.*

College de Frere – *The Catholic elementary school in Jaffa, Israel, where Benny attended and was taught by monks. While the Hinn family was Greek Orthodox by religion, Benny says his schooling made him "an expert on the Catholic life."*

High School Drop-Out – *Georges Vanier Secondary School in Toronto, Canada, where Benny completed only the 11th grade before dropping out. The most standardized version of his conversion story takes place here, at the school library in February 1972.*

Mass Salvations at Schmidt's – *Schmidt's Girls College, an all girls Catholic school, in East Jerusalem, Israel, where Benny claims to have preached in 1976 resulting in the conversions of two to three hundred students along with the nuns who taught them. A Schmidt's College official states Benny's claim is "nonsense, real nonsense."*

Orlando Christian Center – *The church founded and built by Benny in Orlando. The Florida-based charismatic church was founded in 1983 and was later called World Outreach Center and then World Outreach Church. In 2000, Benny resigned as pastor and the church merged with Faith World Church pastored by the Rev. Clint Brown.*

Anointing from the Dead – The grave site of Aimee Semple McPherson, founder of the International Church of the Foursquare Gospel, located at Forest Lawn Cemetery in Glendale, California. Two large kneeling angels at the head and foot of the polished Italian tomb are like a modern Ark of the Covenant. Benny alleges "the anointing has lingered over Aimee's body."

Healings from the Grave – The grave (second from left) of faith healer Kathryn Kuhlman is said by Benny to possess healing power. It is located in a walled section of Forest Lawn Cemetery amongst hundreds of other graves of both celebrities and unrenowned. The marker reads, "Kathryn Kuhlman - I Believe in Miracles Because I Believe in God - February 20, 1976."

The Anointing Flows in Kansas City – *Benny at his Kansas City Miracle Crusade in July 1993, where he continued to proclaim healings from the stage, a practice which he said on national television a few months earlier he would stop because news reports had proven his "healings" bogus. He also said that Jesus appeared to him in his hotel room while in Kansas City.*

Performing for the Assemblies – *Benny entertains the leadership of the Assemblies of God in Springfield, Missouri, with one of his healing campaigns. In 1994, he sought and was given credentials with the denomination. In March 1995, he appeared at the "Signs and Wonders Conference," to respond to complaints leveled against him.*

Benny's Anointing – *Benny claims that God has powerfully anointed him and claims that his "anointing" gives him the power to knock people down, or "slay them in the Spirit" by touching, waving, or blowing on them. He warns critics not to mock his "anointing" and has even pronounced curses on those who do.*

California Television Production Studio – *The World Media Center of Benny Hinn Ministries in Aliso Viejo, California. Benny acquired the facility in the mid-1990s and uses the production studio to tape his television program, "This Is Your Day." In 1999, Benny and his family moved from Orlando to Southern California to be closer to his Media Center.*

About the Authors:

G. Richard Fisher has served as pastor of Laurelton Park Baptist Church in Bricktown, New Jersey, since 1968. He is a member of the Board of Directors of Personal Freedom Outreach (PFO) and the senior researcher/writer for its newsletter publication, *The Quarterly Journal*.

M. Kurt Goedelman founded PFO in 1975 and is the organization's executive director. He and his wife, Angela, handle PFO's ministry operations in the Saint Louis office.

W.E. Nunnally is Professor of Early Judaism and Christian Origins at Evangel University, and Adjunct Professor at Central Bible College and Southwest Missouri State University in Springfield, Missouri.

Stephen F. Cannon has an associate of arts degree in biblical studies from Antioch Baptist Bible College in Marietta, Georgia. His research includes a primary emphasis on aberrational teachings in the Church. He serves as director of PFO's Arizona office.

Paul R. Blizard served on PFO's Board of Directors from 1988 to 1994. He presently serves in full-time ministry work as a Southern Baptist pastor.

The Quarterly Journal

For those with questions about cultic and aberrational issues facing the Christian Church today, *The Quarterly Journal* is a tremendous resource to assist the Christian's spiritual discernment.

In 1981, Personal Freedom Outreach began publishing its quarterly newsletter. This periodical is mailed to those who help to financially support the work of PFO with a minimum annual donation of $20 or more. It carries articles and editorials on current cult-related topics and errant teachings within Christianity, brief news items, personal testimonies, and book reviews.

To receive a sample copy of the current issue of *The Quarterly Journal*, please send $5.00 to cover printing, postage and handling costs. Mail your request to Personal Freedom Outreach, P.O. Box 26062, Saint Louis, MO 63136-0062.